A WORLD BANK COUNTRY STUDY

# Chile

## *The Adult Health Policy Challenge*

The World Bank
Washington, D.C.

Copyright © 1995
The International Bank for Reconstruction
and Development/ THE WORLD BANK
1818 H Street, N.W.
Washington, D.C. 20433, U.S.A.

World Bank Country Studies are among the many reports originally prepared for internal use as part of the continuing analysis by the Bank of the economic and related conditions of its developing member countries and of its dialogues with the governments. Some of the reports are published in this series with the least possible delay for the use of governments and the academic, business and financial, and development communities. The typescript of this paper therefore has not been prepared in accordance with the procedures appropriate to formal printed texts, and the World Bank accepts no responsibility for errors. Some sources cited in this paper may be informal documents that are not readily available.

The World Bank does not guarantee the accuracy of the data included in this publication and accepts no responsibility whatsoever for any consequence of their use. The boundaries, colors, denominations, and other information shown on any map in this volume do not imply on the part of the World Bank Group any judgment on the legal status of any territory or the endorsement or acceptance of such boundaries.

The material in this publication is copyrighted. Requests for permission to reproduce portions of it should be sent to the Office of the Publisher at the address shown in the copyright notice above. The World Bank encourages dissemination of its work and will normally give permission promptly and, when the reproduction is for noncommercial purposes, without asking a fee. Permission to copy portions for classroom use is granted through the Copyright Clearance Center, Inc., Suite 910, 222 Rosewood Drive, Danvers, Massachusetts 01923, U.S.A.

The complete backlist of publications from the World Bank is shown in the annual *Index of Publications*, which contains an alphabetical title list (with full ordering information) and indexes of subjects, authors, and countries and regions. The latest edition is available free of charge from the Distribution Unit, Office of the Publisher, The World Bank, 1818 H Street, N.W., Washington, D.C. 20433, U.S.A., or from Publications, The World Bank, 66, avenue d'Iéna, 75116 Paris, France.

ISSN: 0-0253-2123

**Library of Congress Cataloging-in-Publication Data**

Chile: the adult health policy challenge.
       p.  cm. — (A World Bank country study)
   Includes bibliographical references.
   ISBN 0-8213-3224-4
   1. Medical policy—Chile.  2. Health transition—Chile.
 3. Medical economics—Chile.  I. International Bank for
Reconstruction and Development.  II. Series.
   RA395.C5C48   1995
   362.1'0983—dc20                      95-8630
                                      CIP

# Contents

## *List of Tables*

## List of Boxes

## List of Figures

# PREFACE

In many developing countries, social and economic transformations of the last several decades have contributed to the emergence of a new set of health priorities.[1] While the prevalence of infectious and parasitic diseases has diminished sharply or, as in the case of smallpox, been eradicated, there has been an increase in the relative importance of non-communicable diseases[2] and injuries, which is related mainly to the aging of the population due to the decline in fertility and increase in life expectancy, as well as rapid urbanization and industrialization, changes in life styles, and improved access to, use of, and effectiveness of health care. As a result, non-communicable diseases and injuries are now the leading causes of death in these countries, particularly among the adult age group (15-59 years) and the elderly (age 60 and older).[3] Differences in the natural history of non-communicable diseases (long periods of sickness and disability) and infectious and parasitic diseases (mostly acute episodes of short duration) have also implied an increase in the relative importance of morbidity and disability stemming primarily from cardiovascular disease, cancer, chronic obstructive pulmonary disease, diabetes, mental illness, and injuries. In general, non-communicable diseases and injuries affect low and high socioeconomic groups alike and impose two types of costs on society: they affect an individual's productivity and income-generating potential, and they increase consumption of high-cost health care services. In many developing countries, however, risk factors for non-communicable diseases and injuries are often more prevalent and disease rates are generally higher among the poor.

Chile is a good example of a country that has experienced profound demographic and epidemiological changes in recent decades. As a consequence, non-communicable diseases and injuries are already posing and will continue to pose in the coming decades difficult problems for the health system. Responding effectively to these problems requires a clear understanding of recent and future demographic and epidemiological changes, their possible implications, and possible options for the Chilean health system as the country moves into the 21st Century. Following World Bank country studies on the epidemiological transition in Brazil[4] and China,[5] the primary objective of this study is to analyze the demographic, epidemiological, financial, and institutional aspects of the health transition in Chile and discuss alternative actions for addressing them.

---

1. Jamison, D.T. and Mosley, W.H. 1991. Disease Control Priorities in Developing Countries: Health Policy Responses to Epidemiological Change. American Journal of Public Health 81:15-22.

2. In general, non-communicable diseases are characterized by a long latency period, prolonged clinical course, and debilitating manifestations.

3. Feachem, R.G.A., Kjellstrom, T., Murray, C.J.L., Over, M., and Phillips, M.A. 1992. The Health of Adults in the Developing World. New York: Oxford University Press for the World Bank.

4. World Bank. 1989. Adult health in Brazil: Adjusting to new challenges. Report No. 7807-BR. Washington, D.C.

5. World Bank. 1990. China Long-Term Issues and Options in the Health Transition. Report No. 7965-CHA. Vols.I-II. Washington, D.C.

# *ACKNOWLEDGMENTS*

This study was prepared by Patricio Márquez, Public Health Specialist, Human Resources Division, Department III, Latin America and Caribbean Vice Presidency. It is based on World Bank missions led by Evangeline Javier that visited Chile in 1992 and 1993, in conjunction with the preparation, appraisal, and supervision of the World Bank-supported Technical Assistance and Hospital Rehabilitation Project (TAHRP) and the Health Sector Reform Project (HSRP). The study was prepared in the Human Resources Division of the former Country Department IV (now Country Department I) in the Latin America and Caribbean Vice Presidency. The Chilean Ministry of Health supported the preparation of this study at all stages, providing leadership and invaluable insights.

The study draws heavily on background papers prepared for the World Bank by the following Chilean experts (in alphabetical order):

Cecilia Albala of the Institute of Food Technology and Nutrition;
Sergio Bello of the National Institute of Respiratory Diseases;
María C. Escobar of the Chilean Ministry of Health;
Rony Lenz of FONASA;
Luis Martinez of the Chilean Ministry of Health;
Eduardo Medina of the Chilean Ministry of Health;
Ernesto Medina of the University of Chile School of Public Health;
César Oyarzo of FONASA;
Alfredo Pemjean of the Chilean Ministry of Health;
María Inés Pino of the Chilean Ministry of Health;
Jaime Rozovski of the Catholic University School of Medicine;
Cecilia Sepúlveda of the Chilean Ministry of Health;
Erica Taucher of the Chilean Ministry of Health.

H. Dennis Tolley of Brigham Young University in Utah, United States, constructed the computerized projection model on which future epidemiological scenarios are based. María Isabel Rivara of the Chilean Ministry of Health compiled the data set used in the projection model.

Background papers were also prepared by Renaldo Battista and Matthew Hodge of McGill University Division of Clinical Epidemiology; Enis Baris, André-Pierre Contandriopoulos, and Francois Champagne of the Université de Montréal Département d'Administration de la Santé; and Carlota Rios and Victor Sierra (World Bank Consultants).

In addition, Daniel Joly formerly of the Pan American Health Organization, and Lani Rice Márquez of University Research Corporation reviewed the background papers and provided insightful comments and advice, respectively. Suzanne McQueen provided valuable research assistance. Aracelly Woodall supported in the production of the report.

Detailed comments and guidance on an early draft were provided by Philip Musgrove, Oscar Echeverri, Mary Eming Young, Willy De Geyndt and José-Luis Bobadilla, the Peer Reviewers, and useful feedback was received from Julian Schweitzer, Danny Leipziger, Dean Jamison, Richard Feachem, Brian Abel-Smith, Xavier Coll, Evangeline Javier, and Gunnar Eskeland. Additional comments were provided by the following Chilean experts: Jorge Jiménez, Juan Giaconi, Cristian Baeza, Hernán Montenegro, and Ximena Aguilera. Julio Montt, former Minister of Health of Chile, also supported the preparation of this study. Helena Restrepo of the Pan American Health Organization, Jean Pillet, former World Bank staff member, and José Ruales of the Ecuadorian Ministry of Public Health also provided comments and advice.

The objectives, methodology, findings, and recommendations of the draft report were presented at a one day seminar held at the Pontificia Universidad Católica de Chile on 12 July, 1994. The seminar was organized by Juan Giaconi and Jorge Jiménez, former Ministers of Health, and presided at its opening by Carlos Massad, Minister of Health.

A draft of the report was discussed formally with the Government of Chile on 13 July, 1994, and benefitted from written comments provided by a Ministry of Health commission established by Carlos Massad, Minister of Health. Commission members included: Marcos Vergara, Hugo Salinas, Isabel Rivara, Jaime Sepúlveda, Pedro Crocco, Marisol Concha, Patricio Hurtado, Alberto Muñoz, and Hernán Montenegro.

The World Bank-managed Consultant Trust Funds of the Governments of Canada, Denmark, Finland, and The Netherlands helped to finance the preparation of the background papers commissioned to the Chilean experts. The simulation model for forecasting future health trends and costs was financed by a grant provided by the World Bank's Research Advisory Staff (RAD).

# CURRENCY AND EQUIVALENTS

Currency Unit  =  Chilean Peso (CH$)
US$1.00  =  CH$345 (June 1991)
US$1.00  =  CH$350 (February 1992)
US$1.00  =  CH$432 (October 1993)

CH$1.00  =  US$0.003
CH$1.00  =  US$0.003
CH$1.00  =  US$0.002

## Government Fiscal Year

January 1 - December 31

## Abbreviations and Acronyms

| | |
|---|---|
| AFP | Private Pension Funds (Administradoras de Fondos de Pensiones) |
| AHP | Adult Health Program (Programa de Salud del Adulto del Ministerio de Salud) |
| BCG | Bacillus of Calmette and Guerin (Anti-Tuberculosis Vaccine) |
| BMI | Body Mass Index |
| CDT | Diagnostic and Treatment Center (Centro de Diagnóstico y Tratamiento) |
| CRS | Health Referral Center (Centro de Referencia de Salud) |
| CSF | Central Supply Facility (Central de Abastecimiento) |
| CVD | Cardiovascular Disease |
| DALY | Disability-Adjusted Life Year |
| DPT | Diptheria Pertussis Tetanus Vaccine |
| DRG | Diagnostic-Related Groups |
| FAP | Fee-for-Service System for Reimbursing Hospitals (Facturación por Atención Prestada Integral) |
| FAPEM | Fee-for-Service System for Reimbursing Municipal Health Facilities (Facturación por Atención Prestada en Establecimientos Municipalizados) |
| FNDR | National Fund for Regional Development (Fondo Nacional de Desarrollo Regional) |
| FONASA | National Health Fund (Fondo Nacional de Salud) |

| | |
|---|---|
| GDP | Gross Domestic Product (Producto Geográfico Bruto) |
| HSA | Health Service Area (Servicios de Salud) |
| ICD | International Classification of Diseases |
| IDDM | Insulin Dependent Diabetes Mellitus |
| INE | National Institute of Statistics (Instituto Nacional de Estadística) |
| INP | Instituto de Normalización Previsional |
| ISAPREs | Prepaid Health Insurance Plans (Instituciones de Salud Previsional) |
| ISP | Public Health Institute (Instituto de Salud Pública) |
| MIDEPLAN | Ministry of Planning (Ministerio de Planificación) |
| MOF | Ministry of Finance (Ministerio de Hacienda) |
| MOH | Ministry of Health (Ministerio de Salud) |
| NHS | National Health Service (Servicio Nacional de Salud) |
| NHSS | National Health Services System (Sistema Nacional de Servicios de Salud) |
| NIDDM | Non-Insulin Dependent Diabetes Mellitus |
| PAD | Per Case Payment Associated with Diagnosis (Pago Asociado a Diagnóstico) |
| PAHO | Pan American Health Organization (Oficina Panamericana de la Salud) |
| PNAC | National Supplementary Feeding Program (Programa Nacional de Alimentación Complementaria) |
| PPP | Prospective Fee Schedule (Pagos Prospectivos por Prestación) |
| PPS | Preferred Provider System (Sistema de Libre Elección) |
| SEREMI | Regional Secretariat (Secretaria Regional Ministerial) |
| SERMENA | National Medical Service for Employees (Servicio Médico Nacional) |
| SIGMO | Monitoring and Management Information System (Sistema de Información Gerencial y Monitoreo) |
| SF | Social Fund (Fondo Social) |
| WHO | World Health Organization (Organización Mundial de la Salud) |
| YPLL | Years of Potential Productive Life Lost |

## COUNTRY DATA SHEET

---

Area: 756.95 thou.sq.km          Population (1993): 13.5 mill.          Density (per sq km): 17.8
                                 Rate of Growth: 1.7%

Population Characteristics (1990)                Health (1991)
  Crude birth rate (per 1,000): 23                 Population per physician: 895
  Crude death rate (per 1,000): 7                  Hospital beds per 10,000 persons: 33
  Total fertility rate : 2.6
  Infant mortality (per 1,000): 17
  Life expectancy at birth (years): 72

Income Distribution (1992)                       Access to Potable Water
(share in total income)                          (% of population, 1991)
  Highest 20%: 51.8%                               Urban: 95.2
  Lowest 20%:   6.5%                               Rural: 73.3

Nutrition (1990)                                 Education (1991)
  Per capita calorie intake (cal/day): 2584        Enrollment rate
  Per capita protein intake (gms/day): 65            Primary:  98
                                                     Secondary: 72
                                                     Adult Illiteracy Rate : 8

GNP Per Capita (US$, 1992): 2,726

## OUTPUT, EMPLOYMENT AND PRODUCTIVITY

|                              | Value Added | | Labor Force | | V-A per Worker | |
|                              | 1990 | 1993 | 1990 | 1993 | 1990 | 1993 |
|                              | (% of GDP) | | (% of total) | | (1986=100) | |
|------------------------------|------|------|------|------|------|------|
| Agriculture & Fisheries      | 8.9  | 7.9  | 19.2 | 16.6 | 127.4 | 156.7 |
| Mining                       | 8.9  | 7.8  | 2.3  | 1.8  | 96.1  | 116.5 |
| Industry                     | 17.6 | 17.3 | 16.0 | 16.7 | 94.8  | 100.6 |
| Services                     | 15.0 | 16.0 | 17.7 | 18.6 | 114.0 | 130.3 |
| Financial Services           | 13.1 | 13.6 | 4.5  | 5.8  | 107.1 | 94.1  |
| Transport&Communication      | 7.0  | 7.7  | 6.9  | 7.1  | 107.2 | 126.3 |
| Total/Average                | 100  | 100  | 100  | 100  | 111.5 | 122.8 |

## KEY ECONOMIC INDICATORS

| | 1990 | 1991 | 1992 | 1993 |
|---|---|---|---|---|
| ***GROSS DOMESTIC PRODUCT (% of GDP)*** | | | | |
| GDP at market prices (Mill. of US$) | 30,183 | 33,992 | 41,205 | 43,704 |
| Gross Domestic Investment | 24.7% | 22.2% | 23.7% | 26.5% |
| Consumption | 72.7% | 73.1% | 74.2% | 76.1% |
| Exports GNFS | 33.6% | 32.9% | 30.4% | 27.8% |
| Imports GNFS | 31.0% | 28.2% | 28.4% | 30.1% |
| Gross National Savings | 22.0% | 22.6% | 22.3% | 21.3% |
| | | | | |
| ***PUBLIC FINANCE (% of GDP)*** | | | | |
| Non-Financial Public Sector Surplus | 3.5% | 2.1% | 3.0% | 1.4% |
| Central Government | 0.7% | 1.5% | 2.3% | 0.9% |
| Total Revenues | 22.0% | 23.8% | 24.5% | 23.8% |
| Total Expenditures | 21.3% | 22.3% | 22.2% | 22.8% |
| Public Enterprises | 2.8% | 0.6% | 0.7% | 0.5% |
| Central Bank Loss | -2.2% | -1.1% | -1.2% | -1.0% |
| | | | | |
| ***MONEY*** | | | | |
| M1A Growth | 11.9% | 40.3% | 26.4% | 19.2% |
| Money Base | 97.1% | 84.7% | 71.6% | 38.5% |
| Real Interest Rate on 60-365 days (indexed to UF) | | | | |
| Loans | 13.3% | 8.5% | 8.1% | 9.2% |
| Deposits | 9.4% | 5.4% | 5.3% | 6.4% |
| | | | | |
| ***PRICES*** | | | | |
| CPI Inflation (end of period) | 27.3% | 18.7% | 12.7% | 12.2% |
| Terms of Trade (1986=100) | 111.8 | 111.2 | 110.1 | 112.9 |
| Nominal Exchange Rate (Ch$/US$) | 304.9 | 349.2 | 362.6 | 404.2 |
| Real Exchange Rate (1986=100) | 112.8 | 106.4 | 97.8 | 97.1 |
| Real Wages (December 1982=100) | 104.4 | 109.5 | 114.5 | 118.5 |
| Copper Prices (US cents per pound) | 120.9 | 106.1 | 103.6 | 86.7 |
| | | | | |
| ***BALANCE OF PAYMENTS (Mill. of US$)*** | | | | |
| Trade Balance | 1,273 | 1,576 | 749 | -978 |
| Exports FOB | 8,310 | 8,929 | 9,986 | 9,202 |
| Imports FOB | 7,037 | 7,353 | 9,237 | 10,181 |
| Non-Financial Services (net) | -258 | 36 | -63 | 5 |
| Financial Services (net) | -1,811 | -1,809 | -1,860 | -1,503 |
| Current Account Deficit | -597 | 143 | -743 | -2,092 |
| Foreign Investment | 941 | 450 | 653 | 1,153 |
| Medium and Long-term Capital | 692 | -83 | 290 | 519 |
| Short-term Capital | 1,435 | 447 | 1,940 | 1,091 |
| Errors and Omissions | -103 | 282 | 359 | -94 |
| Overall Balance | 2,410 | 1,284 | 2,369 | 580 |
| Memorandum Items: | | | | |
| Current Account (% of GDP) | -2.1% | 0.5% | -1.8% | -4.8% |
| Stock of Foreign Reserves | 5,358 | 6,641 | 9,009 | 9,759 |
| | | | | |
| ***FOREIGN DEBT*** | | | | |
| Total Debt Stock (Mill. of US$) | 18,576 | 17,355 | 18,945 | 18,714 |
| Debt/GDP (%) | 66.8% | 55.4% | 50.0% | 42.5% |
| Debt Services (% of XGS) | 26.4% | 23.1% | 20.9% | 19.6% |

Sources: The Central Bank of Chile and Ministry of Finance.

# EXECUTIVE SUMMARY

The social and economic transformations of the last several decades have led to profound demographic and epidemiological changes in many developing countries. Increases in the importance of non-communicable diseases and injuries affecting primarily adults and the elderly pose new disease control challenges for health systems that must simultaneously address problems of infectious diseases. This study of adult health in Chile analyzes recent and projected demographic and epidemiological trends and their implications for health care expenditures and intervention programs, including strategies for managing medical technology and containing the escalation of health care costs.

## The Chilean Health Sector and Its Financing

The Chilean health sector is characterized by a multiplicity of public and private providers, although the bulk of curative and preventive services are delivered through the government-managed National Health Service System (NHSS), which is coordinated by the Ministry of Health (MOH). The NHSS covers 60 percent of the population, delivering care in 26 geographically defined Health Service Areas (HSAs) which operate the public hospitals within their boundaries. Chile's well established primary care network is run by municipal governments, which receive resource transfers from the central government to help finance the delivery of primary health services. Insured workers contributing to the National Health Fund (FONASA) and their dependents have the option of private providers under the Preferred Provider System (PPS) which is regularly used by about 13 percent of the population; under this system users pay varying levels of co-payments for generalist and specialist care. Insured workers may also opt out of the NHSS entirely by channeling their obligatory 7 percent health care payroll deductions to one of the private pre-paid health insurance plans called ISAPREs, which cover about 21 percent of the population.

The NHSS depends on the following major revenue sources administered by FONASA: the obligatory payroll deductions, accounting for close to 40 percent of all income; central government contributions, accounting for another 40 percent of income; sale of vouchers to workers using the PPS providers, amounting to 7 percent; user charges in public hospitals, representing 9 percent, and income from other sources 7 percent. FONASA finances the delivery of public hospital services through reimbursement according to a set fee-for-service schedule which is intended to cover all operating costs except salaries, which are paid directly by the MOH. In addition to payment for services, FONASA provides a fixed budget allocation to each HSA to cover administration and certain investment and indirect costs. The municipal-run primary health care network is financed in principle through reimbursement for specific services rendered in each facility, but in practice payments are determined by monthly ceilings on the total amount of fees that FONASA will pay to each municipality. In addition, the municipalities themselves contribute significantly to the financing of services.

Health services provided by the ISAPREs are financed through affiliates' payroll deductions, which are used to pay monthly premiums which vary according to the specific coverage plan, and co-payments at the time of service which vary from 10 to 40 percent of the cost of each service. While the number of ISAPRE beneficiaries has grown rapidly from about 62,000 in 1982 to about 3 million in 1992, the effects of significant market imperfections have limited wider access to the ISAPRE system (e.g., exclusionary clauses denying coverage for certain services), particularly among the elderly.

In 1990, the democratically elected Government began an ambitious national reform program to address imbalances in the public health system which had led to inefficient resource use and poor service quality. Major initiatives are underway to rehabilitate the country's deteriorated public hospital infrastructure and create a new level of specialized ambulatory care facilities to better bridge the gap between primary and hospital care. The reform program also contemplates further decentralization of management responsibility for health services delivery to the HSAs and redirection of the role of the central MOH toward policy development, planning and monitoring. A significant feature of the reform program is the proposal to replace the current fee-for-service resource allocation mechanisms with fixed diagnosis-related payments for hospitals and a capitated system for primary health care facilities. Legislation has also been enacted to strengthen the MOH's regulatory role over the ISAPREs in order to mitigate the effects of certain market imperfections. Collectively these reforms will better enable the NHSS to meet the challenges posed by Chile's changing epidemiological profile.

## Chile's Demographic and Epidemiological Transition

In the past 50 years, Chile has experienced a sharp drop in birth rates and a sustained decline in death rates which have lowered the annual population growth rate to 1.7 percent. As a result, the population age structure has been transformed, with a relative increase in the young adult, middle-aged and elderly populations. These demographic changes have been accompanied by rapid urbanization (85 percent of the population now lives in urban areas) and industrialization of the country and associated lifestyle changes, including reduced risk from infectious diseases. Infant and child health has improved most dramatically, with the contribution of deaths under age 15 to total mortality dropping from 48 percent in 1960 to 9 percent in 1990. The longer life expectancy of the Chilean population (72 years in 1990) has resulted in a shifting disease profile characterized by the predominance of non-communicable diseases and injuries affecting adults and the elderly.

### The rise of non-communicable diseases and their risk factors

The leading non-communicable conditions affecting the Chilean population are cardiovascular disorders, cancer, cirrhosis of the liver, diabetes, chronic obstructive pulmonary disease, and external injuries, which together account for 66 percent of all deaths. Some of these conditions account for about 40 percent of the disease burden of premature mortality as measured by disability-adjusted life years (DALYs). The rise in importance of non-communicable illnesses is reflected in the vastly increased numbers of Chileans dying from these causes. Such increases are of particular public health concern because as the population ages an even greater disease burden may be expected in coming decades.

Trends in cause-specific mortality rates for each major non-communicable disease were analyzed for the past 30 years. Most causes of cardiovascular disease were found to show stable or slightly decreasing mortality rates, though hospitalization rates (which better reflect the burden to the health system of treating non-communicable illnesses) have shown marked increases. Age-adjusted mortality rates for several leading causes of cancer (gallbladder, lung, breast) were found to be on the increase. Mortality rates from accidental injuries have experienced a modest decline, although the rate of hospitalization for injuries has nearly doubled. Chronic Obstructive Pulmonary Disease (COPD), which encompasses a family of illnesses including chronic bronchitis and emphysema, has shown marked increases in mortality rates. Since COPD cannot be cured, this condition in particular adds to the disability burden of the country. Mortality and hospitalization rates for diabetes and cirrhosis have registered steady increases in the past 30 years.

The study also examined trends in the principal risk factors for degenerative illnesses, focussing on smoking, alcohol and drug abuse, hypertension, sedentary lifestyle, dietary patterns, occupational hazards and pollution, which have become important determinants of illness, particularly among low-income groups. The status of major risk factors for non-communicable illnesses and injuries can be summarized as follows:

- Smoking prevalence among adults in Chile is high; approximately 38 percent of men and 25 percent of women smoke. There has been a modest increase in prevalence among females in the past twenty years and a slight decrease in prevalence among men.

- Use of alcohol is widespread, with approximately 15 percent of the adult population estimated to be excessive drinkers or alcoholics.

- Abuse of drugs has shown a gradual increase since the early 1960's, affecting an estimated 3-5 percent of adolescents and young adults, particularly those in the northern regions.

- Hypertension is estimated to be present in 10-16 percent of the adult population.

- Sedentarism is prevalent, particularly among lower income groups and women, as recreational exercise is not a widely accepted habit in Chile.

- Important nutrition-related risk factors include obesity, affecting in particular low-income women, high cholesterol among upper socioeconomic levels, and low calcium intake.

- Air pollution is a significant risk factor for respiratory illnesses among urban dwellers, especially residents of Santiago.

Though the prevalence of many non-communicable disease risk factors is high in Chile, mortality rates from these conditions have still not reached the levels found in industrialized countries. This is because most non-communicable illnesses have a long latency period, such that the clinical manifestations of the disease only become apparent after periods as long as 10 to 30 years after initial exposure to precipitating conditions and risk factors. Current disease trends in Chile are thus the product of the past 20 to 30 years' exposure to risk factors. The rise in prevalence of major risk factors during the past three decades suggests that non-communicable diseases in Chile have still not reached the stage in their natural histories at which their full fatal effects are felt and that these illnesses will continue to grow in prominence and magnitude.

**The projected future burden of disease**

To estimate the burden to the health system of likely future demographic and epidemiological trends, a model was developed to project over the next forty years morbidity and mortality from leading non-communicable illnesses and injuries in Chile, based on current prevalence of risk factors and mortality rates. Two scenarios were considered in the model: a baseline scenario reflecting a continuation of current trends, and an intervention scenario in which risk factor prevalence and age-specific mortality were selectively reduced over time. The baseline and intervention scenarios were compared to estimate the impact that effective disease prevention strategies enacted now could have on future health care requirements.

Within this context, it is important to note that as countries develop, total mortality falls even though the prevalence of some health risk factors increases (e.g., consumption of alcohol, animal fats, and tobacco). The correlation of increasing national wealth and per capita income with a decrease in total mortality has been clearly observed in data world wide. Chile has been the beneficiary of such a reduction in total mortality for the past several decades and would undoubtedly continue to be so. The trend in overall reduction of mortality for the future as Chile continues to develop and increase in wealth was therefore included in the forecast model.

The forecast exercise shows that the number of deaths from six of the leading groups of non-communicable diseases and injuries will continue to increase due to the relative aging of the Chilean population and to growing exposure to major risk factors. The model suggests that aggressive disease prevention strategies, particularly for coronary heart disease and chronic respiratory diseases, will indeed help to slow expected increases in cause-specific mortality, especially among middle-aged groups. The intervention scenario is also expected to reduce total DALYs lost due to various non-communicable conditions and injuries by about 9 percent for males and 7 percent for females. More importantly, the strongly positive effect of the preventive strategy on DALYs saved is obtainable after only the first 10 years of intervention. However, the effect of intervention on some causes of death is not likely to be visible until after at least 20 years.

Despite these constraints on the benefits of non-communicable disease and injury control, the projection model showed that in the future, as the population ages, an even larger number of deaths, illnesses and disability due to specific non-communicable diseases and injuries may occur if effective measures are not introduced to deal with the main risk factors associated with the onset of these conditions. That is, the demographic engine behind the health transition will ensure that the number of non-communicable deaths will rise even if effective measures are taken. The purpose of prevention is to attenuate the rise, to postpone death to later ages, and to shift the cause structure of death away from some readily preventable and untreatable causes such as lung cancer.

## Implications for health care costs

To examine the implications of these trends for public health care spending, the study examined available information on the costs of adult health care, focusing on hospital costs. Total public and private health expenditures in Chile are approximately US$1.7 billion, or 5-6 percent of GDP, a share comparable to that in other middle-income Latin American countries, but below the median of 8-9 percent in OECD countries. Per capita expenditure in health is about US$116. Public health spending in 1992 amounted to about US$952 million or 12.23 percent of total public expenditures, up from US$717 million or 10.66 percent in 1989. In the ISAPRE system, analysis of information from 1986 to 1992 shows that income has more than tripled (284 percent increase), their operating surplus has more than doubled (114 percent increase) and health service delivery costs have more than tripled (325 percent increase). Public expenditures on health account for about 59 percent of total health spending in Chile. Annual expenditures per beneficiary amount to US$100 in the public sector, as contrasted with US$232 per beneficiary spent by the ISAPREs.

Approximately 85 percent of government expenditures on direct health services goes to hospital-based services. Based on average costs for a sample of public facilities of varying complexity, the study estimated average cost per bed day in public hospitals at US$28. In 1990, some 7,981,000 days of hospital care (about 75 percent of the total) were provided to individuals aged 15 and older, at a total cost of over US$293,720,000.

To examine the future financial burden of adult health services, the study projected costs over the next 40 years, based on the rates of hospitalization resulting from the projected prevalence of risk factors and rates of disease-specific morbidity and mortality. Without taking into account cost increases due to more intensive use of technology and other resources, medical care costs in the public sector can be expected to rise about 13 percent by the year 2000 and 38 percent by the year 2030, just as a result of an increase in the number of adults and elderly seeking care and of changes in the disease profile. In view of the above, these figures undoubtedly underestimate the possible increase in health care costs in the Chilean public health system. The incorporation of new technology would in the future compound the pressures brought on the system by the previously described demographic changes. If the current cost increases in the ISAPRE system continue, they will only exacerbate the future escalation of total health care costs. Moreover, it should be expected that as income levels rise in the future, there will be an ever-expanding appetite for more health services, as patients expect to raise their quality of life through medical care, further increasing the total health care bill.

When a successful disease prevention scenario (i.e., which reduces the prevalence of risk factors and lowers age-specific mortality rates) is simulated, total health care costs are lowered by about 10 percent or about US$40 million by the Year 2030, some US$1 million per year in savings. More importantly, over US$27 million or more than half (68 percent) of the total 40-year savings are accrued after the first ten years of intervention.

Nevertheless, the future costs of health care are somewhat ominous. The demographic and epidemiological trends analyzed in this study are likely in the future to raise financing problems for both public and private health programs in Chile since they have traditionally been financed on a "pay-as-you-go" basis in which current contributions are used to meet current expenditures. Early planning efforts would offer the opportunity to prefund, on an individual or social basis, higher consumption of services which otherwise would be financially burdensome if the entire cost had to be paid upon their delivery. For public sector beneficiaries (i.e., FONASA's affiliates), this would mean beginning to set aside now a portion of the payroll deduction earmarked for health, in order to cover anticipated future long-term care costs. As a result, a policy issue facing FONASA is whether the current payroll deduction is adequate to meet long-term care needs. In order to determine whether adequate financing is available in light of the epidemiological transition further simulation work should be conducted to examine likely future revenues and expenditures in the NHSS. In the private sector, advanced "savings" approaches similar to Individual Retirement Accounts (IRAs) need to be considered, particularly for providing and financing nursing home and advanced home health care, which remain a gap in the Chilean health system.

The urgency of developing alternative financing schemes for long-term care needs will increase in direct relation to the aging of the Chilean population. Otherwise, Chile may likely face an almost paradoxic attempt to contain health care costs while expanding benefits to a population increasing in numbers and longevity.

**The need for prevention now**

Many non-communicable illnesses and injuries are preventable through carefully designed interventions to address known risk factors. The long latency of these diseases means, however, that risk factor interventions initiated now will only begin to exert effects on mortality in future decades. The high current prevalence of some risk factors, coupled with the progressive aging of the Chilean population, means that unless some aggressive steps are taken, Chile can expect explosive growth in the demand for medical services to treat non-communicable illnesses in the coming years. This justifies the immediate implementation, or in some cases, strengthening of preventive measures, particularly those aimed at modifying risk factors among adolescents and young adults.

The current health sector reforms underway in Chile are almost exclusively reforms of curative health services. It is now timely to consider parallel reforms and upgrading of preventive health services. There are three main reasons why reforms affecting preventive services should go hand-in-hand with reforms of curative services:

(a) Reallocation of resources from curative to preventive services would, in general, enhance equity, since the major risk factors for disease are more prevalent among the poor, who therefore benefit disproportionately from investments in prevention.

(b) Reallocation of resources from curative to preventive services would, in general, enhance efficiency because preventive interventions tend to be more cost-effective (in terms of $ per DALY gained) than curative interventions.

(c) The reform of curative services provides specific opportunities to incorporate incentives for prevention, both for medical professionals and for the general population. For example, the reform of the National Health Service in the United Kingdom allowed the contracts of general practitioners to be modified to incorporate financial incentives for health promotion and screening.

### Intervention Programs: Successes and Limitations of Current Efforts

The study assessed current programs and activities carried out in Chile to prevent and manage non-communicable illnesses and injuries affecting the adult population and identified areas that need to be strengthened or expanded. Programs and interventions to reduce non-communicable illnesses and injuries may be grouped into three categories, according to their focus (individual vs. population) and location (clinical setting, work place, community). **Health promotion** refers to primary prevention strategies related to lifestyles and behaviors and may utilize a variety of methods ranging from individual counseling to public information campaigns to taxes on cigarettes and alcohol. **Health protection** encompasses actions related to the environment or which provide protection to large segments of the population, involving a community-wide rather than an individual focus. **Disease prevention** includes screening, counseling, immunization, and prophylactic interventions for individuals in clinical settings.

Most of the activities examined are directed by the MOH, which is responsible for carrying out health promotion and disease prevention activities, as well as enforcing occupational health and safety. Several other Government-sponsored commissions and agencies deal with environmental pollution and injury control.

**Health promotion and disease prevention**

The bulk of the NHSS's non-communicable disease prevention and health promotion efforts are clustered under the MOH's Adult Health Program (AHP). Currently, the AHP includes the following subprograms: Tuberculosis, Sexually Transmitted Diseases, AIDS, Cholera, Hypertension, Diabetes and Epilepsy. In addition to these, two independent non-communicable illness programs also exist in the MOH: Cancer and Mental Health.

The AHP was revised in 1991 to propose, for the first time, integrated control measures, i.e., control of risk factors common to many non-communicable diseases, such as cardiovascular disease, hypertension, diabetes and cancer. The AHP has supported activities such as anti-smoking public information and education campaigns. Also, a series of health promotion activities supported by non-governmental organizations (NGOs) have been carried out (e.g., pilot projects against smoking in the primary and secondary schools and against alcohol abuse among adolescents). With respect to specific subprograms, major improvements have been made in the past two years to standardize diagnostic and therapeutic guidelines and to increase coverage and diagnostic reliability of cervical cancer screening. The National Chemotherapy Program has improved and help to standardize cancer treatment. The mental health program is well integrated with other health services and works in coordination with other social services agencies.

However, implementation of adult-health related programs has been hampered by lack of operational funds and personnel; as a result, activities have not been continuous or systematic and have not been implemented consistently throughout the country. Despite some improvements since 1991, the current structure of activities related to adult health in Chile is fragmented, impeding the dissemination of guidelines and standards and the organization of comprehensive control efforts. Coverage of some programs, such as hypertension, remains low, and there are no programs to address certain problems of unquestionable importance, such as breast cancer and injuries, the latter being the leading cause of death among adolescents and young adults.

The public health system's infrastructure for secondary and tertiary prevention is also limited. Public hospitals, particularly outside of Santiago, lack basic diagnostic and treatment equipment and suffer from shortages of specialized personnel, resulting in common delays in treatment, especially for radiation therapy, chemotherapy and supporting laboratory services. The growing aged population will only exacerbate this problem by increasing the demand for diagnostic and treatment services.

Intersectoral coordination, particularly with the education sector, is limited. A coordinated public information campaign using mass media, which was used quite effectively in the fight against cholera, has not been enlisted to combat non-communicable disease risk factors, except for smoking.

## Health protection

Occupational health and safety has been the focus of numerous Chilean laws since 1916 which have mandated employer coverage of occupational diseases and accidents occurring to their employees and set standards for sanitation and safety in the work place. The country also has extensive national and sectoral legislation governing the protection of the environment.

Chile has establish a fairly broad legal framework for injury prevention, including traffic regulations, obligatory use of seat belts, and driver tests prior to the issuance of licenses. The National Environment Commission (CONAMA), an inter-agency body, was established in 1990 and has developed a strategic plan to reduce pollution in the Santiago Metropolitan Region. The measures that have been taken thus far by the Government are in line with those that are needed, though they should be accelerated. An ongoing project is designed to strengthen CONAMA's key functions to enable it to play a catalytic role in defining environmental policies.

Very little information is available on the prevalence of occupational exposure to hazardous and carcinogenic substances, and awareness of occupational risks on the part of both workers and managers is limited. Basic environmental data are either lacking or collected independently by each sector and are not compiled in an integrated manner to facilitate planning and monitoring.

### Policy Recommendations

The report analyzes the implications of Chile's changing demographic and epidemiologic profile and makes recommendations for five major areas of concern to policymakers: the consolidation of current reforms in the delivery of health care services; strengthening health promotion, disease prevention, and health protection programs and interventions; the efficient use of critical health care inputs; containing health care costs; and regulation of health care. Specific recommendations are summarized in boxes and categorized as either short-term (i.e., to be implemented over the next five years, during the life of the MOH's Health Sector Reform Project) or medium-term (should be carried out over the next 5-10 years).

### A. Consolidation of current reforms for reorganizing, improving, and managing the delivery of health care services

The deteriorated condition of much of the country's public hospital infrastructure and equipment compromises the public sector's ability to meet the clinical needs of those persons already suffering from non-communicable illnesses and injuries, and without significant improvement now, the country will be ill-equipped to meet the needs of the increasing numbers of persons with non-communicable conditions and injuries that were projected by the forecast model. The public hospital infrastructure must be revamped and the quality of public hospital services upgraded. The MOH's Technical Assistance and Hospital Rehabilitation (TAHRP) and Health Sector Reform (HSRP) Projects, as well as those financed by other multilateral and bilateral agencies provide a mechanism for advancing this agenda. A key aspect of the reforms is a redefinition of the role of the MOH and the concomitant decentralization of the management of health services delivery to the HSAs.

| Recommendations for Consolidating Reforms in the Delivery of Health Services | |
|---|---|
| | Short Term (Next Five Years) |
| Upgrading infrastructure | • Ambulatory referral and diagnostic and treatment centers should be established as proposed under the MOH's HSRP to make specialized services more widely available and reduce the use of higher cost hospital-based services.<br><br>• The MOH, when procuring new medical equipment, should consider emphasizing the availability of cost-effective technologies to support timely diagnosis and treatment of non-communicable illnesses and injuries. |
| Redefining the role of the MOH | • The MOH should consider strengthening its management information and epidemiological monitoring systems for guiding efforts to improve health services efficiency and effectiveness and resource allocation decisions.<br><br>• Annual service provision agreements between the MOH and the HSAs should be structured as proposed under the MOH's HSRP to provide a mechanism for periodic, systematic review of the quality, effectiveness and efficiency of services, and to ensure that goals of equity and efficiency are being achieved.<br><br>• The MOH should consider providing training and technical assistance to its staff to develop the capacity to undertake technology assessments and cost-effectiveness analysis in order to increase the efficiency and effectiveness of the resource allocation process, as well as to the HSAs to develop their own internal capacity to prepare budgets, monitor expenditures, and assess productivity, effectiveness, and quality. |

## B. Strengthening health promotion, disease prevention and health protection programs and interventions

Currently, activities to combat non-communicable illnesses and their risk factors are fragmented among different MOH programs which do not control the resources needed to implement the programs they plan. This situation has resulted in important gaps in adult health program priorities (e.g., lack of focus on cardiovascular disease, breast cancer) and impeded the dissemination of standards and guidelines and the organization of integrated control efforts. Similarly, health protection activities related to occupational health and environmental contamination are diffused among various government agencies and have been constrained by lack of coordination and data for decision-making.

It is recommended that the Chilean Government should adopt an aggressive, multisectoral approach to reducing common risk factors throughout the population, focussing on smoking, dietary and nutritional habits, sedentarism, alcohol and drug use, and mental health. In view of Chile's epidemiological profile and the potential impact of available treatments, the priority areas for early secondary prevention and diagnosis should be cardiovascular diseases, cancer and diabetes, to prevent or slow the progression of disabling complications and death.

Preventive strategies should address the control of multiple risk factors and should target the social environment to facilitate and create greater support for individual decisions to make healthy lifestyle choices. Strategies should be targeted to specific population groups on whom they can have the greatest impact. For many risk factors that are difficult to modify once they are firmly established, this means channeling resources toward primary prevention activities among school-age children and adolescents.

The MOH will need to continue to exercise a leadership role while finding ways to strengthen coordination with other ministries and government institutions, particularly the Ministry of Education. By the same measure, the MOH must find ways to enlist greater cooperation and participation of the private sector (i.e., ISAPREs, NGOs, private practitioners) in health education concerning non-communicable disease risk factors. Given the decentralized nature of the Chilean health system, the role of the MOH should be to foster the development and implementation of appropriate and timely disease prevention efforts by local governments, HSAs, municipal health authorities, NGOs, and practitioners.

| Recommendations for Strengthening Health Promotion and Protection And Disease Prevention Strategies | |
|---|---|
| | Short Term (Next Five Years) |
| Reform MOH program structure/roles | • The MOH should consider strengthening its approach for managing non-communicable illnesses and injuries to facilitate greater integration of prevention strategies and coordination of resources to address multiple risk factors. <br><br> • The definition of program priorities should be considered on the basis of the magnitude of the problem (both prevalence and severity), susceptibility to modification, and the technical and economic feasibility of the interventions proposed (i.e., cost-effectiveness). <br><br> • The MOH should consider strengthening its capabilities to collect and monitor data on occupational and environmental risks to guide planning and priority-setting. |
| Adopt multiple risk factor strategy and enhance current efforts | • Comprehensive health information campaigns, which emphasize the benefits of risk factor modification (e.g., smoking cessation during pregnancy), should be considered. <br><br> • The MOH should consider forging stronger links with other Ministries, NGOs and private providers for developing and implementing education and intervention strategies and ensuring that financing mechanisms provide appropriate incentives for such services. <br><br> • The MOH should consider expanding efforts in the early detection of hypertension and diabetes and testing of alternative strategies to increase compliance with treatment regimens. <br><br> • The MOH should consider expanding coverage of cervical cancer screening and the upgrading of capabilities for cytological diagnosis. <br><br> • The MOH should consider disseminating information on breast cancer self-diagnosis and offer breast cancer screening for high risk groups. |

| Recommendations for Strengthening Health Promotion and Protection And Disease Prevention Strategies | |
| --- | --- |
| | Short Term (Next Five Years) |
| Strengthen multisectoral coordination | • With respect to non-occupational injuries, the MOII should consider playing a leadership role in injury prevention initiatives and ensuring coordination with police and judicial agencies as well as with its own alcohol and drug programs. The successful model of inter-agency coordination used for pollution control in Metropolitan Santiago should be considered for the prevention of injuries.<br><br>• The launching of a national constituency-building initiative on health prevention and promotion priorities should be considered to raise public awareness of individual, community, and societal responsibilities in health. To this end, the following steps should be considered: (a) the development of national health goals, including specific targets for selected preventable conditions and their risk factors; (b) the creation of popular and political consensus on these goals; and (c) the development of a plan to achieve these goals, incorporating regulation, public education, and appropriate incentives to individuals, businesses, and providers.<br><br>• The Government, with private sector support, should consider establishing a funding mechanism (e.g., demand-driven fund) to channel resources to implement cost-effective interventions and facilitate funding of intersectoral activities (e.g., smoking cessation programs, education campaigns to prevent sexually transmitted diseases, including AIDS). The fund would allocate resources to public agencies, NGOs, private providers, and community groups. |

| | Recommendations for Strengthening Health Promotion and Protection And Disease Prevention Strategies |
|---|---|
| | **Medium Term** (In Five to Ten Years) |
| Strengthen multisectoral coordination | • The establishment of a mechanism to gather, on an ongoing basis, comprehensive data on the prevalence of risk factors and non-communicable illnesses and on the characteristics of groups at highest risk and to use such information for targeting interventions, should be considered.<br><br>• The establishment of programs to carry out targeted occupational health activities in high-risk industries should be considered at the HSA level and training provided to HSA personnel to implement monitoring and educational activities.<br><br>• The Government should consider supporting the establishment of systems to track and evaluate the link between environmental exposures and diseases. To this end, it should consider ways to encourage health professionals to work closely with agencies involved with pollution control. |

## C. Increasing the efficient use of medical inputs: technology, drugs and personnel

The treatment of non-communicable illnesses is characterized by the intensive use of technological inputs, including specialized personnel, sophisticated equipment, and drugs. Experience in Chile and OECD countries has shown that these inputs are a major source of cost escalation for health care. Because of the projected rapid growth in the demand for adult health services, limits on health care resources will place increasing pressure to enhance efficiency in the use of these inputs. Given the sizeable share of health resources that are channeled to private providers, an issue for the Government is how to manage competition and/or coordination with the private sector with respect to the acquisition of sophisticated medical equipment in order to avoid duplication and to contain the escalation of health care costs resulting from the increasingly intensive use of technological inputs.

Rising drug costs and the predominance of pharmaceutical therapies in the management of many non-communicable conditions affecting adults dictate that the MOH must also identify ways of controlling drug expenditures while at the same time improving the availability of efficacious drugs for early treatment and management.

Finally, another issue that merits in-depth assessment is the current skewed health personnel mix. Chile's physician market is characterized by a low number of general practitioners and a growing supply of specialists. A related issue is the geographical maldistribution of physicians and the low number of nurses vis-a-vis the evolving needs of the primary care system.

| Recommendations for Increasing the Efficient Use of Medical Inputs | |
|---|---|
| | Short Term<br>(Next Five Years) |
| Medical technology | • The Government should consider revising the methodology used for the acquisition of sophisticated medical technology to incorporate efficiency, equity, cost control and long-term maintenance concerns.<br><br>• The MOH should consider mechanisms for promoting the participation of the HSAs and of practitioners in identifying technology needs and priorities and in assessing effectiveness of practices and technologies. To this end, the medical technology inventory conducted in 3 HSAs could be extended to the entire country, to serve as the baseline for future procurement decisions.<br><br>• The MOH should consider developing mechanisms to leverage government investment in medical technology to generate additional revenues through the sale of excess diagnostic and therapeutic capacity in public facilities to private providers.<br><br>• In those areas where private institutions already possess sophisticated medical technology unavailable in public facilities, ways should be considered to encourage public providers to purchase services from private providers to avoid duplication. |

| Recommendations for Increasing the Efficient Use of Medical Inputs | |
|---|---|
| | **Short Term** (Next Five Years) |
| Pharmaceuticals | • The MOH should consider placing added attention to the design and implementation of policies and strategies to improve the selection, procurement and use of pharmaceuticals. Special emphasis should be given to promoting the use of generic equivalents.<br><br>• The development of a public information campaign should be considered to educate providers and consumers about the efficacy of generic drugs. |
| Health personnel | • The continuation of MOH-administered scholarship programs for young physicians who have served in rural areas should be considered as a way to provide incentives for recent medical graduates to locate in underserved areas.<br><br>• Health promotion and disease prevention strategies should give explicit consideration to the use of nurses and auxiliary personnel in providing care related to non-communicable illnesses. The MOH should consider developing incentives to encourage the training and employment of nurses and auxiliary personnel to fulfill these roles. |
| | **Medium Term** (In Five to Ten Years) |
| Medical technology | • The development of a broader structure for medical technology assessment which incorporates views of the MOH, the Ministry of Planning and the Ministry of Finance along with private sector agencies, private practitioners and consumer advocates, should be considered.<br><br>• Given the well developed public/private mix in Chile for the financing and delivery of health services, the feasibility of establishing integrated high technology reference programs for certain specialized procedures should be considered. |
| Health personnel | • Medical schools should consider giving greater importance to the training of general practitioners that can better respond to the country's health care needs and demands. |

### D. Containing health care costs

The rising demand for medical care engendered by the projected relative increase in persons suffering from non-communicable diseases will further strain public sector health resources and create resource allocation tensions between health promotion and protection efforts on one hand, and treatment and rehabilitation services on the other. It is imperative that Chile begin implementing strategies now that will contain health care costs and mitigate the financial burden of the increased demand for health services. In addition, wider cost recovery in public sector facilities is needed to mobilize additional resources to complement budgetary allocations.

| Recommendations for Containing Health Care Costs | |
| --- | --- |
| | Short Term <br> (Next Five Years) |
| Financing mechanisms | • It is recommended that the Government continue to implement proposed reforms in health care financing mechanisms to use a prospective payment based on overall treatment of a diagnosis at the hospital level and capitated payments for primary health care services. These reforms would likely help link the planning process to resource allocation in the production and delivery of health services and provide incentives for increased efficiency and productivity at the decentralized service delivery levels. <br><br> • Chilean policymakers should consider examining in more depth the experience of OECD countries with diagnostic-related groups (DRGs) and global budget instruments to identify ways of overcoming pitfalls in implementing these types of reimbursement systems. <br><br> • Reforms in health care financing should also consider the likely future demand for long-term care and advanced home health care and how such services will be financed both in the public and private systems. In order to determine whether adequate financing is available in light of the epidemiological transition, further simulation work on likely future revenues and expenditures in the health system as a whole should be considered. |

| Recommendations for Containing Health Care Costs | |
|---|---|
| | **Short Term**<br>(Next Five Years) |
| Increasing efficiency | • Disease prevention and management strategies should consider allocating resources to those interventions proven to be cost-effective. Efficiency criteria should receive greater explicit treatment in decision-making about resource allocation and technology acquisition.<br><br>• Since standardized cost-effectiveness data for most health interventions are lacking in Chile, the NHSS should consider gathering reliable local data to assess the cost-effectiveness of health interventions and use such data in resource allocation decisions.<br><br>• The ISAPRE system should consider assessing the underlying factors of cost escalation and devise strategies to better control health care costs. |
| Cost recovery | • The revision of existing fee schedules for services to reflect actual production costs should be considered. The NHSS should consider establishing a mechanism for periodic updating of price lists to take into account inflation and changes in production costs.<br><br>• The redefinition of the boundaries of the four income categories used to classify FONASA beneficiaries should be considered so that those who cannot afford copayments effectively do not pay them and those who can afford them do. Given the current low level of cost recovery, the overall effect would be to increase financing through copayments but drawing from a wider, more equitable base.<br><br>• The revision of the rules governing cost recovery at the individual hospital level should be considered to ensure that undue restrictions and disincentives are removed. The introduction of a mechanism for redistributing some portion of revenues from "high profit" hospitals to those where cost recovery potential is not as great should be considered.<br><br>• The strengthening of cost recovery by the public system for services rendered to ISAPRE patients should be considered. |

| Recommendations for Containing Health Care Costs | |
| --- | --- |
| | Medium Term<br>(In Five to Ten Years) |
| Financing mechanisms | • It should be considered that early planning efforts would offer the opportunity for prefunding, on an individual or social basis, higher consumption of services than would be difficult to afford if the entire cost had to be paid upon their delivery. Ways should be considered to begin to develop the financing needed to cover future health care costs, perhaps considering new schemes based on a prefunded system in the public sector or advanced "savings" approaches in the private sector, particularly for providing and financing long-term care and advanced home health care, which are still a gap in the Chilean health system. |

### E. Enhancing the regulation of health care

For many of the adult health problems discussed in this report, the intervention strategies used by the MOH have not fully utilized the range of mechanisms available to promote and protect health and prevent non-communicable disease, particularly those regulatory measures which extend beyond the traditional boundaries of the health sector. In areas such as occupational health and safety where adequate legislation already exists, the MOH's efforts at enforcement of laws have often lacked the necessary resources.

The rapid growth in number of beneficiaries and total expenditures of the ISAPREs underscore the increasingly predominant role that the private health insurance plans will have in responding to Chile's emerging epidemiological profile. Pressures to contain costs have resulted in some cost-shifting to the public sector.

| Recommendations for Enhancing the Regulation of Health Care | |
| --- | --- |
| | Short Term<br>(Next Five Years) |
| Expand Use of Regulatory Tools and Enforcement | • Greater use of fiscal and regulatory tools to control tobacco and alcohol use, including taxes on cigarettes and greater restrictions on cigarette and alcohol advertising, should be considered.<br><br>• The extension of laws and their strict enforcement for promoting widespread use of seat belts in cars and helmets when riding motorcycles, as well as to deter driving under the influence of alcohol and drugs, should be considered. |

| Recommendations for Enhancing the Regulation of Health Care | |
|---|---|
| | Short Term (Next Five Years) |
| **Regulation of the private sector** | • Discouragement of cost-shifting to the public sector, such as from denial of coverage or benefits to persons with pre-existing conditions, through enactment of proposed reforms of the ISAPRE Law and the elimination of existing public subsidies to the ISAPREs, should be considered. Also, a risk structure equalization scheme should be considered for the ISAPRE system as a whole (e.g., ISAPREs with low-risk/high-income memberships would subsidize those with high-risk/low-income profiles) to remove the economic incentive to discriminate among potential affiliates, and to control costs due to external factors, such as the risk structure of individual ISAPREs' memberships. |
| | Medium Term (In Five to Ten Years) |
| **Expand Use of Regulatory Tools and Enforcement** | • It is recommended that the Government more actively enforce compliance with existing occupational safety legislation.<br><br>• The MOH should consider, in cooperation with the HSAs, increasing its efforts to educate and inform managers and workers about occupational health risks and protective measures, as well as helping small firms set up and implement occupational health programs.<br><br>• Revisions in the primary law covering Occupational Health (Law No. 16.744) should be considered as a way to extend its coverage to workers currently not protected. |

## RESUMEN EJECUTIVO

Las transformaciones sociales y económicas de las ultimas décadas han llevado a profundos cambios demográficos y epidemiológicos en muchos países en desarrollo. El aumento de la importancia de las enfermedades no transmisibles y de las lesiones por accidentes que afectan principalmente a los adultos y a los ancianos, impone nuevos retos a los sistemas de salud en relación al control de enfermedades. Este estudio sobre la salud del adulto en Chile analiza las tendencias demográficas y epidemiológicas recientes y futuras, y sus implicaciones en los costos de los servicios de salud y en los programas de intervención, incluyendo estrategias para el manejo de la tecnología médica y para controlar los gastos en salud.

### El Sector Salud Chileno y su Financiamiento

El sector salud de Chile se caracteriza por una multiplicidad de proveedores públicos y privados, aunque el grueso de los servicios curativos y preventivos se entregan a través del Sistema Nacional de Servicios de Salud (SNSS) que es coordinado por el Ministerio de Salud (MS). El SNSS cubre el 60 por ciento de la población, entregando atención médica en 26 Servicios de Salud (SS) o sistemas regionales de salud ubicados a lo largo del país, que operan los hospitales públicos. La bien establecida red de atención primaria en Chile es manejada por los municipios, los que reciben una transferencia de recursos del gobierno central para ayudar a financiar la entrega de servicios básicos de salud. Los empleados públicos y privados contribuyen al Fondo Nacional de Salud (FONASA) y tienen la opción de obtener junto con sus dependientes atención privada a través del Sistema de Libre Elección (SLE) que normalmente es usado por un 13 por ciento de la población; bajo este sistema los usuarios pagan varios niveles de co-pagos para la atención general y especializada. Los empleados públicos y privados pueden también optar a salir enteramente fuera del SNSS, canalizando su 7 por ciento obligatorio deducido de su salario, para financiar la compra de uno de los planes de salud ofertados por los múltiples seguros de salud privados o ISAPRE, que cubren a alrededor del 21 por ciento de la población.

El SNSS depende de las siguientes fuentes de ingreso administradas por FONASA: la deducción obligatoria de los salarios (7 por ciento), que alcanza a casi el 40 por ciento de todo el ingreso; contribuciones del gobierno central, que alcanzan a otro 40 por ciento; venta de bonos a los trabajadores que usan el sistema SLE, que alcanza al 7 por ciento; cargos a los usuarios en hospitales públicos, que representan el 9 por ciento; y entradas de otras fuentes, 7 por ciento. FONASA financia la entrega de servicios en los hospitales públicos mediante reembolsos de acuerdo a un esquema de pago por servicio que pretende cubrir todos los costos operacionales excepto salarios, los que son pagados directamente por el MS. Además del pago por servicios, FONASA proporciona un presupuesto fijo adicional a cada SS para cubrir los costos de administración y ciertas inversiones y costos indirectos. La red de atención primaria municipal se financia en principio a través de reembolsos por servicios específicos entregados en cada establecimiento, pero en la práctica los pagos están determinados por topes mensuales sobre la cantidad total de los pagos que FONASA le pagará a cada muncipalidad. Además, las municipalidades mismas contribuyen con sus propios ingresos al financiamiento de los servicios de salud.

Los servicios de salud que proporcionan las ISAPRE están financiados por el descuento obligatorio del salario de sus afiliados, el que se usa para pagar primas mensuales que varían de acuerdo a los beneficios incluidos en los planes de salud, y co-pagos al momento del servicio que varían de 10 a 40 por ciento del costo de cada servicio. Mientras que el número de beneficiarios de las ISAPRE ha crecido rápidamente desde alrededor de 62.000 en 1982 a cerca de 3 millones en 1992, los efectos de importantes imperfecciones del mercado han limitado un mayor acceso al sistema de ISAPRE (por ejemplo, ciertas cláusulas de exclusión niegan cobertura por ciertos servicios), particularmente entre personas de mayor edad.

En 1990, el gobierno electo democráticamente empezó un ambicioso programa de reforma para confrontar los desbalances en el sistema de salud pública que llevó al uso ineficiente de recursos y a una mala calidad de los servicios. Estas iniciativas están encaminadas a rehabilitar la deteriorada infraestructura hospitalaria del país y a crear un nuevo nivel de atención especializada de tipo ambulatorio a fin de cubrir mejor la brecha entre atención primaria y la atención hospitalaria. El programa de reformas también contempla una mayor descentralización de responsabilidades en el manejo de la entrega de servicios de salud, y un cambio en el rol del MS a nivel central para concentrarlo en la formulación, normatización, y supervisión de las políticas de salud a nivel nacional. Un aspecto significativo del programa de reforma es la propuesta de reemplazar el sistema actual de "pago por servicio" para la asignación de recursos dentro del SNSS, por pagos fijos en relación con el diagnóstico para los hospitales y un sistema de capitación para los establecimientos de atención primaria. También se ha preparado legislación para reforzar el rol regulador del MS sobre las ISAPRE a fin de eliminar ciertas imperfecciones en ese mercado. En forma colectiva, estas reformas permitirán al SNSS responder al reto impuesto por el cambiante perfil epidemiológico.

## Transición Demográfica y Epidemiológica

En los pasados cincuenta años, Chile ha experimentado una marcada baja en las tasas de nacimiento y una declinación mantenida en las tasas de mortalidad, lo que ha disminuido la tasa anual de crecimiento de la población a 1.7 por ciento. Como resultado, la estructura etaria de la población se ha transformado, con un aumento relativo en la población de adultos jóvenes, de edad mediana, y ancianos. Estos cambios demográficos han sido acompañados por una rápida urbanización (85 por ciento de la población vive en áreas urbanas) e industrialización del país, y por los cambios en los estilos de vida, incluyendo un menor riesgo de enfermedades infecciosas. La salud de lactantes y pre-escolares ha mejorado en forma espectacular, y las muertes bajo los 15 años han contribuido a la mortalidad total en una forma decreciente (de 48 por ciento en 1960 a 9 por ciento en 1990). La mayor expectativa de vida de la población Chilena (72 años en 1990) ha dado por resultado un cambio en el perfil de salud de la población caracterizado por el predominio de las enfermedades no transmisibles y lesiones por accidentes afectando a los adultos y a los ancianos.

**El aumento de las enfermedades no transmisibles y sus factores de riesgo**

Las principales condiciones no transmisibles que afectan a la población Chilena son los desórdenes cardiovasculares, cáncer, cirrosis hepática, diabetes, enfermedad pulmonar obstructiva crónica, y lesiones por accidentes, los que juntos corresponden al 66 por ciento de las muertes. Algunas de estas condiciones son responsables por más del 40 por ciento de la carga de la enfermedad impuesta por la mortalidad prematura, de acuerdo a lo medido por años de vida ajustados por discapacidad (AVAD). El aumento en la importancia de las enfermedades no transmisibles se refleja en el creciente número de Chilenos que mueren por estas causas. Tales aumentos son una especial preocupación de salud pública porque a medida en que la población envejece es de esperar una carga de enfermedad todavía mayor en las décadas venideras.

Este estudio analizó las tendencias en los pasados 30 años de las tasas de mortalidad para cada una de las principales enfermedades no transmisibles y las lesiones por accidentes. Se encontró que la mayoría de las enfermedades cardiovasculares mostraron tasas de mortalidad estables o levemente decrecientes, aunque las tasas de hospitalización (que son las que mejor reflejan el peso para el sistema de salud del tratamiento de las enfermedades no transmisibles) han mostrado marcados aumentos. Se encontró que las tasas de mortalidad por edad para algunas de las causas principales de cáncer (vesícula biliar, pulmón, mama) estaban en aumento. Las tasas de mortalidad debido a lesiones por accidentes han experimentado una leve baja, aunque la tasa de hospitalización por lesiones por accidentes casi se ha doblado. La enfermedad pulmonar obstructiva crónica (EPOC), que incluye toda una familia de enfermedades pulmonares como la bronquitis crónica y la enfisema, ha mostrado una marcada alza en las tasas de mortalidad. Ya que la EPOC no es curable, esta condición en particular aumenta la carga de discapacidad del país. Las tasas de mortalidad y de hospitalización de la diabetes y la cirrosis hepática han registrado aumentos constantes en los pasados 30 años.

El estudio también examinó las tendencias en los principales factores de riesgo asociados con las enfermedades no transmisibles, con enfoque en el abuso en el consumo del tabaco, el alcohol y las drogas, la hipertensión, la vida sedentaria, los patrones dietéticos, los riesgos ocupacionales y la contaminación ambiental, los que han llegado a ser importantes determinantes de la morbi-mortalidad en Chile, particularmente entre grupos de bajo ingreso. La prevalencia de los principales factores de riesgos asociados con las enfermedades no transmisibles y de las lesiones por accidentes se puede resumir como sigue:

-   La prevalencia del hábito de fumar en adultos en Chile es alta; aproximadamente 38 por ciento de hombres y 25 por ciento de mujeres fuman. Ha habido un pequeño aumento en la prevalencia entre mujeres en los pasados veinte años y una leve declinación en la prevalencia entre hombres.

- El uso del alcohol está muy extendido, estimándose que aproximadamente un 15 por ciento de la población de adultos son bebedores excesivos o alcohólicos.

- El abuso de drogas ha mostrado un aumento gradual desde comienzos de la década de los 60, estimándose que afecta a un 3-5 por ciento de los adolescentes y adultos jóvenes, particularmente en las regiones del norte.

- Se estima que la hipertensión arterial está presente en 10-16 por ciento de la población adulta.

- El sedentarismo tiene especial prevalencia entre los grupos de menores ingresos y en mujeres, ya que el ejercicio recreacional no es un hábito ampliamente aceptado en Chile.

- Factores de riesgo importante relacionados con la nutrición incluyen obesidad, que afecta en particular a las mujeres de bajos recursos, colesterol alto entre los niveles socioeconómicos altos, y baja ingesta de calcio.

- La contaminación ambiental es un factor de riesgo significativo para enfermedades respiratorias entre los habitantes urbanos, especialmente entre los residentes de Santiago.

Aunque la prevalencia de muchos factores de riesgo para las enfermedades no transmisibles es alta en Chile, las tasas de mortalidad por estas condiciones no han alcanzado todavía los niveles que se encuentran en los países industrializados. Esto se debe a que la mayoría de las enfermedades no transmisibles tienen un período de latencia largo, de modo que las manifestaciones clínicas de las enfermedades sólo se harán aparentes luego de períodos largos que fluctúan entre 10 y 30 años, después de la exposición inicial a factores de riesgo. Las tendencias de las enfermedades actuales en Chile son, por tanto, el producto de los pasados 20 a 30 años de exposición a factores de riesgo. El aumento en la prevalencia de los principales factores de riesgo durante las pasadas tres décadas sugiere que las enfermedades no transmisibles en Chile no han alcanzado todavía la etapa en sus historias naturales en la cual todos sus efectos fatales se hacen sentir y que dichas enfermedades continuarán creciendo en magnitud y prominencia.

## La futura carga de la enfermedad

Para estimar la carga para el sistema de salud de las probables tendencias demográficas y epidemiológicas futuras, se desarrolló un modelo para proyectar, para los próximos cuarenta años, la morbilidad y mortalidad por las principales enfermedades no transmisibles y las lesiones por accidentes en Chile. Este modelo esta basado en la actual prevalencia de factores de riesgo y tasas de mortalidad. En el modelo se consideraron dos escenarios: un escenario de base, reflejando una continuación de las tendencias actuales, y un escenario de intervención, en el cual la prevalencia de los factores de riesgo y la mortalidad específica por edad fueron reducidas selectivamente a través del tiempo. El escenario base y el escenario optimista fueron comparados a fin de estimar el impacto que posibles estrategias de prevención de las enfermedades podría tener en los futuros requerimientos de los servicios de salud.

Dentro de este contexto, es importante notar que en la medida que los países se desarrollan, la mortalidad general baja, a pesar de que aumenta la prevalencia de ciertos factores de riesgo (por ejemplo, consumo de alcohol y alimentos altos en grasa, y tabaco). La relación que existe entre la riqueza nacional y el ingreso por habitante con una disminución del total de la mortalidad se puede observar claramente en las estadísticas a nivel mundial. Chile se ha beneficiado en las últimas décadas en la reducción de la mortalidad y sin duda continuará haciéndolo. A manera global está previsto en el modelo que la tendencia observada en Chile a la reducción de la mortalidad se mantendrá en el futuro a medida que el país continúe desarrollándose y aumentando en riqueza.

Las proyecciones muestran que la mortalidad, para seis de las principales enfermedades no transmisibles y lesiones por accidentes, continuará creciendo debido al envejecimiento relativo de la población Chilena y a la creciente exposición a los principales factores de riesgo. El modelo sugiere que estrategias agresivas para la prevención de las enfermedades, especialmente para la enfermedad coronaria y las enfermedades respiratorias crónicas, ayudarán a hacer más lentos los esperados aumentos en la mortalidad, especialmente entre los grupos de edad media. También se espera que las intervenciones reduzcan las pérdidas en términos de AVAD debidas a varias condiciones no transmisibles, en alrededor del 9 por ciento para los hombres y 7 por ciento para las mujeres. Más importante, el efecto fuertemente positivo de la estrategia preventiva en los AVAD salvados se obtiene después de los primeros 10 años de intervención. Sin embargo, el efecto de las intervenciones sobre algunas causas de muerte probablemente no será visible sino después de al menos 20 años.

A pesar de estas restricciones sobre los beneficios del control de las enfermedades no transmisibles, el modelo de proyección mostró que, en el futuro, a medida que la población envejece, puede producirse un mayor número de muertes, enfermedades e incapacidades si no se toman medidas efectivas para controlar los principales factores de riesgo asociados con el inicio de las condiciones no transmisibles.

## Implicaciones sobre los costos de los servicios de salud

Para examinar las implicaciones de estas tendencias en los costos de los servicios de salud, el estudio revisó la información disponible sobre los costos de los servicios hospitalarios. Los gastos totales de salud pública y privada en Chile son de aproximadamente US$1.7 mil millones, ó 5-6 por ciento del producto nacional bruto, una proporción comparable a la de otros países latinoamericanos de ingresos medianos, pero menor que la media de 8-9 por ciento en los países desarrollados. El gasto en salud por habitante es de alrededor de US$116. El gasto público en salud ascendió en 1992 a alrededor de US$952 millones o 12.23 por ciento del gasto público total, encima de los US$717 millones o 10.66 por ciento del gasto público total en 1989. En el sistema ISAPRE, un análisis de la información desde 1986 a 1992 muestra que los ingresos se han más que triplicado (284 por ciento de aumento), el excedente operacional se ha más que doblado (114 por ciento de aumento) y los gastos de entrega de servicios de salud se han más que triplicado (325 por ciento de aumento). Los gastos públicos en salud corresponden a alrededor del 59 por ciento de todo el gasto en salud en Chile. Los gastos anuales por beneficiario llegan a US$100 en el sector público, en contraste con los US$232 por beneficiario que gastan las ISAPRE.

Aproximadamente el 85 por ciento del gasto público en prestaciones directas de salud se destinan a los servicios hospitalarios. En base al promedio de costos de una muestra de instituciones públicas de variada complejidad, el estudio estimó un costo promedio por día-cama en hospitales públicos de US$28. En 1990 alrededor de 7.981.000 días de atención hospitalaria (alrededor del 75 por ciento del total) fue proporcionada a personas mayores de 15 años, a un costo total de más de US$293 millones.

Para examinar el peso futuro del costo de los servicios de salud para adultos, el estudio proyecto costos para los próximos 40 años, basados en las tasas de morbilidad y mortalidad de enfermedades específicas. Sin tomar en cuenta los posibles aumentos en los costos debido al uso más intensivo de tecnología y otros insumos médicos, se puede esperar que los costos de los servicios de salud en el sector público aumenten alrededor del 13 por ciento para el año 2000 y 38 por ciento para el año 2030, sólo como resultado de un aumento en el número de adultos que demanden una mayor cantidad de servicios de salud asociado al cambiante perfil de la morbilidad.

En vista de lo anterior, sin duda estas figuras desestiman el posible incremento de los costos del cuidado de salud, dentro del sistema público de salud en Chile. La incorporación de nueva tecnología dará lugar a que en el futuro se incrementen las presiones que el sistema acarea a causa de los cambios demográficos y epidemiológicos previamente descritos. Si el actual aumento de costos en el sistema de ISAPRE continua, ello únicamente exacerbará la futura escalada del costo total del cuidado de salud. Por otra parte, debe esperarse que, en la medida de que los niveles de ingreso se eleven en el futuro, se seguirá incrementando la demanda por más servicios de salud, ya que los pacientes esperarán mejorar su calidad de vida, por medio del cuidado médico, lo que elevará el costo de salud.

Si se simula un escenario exitoso de prevención de la enfermedad (el cual reduce la prevalencia de factores de riesgo y disminuye las tasas de mortalidad en grupos de edad específicos), los costos totales de la atención de salud disminuyen en alrededor del 10 por ciento o alrededor de US$40 millones para el año 2030, o sea US$1 millón de ahorro por año. Más importante, cerca de US$27 millones o más de la mitad (68 por ciento) de los ahorros totales en los 40 años se obtienen en los primeros 10 años de intervención. No obstante, los costos futuros del cuidado de salud son alarmantes. Las tendencias demográficas y epidemiológicas analizadas en este estudio probablemente causarán problemas financieros, tanto para los programas de salud públicos como privados en Chile ya que tradicionalmente han estado financiados sobre la base de un sistema en el cual las contribuciones presentes se usan para cubrir los gastos corrientes. Para determinar si el financiamiento disponible es apropiado, de acuerdo a la transición epidemiológica, se necesitan hacer mas simulaciones de los ingresos y de los gastos del sector salud. Planes tempranos de ahorro ofrecerán la oportunidad de pagar por adelantado, ya sea a nivel individual o social, un consumo más alto de servicios de salud, que si tuvieran que ser pagados en el momento de obtención del servicio constituirían una carga financiera considerable. Para los beneficiarios del sector público (los miembros de FONASA) eso representaría el separar una porción de sus contribuciones basadas en la deducción salarial para salud, para poder cubrir por anticipado los costos futuros de las atenciones de salud de larga duración. Como resultado, FONASA tendrá que discernir si la deducción del 7 por ciento de los salarios es la cantidad adecuada para financiar las necesidades de atención de largo término. Para eso, una evaluación minuciosa es necesaria para poder determinar si la raíz del problema son las fluctuaciones del consumo de corto término, que van a ser compensadas a lo largo del tiempo por una redistribución interna de los fondos, y en consecuencia, financiada por la deducción del salario del 7 por ciento, o si el problema tiene que ver con el costo global del sistema dado el nuevo perfil epidemiológico, que no puede ser financiado con la contribución actual del 7 por ciento del salario. En el sector privado, sistemas de ahorro anticipado, similar a las cuentas de retiro individual, debe ser considerado especialmente para proveer y financiar cuidados a largo plazo, lo que todavía es un vacío en el sistema de salud Chileno. La urgencia de desarrollar sistemas alternativos de financiamiento para cuidados a largo plazo aumentará en forma directamente proporcional al envejecimiento de la población Chilena. Adicionalmente, medidas para fortalecer la responsabilidad personal del cuidado de la salud deben ser promovidas, de no ser así Chile podría encarar un paradójico intento de contener los costos de salud, mientras extiende los beneficios a una población que aumenta en número y longevidad.

## La necesidad de la prevención de las enfermedades

Muchas enfermedades no transmisibles y lesiones por accidentes se pueden prevenir por medio de intervenciones cuidadosamente diseñadas, dirigidas a los factores de riesgo conocidos. La larga latencia de estas enfermedades significa, sin embargo, que las intervenciones en los factores de riesgo iniciadas ahora sólo empezarán a tener efecto en la mortalidad en las décadas futuras. La alta prevalencia actual de algunos factores de riesgo, junto con el progresivo envejecimiento de la población Chilena significa que, a menos que se den algunos pasos agresivos, Chile puede esperar un crecimiento explosivo de la demanda por servicios médicos para tratar enfermedades no transmisibles en los años venideros. Esto justifica la implementación inmediata, o en algunos casos, el reforzamiento de medidas preventivas, particularmente aquellas destinadas a modificar los factores de riesgo entre los adolescentes y los adultos jóvenes.

Las reformas del sector que se están ejecutando en Chile afectan casi exclusivamente a la prestación de servicios curativos. Conviene considerar reformas paralelas y mejoras en la provisión de servicios preventivos. Hay tres razones por las que las reformas de los servicios preventivos deben acompañar a las reformas en la prestación de servicios curativos:

(a) La redistribución de recursos de los servicios curativos a los preventivos permitirán mejorar la equidad ya que los factores de riesgo asociados a las enfermedades no transmisibles son más prevalentes entre los pobres, quienes se beneficiarán más de las inversiones que se hagan en prevención.

(b) La redistribución de recursos de los servicios curativos a los preventivos, en general, permitirá aumentar la eficiencia, puesto que las intervenciones preventivas tienden a tener un mejor costo-efectividad (en términos de US dólares por AVAD ganado), que las intervenciones de tipo curativas.

(c) La reforma del sistema curativo provee específicamente oportunidades para incorporar incentivos de prevención, tanto para profesionales en medicina como para la población en general. Por ejemplo, la reforma del Servicio Nacional de Salud en Gran Bretaña permitió que los contratos de los médicos generales se modificaran con la incorporación de incentivos de carácter financiero para fomentar actividades de promoción de la salud, como por ejemplo, los exámenes periódicos de detección precoz.

### Programas de Intervención: Exitos y Limitaciones de los Esfuerzos Actuales

El estudio evaluó los programas actuales y las actividades llevadas a cabo en Chile para prevenir y manejar las enfermedades no transmisibles y las lesiones por accidentes que afectan a la población adulta e identificó áreas que necesitan ser reforzadas o expandidas. Los programas e intervenciones para reducir las enfermedades crónicas no transmisibles y las lesiones por accidentes pueden agruparse en tres categorías, de acuerdo a su enfoque (individual vs. poblacional) y ubicación (localización clínica, lugar de trabajo, comunidad). La promoción de la salud se refiere a estrategias de prevención primaria relacionadas a los estilos de vida y puede utilizar una variedad de métodos que van desde consejo individual a campañas de información pública y a impuestos sobre los cigarrillos y el alcohol. La protección de la salud comprende acciones relacionadas al entorno o las que proporcionan protección a grandes segmentos de la población, involucrando a la comunidad como un todo más que a individuos. La prevención de la enfermedad incluye la detección precoz, consejos, inmunizaciones e intervenciones profilácticas en campos clínicos en forma individual.

La mayoría de las actividades examinadas son dirigidas por el MS, que es el ente responsable de realizar las actividades de promoción de la salud y prevención de la enfermedad, así como de reforzar la salud ocupacional. Varias otras comisiones respaldadas por el gobierno y otras agencias se preocupan de la contaminación ambiental y el control de los accidentes.

## Promoción de la salud y prevención de la enfermedad

El grueso de los esfuerzos del SNSS para la prevención de las enfermedades no transmisibles y la promoción de la salud se agrupan bajo el Programa para la Salud del Adulto (PSA) del MS. Actualmente, el PSA incluye los siguientes subprogramas: tuberculosis, enfermedades de transmisión sexual, SIDA, cólera, hipertensión, diabetes y epilepsia. Además, también existen en el MS dos programas independientes de enfermedades no transmisibles: cáncer y enfermedades mentales.

El PSA fue revisado en 1991 a fin de proponer, por primera vez, medidas de control integradas, por ejemplo, control de los factores de riesgo comunes a muchas enfermedades no transmisibles tales como las enfermedades cardiovasculares, la hipertensión, la diabetes y el cáncer. El PSA ha respaldado actividades tales como información pública contra el tabaquismo y campañas educacionales. Asimismo, una serie de actividades de promoción de la salud respaldadas por organizaciones no gubernamentales (ONG) se han llevado a cabo (por ejemplo, proyectos piloto contra el cigarrillo en colegios de educación básica y media y contra el abuso del alcohol entre los adolescentes). Con respecto a subprogramas específicos, en los últimos dos años se han hecho grandes esfuerzos para estandarizar lineamientos diagnósticos y terapéuticos y para aumentar la cobertura y confiabilidad diagnóstica de la detección precoz del cáncer del cuello cervico-uterino. El Programa Nacional de Quimioterapia ha mejorado y ayudado a estandarizar el tratamiento del cáncer. El programa de salud mental está bien integrado con otros servicios de salud y funciona en coordinación con otras agencias de servicio social.

Sin embargo, la implementación de programas relacionados con la salud del adulto se ha visto dificultada por la falta de recursos; como resultado, las actividades no han sido continuas o sistemáticas y no se han implementado adecuadamente a través del país. A pesar de algunas mejoras desde 1991, la estructura actual de las actividades relacionadas con la salud del adulto en Chile está fragmentada, impidiendo la diseminación de lineamientos y normas y la organización de esfuerzos de control comprensivos. La cobertura de algunos programas tales como el programa para el control de la hipertensión, permanece baja y no hay programas que se dirijan a ciertos problemas de incuestionable importancia como el cáncer de la mama y las lesiones por accidentes, siendo éste último la principal causa de muerte entre adolescentes y adultos jóvenes.

La infraestructura del sistema de salud pública para prevención secundaria y terciaria es también limitada. Los hospitales públicos, particularmente fuera de Santiago, carecen de equipo básico para diagnóstico y tratamiento y sufren de falta de personal especializado, lo que da por resultado retrasos en los tratamientos, especialmente en la terapia de radiación, quimioterapia y servicios de apoyo de laboratorio. La creciente población en la tercera edad sólo exacerbará este problema al aumentar la demanda de servicios de diagnósticos y de tratamiento.

La coordinación intersectorial, particularmente con el sector educacional, es limitada. No se ha hecho uso de una campaña pública, coordinada, utilizando medios masivos, como la que fue usada con gran efectividad en la lucha contra el cólera, para combatir los factores de riesgo asociados a las enfermedades no transmisibles, excepto la campaña contra el tabaquismo.

## Protección de la salud

La salud ocupacional han sido el foco de numerosas leyes en Chile desde 1916, que han exigido cobertura del empleador para enfermedades ocupacionales y accidentes que ocurran a sus empleados y han fijado estándares sanitarios y de seguridad en el lugar de trabajo. El país tiene también extensa legislación nacional y sectorial que regula la protección del ambiente.

Chile ha establecido un amplio marco legal para la prevención de accidentes, incluyendo regulaciones de tránsito, uso obligatorio del cinturón de seguridad y exámenes a los conductores antes de otorgar licencia para conducir. La Comisión Nacional del Ambiente (CONAMA) se estableció en 1990 y ha desarrollado un plan estratégico para reducir la contaminación del aire en la Región Metropolitana de Santiago. Las medidas que se han tomado hasta ahora están de acuerdo con lo que se necesita, aunque deberían acelerarse. Hay un proyecto en marcha diseñado para reforzar la capacidad institucional de CONAMA.

Hay muy poca información disponible sobre la prevalencia de los factores de riesgo ocupacionales (por ejemplo, substancias carcinogénicas). Los datos básicos ambientales no existen, o son recolectados independientemente por cada sector.

## Recomendaciones de Política

En el presente estudio se analiza el reto que implica el cambiante perfil demográfico y epidemiológico de Chile y se hacen recomendaciones con respecto a cinco esferas principales de interés para los encargados de formular políticas: la consolidación de las reformas actuales en la prestación de servicios de salud; el fortalecimiento de los programas e intervenciones de promoción y protección de la salud y de prevención de las enfermedades; el uso eficiente de insumos críticos para la atención de salud; el control de los costos de la atención de salud, y la reglamentación de ésta. Las recomendaciones concretas se resumen en recuadros y se clasifican como de corto plazo (por ejemplo, las que podrían ser ejecutadas dentro de los próximos cinco años) o a mediano plazo (las que podrían realizarse dentro de los próximos cinco a diez años).

## A. Consolidación de las reformas actuales para la reorganización y la mejora de la prestación de servicios de salud

El mal estado en que está gran parte de la infraestructura y el equipo de los hospitales estatales del país menoscaba la capacidad del sector público para satisfacer las necesidades clínicas de las personas que ya padecen enfermedades no transmisibles, y si no se hacen cuanto antes mejoras significativas, el país estará mal equipado para hacer frente a las necesidades de un número creciente de personas con dolencias no transmisibles que se prevé en el modelo de proyección. Es preciso mejorar la infraestructura de los hospitales estatales y la calidad de los servicios que prestan. Los Proyectos de Asistencia Técnica y Rehabilitación Hospitalaria y de Reforma del Sector de Salud del MS, que cuentan con el apoyo financiero del Banco Mundial, así como los financiados por otros organismos multilaterales y bilaterales proporcionan un mecanismo para la realización de estas tareas. Un aspecto clave de las reformas es una nueva definición del papel del MS y la descentralización concomitante de la gestión administrativa hacia los SS.

| Recomendaciones para la consolidación de las reformas en la prestación de servicios de salud | |
|---|---|
| | A corto plazo (próximos cinco años) |
| Mejora de la infraestructura | • Podrían establecerse los centros ambulatorios de diagnóstico y de tratamiento previstos en el Proyecto de Reforma del Sector de Salud del MS a fin de ampliar la disponibilidad de servicios especializados y reducir el uso de servicios más costosos en los hospitales.<br><br>• Al comprar equipo nuevo se podría insistir en la adquisición de tecnologías con alto costo-efectividad, para apoyar el diagnóstico y el tratamiento oportunos de enfermedades no transmisibles y lesiones por accidentes. |
| Nueva definición del papel del Ministerio de Salud | • Es preciso fortalecer los sistemas de información para la administración y de vigilancia epidemiológica del MS, a fin de permitirle orientar sus esfuerzos hacia la mejora de la eficacia y la eficiencia de los servicios de salud y de las decisiones en materia de asignación de recursos.<br><br>• Los acuerdos anuales de prestación de servicios propuestos entre el MS y los SS podrían estructurarse de forma que se prevea en ellos un mecanismo para el examen periódico y sistemático de la calidad, la eficacia y la eficiencia de los servicios con el fin de asegurar que se logren los objetivos de equidad y eficiencia.<br><br>• Podría proporcionarse capacitación y asistencia técnica al personal del MS para que pueda llevar a cabo un análisis de la eficacia en función de los costos encaminados a mejorar la eficiencia en el proceso de asignación de recursos, así como también al de los SS, a fin de desarrollar su propia capacidad interna para preparar presupuestos, controlar los gastos y evaluar la productividad y la calidad. |

## B. Fortalecimiento de los programas e intervenciones de promoción y protección de la salud y de prevención de las enfermedades

Actualmente, las actividades destinadas a combatir la enfermedades no transmisibles y sus factores de riesgo están fragmentadas entre diferentes programas del MS que no tienen control sobre los recursos necesarios para poner en práctica los planes que elaboran. Esta situación ha dado como resultado deficiencias importantes en las prioridades de los programas de salud para adultos (por ejemplo, falta de concentración en las enfermedades cardiovasculares, el cáncer de mama, etc.) y han dificultado la difusión de normas y directrices y la organización de esfuerzos integrados de control. De manera análoga, las actividades de protección de la salud relacionadas con la salud ocupacional y la contaminación del medio ambiente están divididas entre varios organismos gubernamentales y se han visto limitadas por la falta de coordinación y de datos para la adopción de decisiones.

Se recomienda que el gobierno de Chile adopte un enfoque multisectorial para reducir factores de riesgo comunes en toda la población, concentrando la atención en el hábito de fumar, los hábitos alimentarios, la falta de actividad física, el consumo de alcohol y de drogas y la salud mental. Dado el perfil epidemiológico de Chile y el impacto potencial de los tratamientos disponibles, las esferas prioritarias para la prevención secundaria y el diagnóstico oportuno deberían ser las enfermedades cardiovasculares, el cáncer y la diabetes, con el objetivo de prevenir o detener la progresión de complicaciones incapacitantes y las defunciones.

En las estrategias de prevención se debe procurar controlar los factores de riesgo múltiples y concentrar la atención en un medio social que facilite y apoye las decisiones individuales de vivir de manera más saludable. Las estrategias deberían orientarse hacia los grupos de población específicos en que pueden tener mayor impacto. En el caso de muchos factores de riesgo que son difíciles de modificar una vez firmemente establecidos, esto implica encauzar los recursos hacia actividades de prevención primaria entre los niños en edad escolar y los adolescentes.

El MS deberá seguir teniendo una función rectora mientras se encuentran formas de fortalecer la coordinación con otros ministerios e instituciones gubernamentales, en particular el Ministerio de Educación. De manera análoga, el MS debe hallar formas de aumentar la cooperación y la participación del sector privado (por ejemplo, las ISAPRE, las organizaciones no gubernamentales, los médicos particulares) en las actividades de educación de salud sobre los factores de riesgo para las enfermedades no transmisibles. Dada la naturaleza descentralizada del sistema de salud Chileno, el papel del MS sería el de promover el desarrollo y la ejecución de estrategias de prevención de las enfermedades no transmisibles por parte de los gobiernos locales, los SS, las autoridades municipales, las ONGs y los profesionales de la salud.

| Recomendaciones para la promoción y la protección de la salud y estrategias para la prevención de las enfermedades | |
| --- | --- |
| | **A corto plazo**<br>**(próximos cinco años)** |
| Reforma de la estructura de los programas del Ministerio de Salud y de sus funciones | • El Ministerio de Salud podría fortalecer su enfoque para el manejo de las enfermedades no transmisibles y las lesiones por accidentes a fin de facilitar una mayor integración de las estrategias de prevención y una mejor coordinación de los recursos para hacer frente a los factores de riesgo múltiples.<br><br>• Las prioridades de los programas podrían seleccionarse sobre la base de la magnitud de los problemas (prevalencia y gravedad), las posibilidades de modificación y la viabilidad técnica y económica de las intervenciones propuestas (es decir, la eficacia en función de los costos).<br><br>• El Ministerio de Salud podría fortalecer su capacidad para reunir datos sobre riesgos ocupacionales y ambientales a fin de orientar la planeación y el establecimiento de prioridades. |
| Adopción de una estrategia para encarar los factores de riesgo múltiples, y mejora de los esfuerzos actuales | • Podrían iniciarse campañas amplias de información sanitaria en que se haga hincapié en los beneficios de la modificación de hábitos que constituyen factores de riesgo (por ejemplo, dejar de fumar durante el embarazo).<br><br>• El Ministerio de Salud podría establecer vínculos más estrechos con otros ministerios, con las organizaciones no gubernamentales y con los médicos y otros proveedores de atención sanitaria particulares a fin de elaborar y aplicar estrategias de educación e intervención y de asegurar que los mecanismos de financiación proporcionen incentivos apropiados para la prestación de esos servicios. |

| Recomendaciones para la promoción y la protección de la salud y estrategias para la prevención de las enfermedades | |
|---|---|
| | • El Ministerio de Salud podría ampliar los esfuerzos de detección precoz de la hipertensión y la diabetes y ensayar distintas estrategias para mejorar el cumplimiento de los regímenes de tratamiento.<br><br>• El Ministerio de Salud podría ampliar la cobertura de las campañas de detección del cáncer cervico-uterino y continuar mejorando la capacidad de diagnóstico citológico.<br><br>• El Ministerio de Salud podría difundir información sobre la detección del cáncer de mama por la propia paciente y ofrecer servicios de diagnóstico de esta enfermedad a los grupos de alto riesgo. |
| Fortalecimiento de la coordinación multisectorial | • Con respecto a las lesiones no ocupacionales, el Ministerio de Salud podría tomar la iniciativa en la prevención de éstas y asegurar la coordinación con la policía y los organismos judiciales, así como con sus propios programas contra el alcoholismo y el uso de drogas. Para la prevención de las lesiones podría adoptarse el modelo exitoso de coordinación interorganizacional utilizado para el control de la contaminación en el área metropolitana de Santiago.<br><br>• Podría lanzarse una campaña nacional de difusión de la necesidad de prevenir enfermedades no transmisibles y reducir los costos de la atención de salud a fin de despertar la conciencia del público sobre la responsabilidad individual, comunitaria y social en materia de salud y promover un uso más eficiente de los recursos. Para ese fin, podrían considerarse los siguientes pasos: (a) la definición de objetivos nacionales de salud, incluyendo metas para enfermedades prevenibles y sus factores de riesgo; (b) establecer un consenso popular y político amplio sobre esos objetivos nacionales de salud; y (c) el desarrollo de un programa para alcanzar esos objetivos, incorporando la regulación en salud, la educación comunitaria y los incentivos apropiados a los individuos, las compañías y los profesionales de la salud. |

| Recomendaciones para la promoción y la protección de la salud y estrategias para la prevención de las enfermedades | |
|---|---|
| | • El gobierno, con apoyo del sector privado y de la comunidad, podría establecer un mecanismo de financiación (por ejemplo, un fondo supeditado a la demanda) para encauzar recursos hacia la aplicación de medidas eficaces y de alto costo efectividad y facilitar la financiación de actividades intersectoriales (por ejemplo, programas para dejar de fumar, campañas de educación para prevenir las enfermedades de transmisión sexual, incluyendo el SIDA). El fondo asignaría recursos a los organismos estatales, organizaciones no gubernamentales, médicos y proveedores de atención de salud particulares y agrupaciones comunitarias. |
| | **A mediano plazo** <br> **(dentro de cinco a diez años)** |
| Fortalecimiento de la coordinación·multisectorial | • Podría establecerse un mecanismo para recolectar en forma permanente datos sobre la prevalencia de factores de riesgo y enfermedades no transmisibles y sobre las características de los grupos de más alto riesgo, y para utilizar esa información a la hora de determinar los beneficiarios de las intervenciones. <br><br> • Podrían establecerse a nivel de los SS programas para llevar a cabo actividades específicas de salud ocupacional en las industrias de alto riesgo, y darse capacitación al personal de esos Servicios para llevar a cabo actividades de seguimiento y educación. <br><br> • El gobierno podría apoyar el establecimiento de sistemas para vigilar y evaluar los vínculos entre la exposición en el medio ambiente y las enfermedades. Con este fin, podría alentarse a los profesionales de la salud a que trabajen en estrecha cooperación con los organismos que se ocupan de reducir la contaminación ambiental. |

### C. Uso eficiente de los insumos médicos: tecnologías, medicamentos y personal

El tratamiento de las enfermedades no transmisibles se caracteriza por el uso intensivo de insumos médicos, a saber, personal especializado, equipo sofisticado y medicamentos. La experiencia en Chile y en los países de la OCDE ha demostrado que estos insumos son una causa importante del aumento de los costos de la atención de salud. A causa del rápido crecimiento que se prevé de la demanda de servicios de salud para adultos, la limitación de los recursos destinados a la atención de salud creará una presión cada vez mayor para mejorar la eficiencia en el uso de esos insumos. Dada la proporción considerable de los recursos de salud que se encauza hacia los proveedores de atención de salud particulares, el gobierno debe encarar la cuestión de cómo manejar la competencia y/o la coordinación con el sector privado, en lo que respecta a la adquisición de equipo médico complejo, a fin de evitar la duplicación en las inversiones y contener la escalada de los costos de la atención de salud que entraña el uso cada vez más intensivo de la tecnología médica.

El aumento del costo de los medicamentos y el predominio de terapias con fármacos, en el tratamiento de muchas dolencias no transmisibles que afectan a los adultos, hacen necesario que el MS establezca también formas de controlar los gastos en medicamentos, al mismo tiempo que se aumenta la disponibilidad de fármacos eficaces para el tratamiento precoz.

Por último, otra cuestión que merece una evaluación a fondo es la composición actual del personal de salud. El mercado médico en Chile se caracteriza por un número reducido de médicos generales y una cantidad creciente de especialistas. Un problema conexo es la mala distribución geográfica de los médicos y el pequeño número de enfermeras, en relación con las necesidades cambiantes del sistema de atención primaria.

| Recomendaciones para mejorar el uso eficiente de los insumos médicos | |
|---|---|
| | **A corto plazo (dentro de los próximos cinco años)** |
| Tecnología médica | • Podría revisarse la metodología que utiliza el gobierno para orientar la adquisición de tecnología médica sofisticada a fin de incorporar elementos de eficiencia, equidad, control de costos y mantenimiento a largo plazo. La adquisición de una cantidad considerable de equipo médico que se contempla en el marco de los proyectos de inversión en marcha podría orientarse de acuerdo con este nuevo criterio. |

| Recomendaciones para mejorar el uso eficiente de los insumos médicos | |
| --- | --- |
| | • Podrían crearse mecanismos para hacer que los SS y los médicos participen en el proceso de identificación de las necesidades y prioridades tecnológicas y en la evaluación de la eficacia de las prácticas médicas y las tecnologías. <br><br> • El Ministerio de Salud podría desarrollar mecanismos para asegurar que las nuevas inversiones en tecnologías médicas generen recursos adicionales para el SNSS mediante el cobro por los servicios de diagnóstico y de tratamiento en los establecimientos asistenciales públicos a los afiliados de las ISAPRE. <br><br> • En las esferas en que las instituciones privadas ya cuentan con tecnologías médicas sofisticadas de que no se dispone en las instituciones públicas, podría alentarse a éstas a contratar servicios a proveedores particulares a fin de evitar la duplicación en las inversiones en equipo médico. |
| Productos farmacéuticos | • El Ministerio de Salud podría concentrar la atención en el diseño y aplicación de políticas y estrategias para mejorar la selección, adquisición y uso de productos farmacéuticos. Debe hacerse hincapié en la promoción del uso de equivalentes genéricos. <br><br> • Podría emprenderse una campaña de información pública para educar a los proveedores y consumidores sobre la eficacia de los medicamentos genéricos. |

| Recomendaciones para mejorar el uso eficiente de los insumos médicos | |
|---|---|
| Personal de salud | • Podrían mantenerse los programas de becas del Ministerio de Salud para médicos jóvenes que han prestado servicios en zonas rurales a fin de proporcionar incentivos para que los médicos recién graduados ejerzan en zonas subatendidas.<br><br>• En las estrategias de promoción de la salud y prevención de las enfermedades podría considerarse, en forma explícita, el empleo de personal de enfermería para la atención sanitaria relacionada con enfermedades no transmisibles. El Ministerio de Salud podría crear incentivos para alentar la capacitación y el empleo de personal de enfermería para desempeñar esas funciones. |
| | **A mediano plazo**<br>**(dentro de cinco a diez años)** |
| Tecnología médica | • Podría crearse un mecanismo más amplio para la evaluación de la tecnología médica en el que se consideren las opiniones de los Ministerios de Salud, Planificación y Hacienda, así como las de los organismos del sector privado.<br><br>• Dada la mezcla pública/privada en Chile para la financiación y la prestación de servicios de salud, el gobierno podría estudiar la viabilidad de establecer programas integrados de alta tecnología para ciertos procedimientos especializados. |
| Personal de salud | • El Ministerio de Salud podría alentar a las facultades de medicina a que den más importancia a la formación de médicos generales, que puedan responder mejor a las necesidades y demandas en materia de salud del país. |

### D. Contención de los costos de la atención de salud

La creciente demanda de atención médica, generada por el aumento relativo que se prevé de las personas con enfermedades no transmisibles, incrementará la presión sobre los recursos del sector de salud y creará tensiones con respecto a la asignación de éstos entre los programas de promoción y protección de la salud, por un lado, y los servicios de tratamiento y rehabilitación, por otro. Es imperativo que en Chile se empiecen ya a poner en práctica estrategias para contener los costos de la atención de salud y reducir la carga financiera que impone la mayor demanda de servicios de salud. Además, es preciso aumentar la recuperación de los costos en los establecimientos asistenciales públicos sobre una base más amplia y equitativa para movilizar recursos adicionales que permitan complementar las asignaciones presupuestarias.

| Recomendaciones para contener los costos de la atención de salud | |
| --- | --- |
| | **A corto plazo** <br> **(dentro de los próximos cinco años)** |
| Mecanismos de financiamiento | • Se recomienda que el gobierno siga aplicando las reformas propuestas a los mecanismos de financiamiento de la atención de salud y utilice pagos relacionados con el tratamiento global de un diagnóstico a nivel hospitalario y pagos por capitación para los servicios de atención primaria de salud. Estas reformas podrían ayudar a vincular el proceso de planificación con la asignación de recursos en la producción y prestación de servicios de salud y proporcionarán incentivos para aumentar la eficiencia y la productividad en los niveles descentralizados de prestación de los servicios. <br><br> • Para la formulación de las políticas de salud en Chile se podría examinar más a fondo la experiencia de los países de la OCDE con la utilización de mecanismos de pago asociados al tratamiento global de un diagnóstico e instrumentos globales de presupuestación a fin de identificar maneras para superar las dificultades en la aplicación de esta clase de sistemas de reembolso. |

| Recomendaciones para contener los costos de la atención de salud | |
|---|---|
| | • En las reformas del financiamiento de la atención de salud se podría tener también en cuenta la probable demanda futura de la atención de largo alcance y la forma en que se financiarán esos servicios en el sistema estatal y el sistema privado. Para determinar si el financiamiento disponible es adecuado, en vista de la transición epidemiológica, se tienen que hacer más simulaciones sobre los ingresos y gastos del sistema de salud en el futuro. |
| Aumento de la eficiencia | • En las estrategias de prevención y tratamiento de las enfermedades no transmisibles los recursos se podrían orientar hacia las intervenciones que han demostrado ser más costo eficaces. En la adopción de decisiones sobre la asignación de recursos y la adquisición de tecnologías podrían tenerse en cuenta más explícitamente los criterios de costo-eficiencia. <br><br> • Dado que en Chile no hay datos estandarizados sobre la eficacia en función de los costos de la mayoría de las intervenciones en salud, en el SNSS se podría empezar a reunir datos locales confiables para efectuar dicha evaluación y utilizar esos datos en las decisiones sobre la asignación de los recursos. <br><br> • El sistema de las ISAPRE podría evaluar los factores causantes del aumento de los costos e idear estrategias para controlar mejor los costos de la atención de salud. |
| Recuperación de los costos | • Podrían revisarse las actuales tarifas de los servicios públicos a fin de reflejar los costos de producción reales. El SNSS podría establecer un mecanismo para actualizar periódicamente las listas de precios para tomar en cuenta la inflación y las variaciones en los costos de producción. |

| Recomendaciones para contener los costos de la atención de salud | |
|---|---|
| | • Podrían ajustarse los límites de las cuatro categorías de ingresos para la clasificación de los beneficiarios del FONASA a fin de que aquellos que no pueden pagar los co-pagos no lo hagan y los que si puedan abonarlo lo efectúen. Dada la baja recaudación a través de la recuperación de costos, el efecto general sería el de aumentar el financiamiento a partir de los co-pagos, pero recuperando costos a partir de una base más amplia y equitativa.<br><br>• Podrían revisarse las normas que rigen la recuperación de los costos a nivel de cada hospital a fin de garantizar que se eliminen las restricciones y los desincentivos indebidos. Podría crearse un mecanismo para redistribuir parte de los ingresos que perciben los hospitales "de alto rendimiento" a aquellos que tienen menos posibilidades de recuperar los costos.<br><br>• El sistema estatal podría mejorar la recuperación del costo de los servicios brindados a los afiliados de las ISAPRE. |
| | **A mediano plazo**<br>**(dentro de cinco a diez años)** |
| Mecanismos de financiamiento | • Esfuerzos de planificación temprana, podrían ofrecer la oportunidad de financiar por adelantado, sobre una base individual o social, un consumo más alto de servicios que serían difíciles de financiar si su costo total debiera ser abonado en el momento de recibir el servicio. Se podría explorar formas de empezar a acumular los fondos necesarios para cubrir el costo de la atención de salud en el futuro. En el sector privado, tal vez podría considerarse la posibilidad de utilizar un mecanismo equivalente a los fondos de jubilación individuales o medios similares, a fin de reducir la carga futura, especialmente para la atención prolongada. |

## E. Mejora de la reglamentación de la atención de salud

Para muchos de los problemas de salud que afectan a los adultos que se examinan en este estudio, en las estrategias de intervención empleadas por el MS no se ha utilizado todavía toda la gama de mecanismos existentes para promover y proteger la salud y prevenir las enfermedades no transmisibles, en particular las medidas de reglamentación que transcienden las fronteras tradicionales del sector de salud. En esferas como la salud ocupacional, donde ya existe legislación adecuada, los esfuerzos del MS para hacer cumplir las leyes no han contado muchas veces con los recursos necesarios.

El rápido aumento del número de beneficiarios y de los gastos totales de las ISAPRE ponen de relieve el papel cada vez más preponderante que tendrán los planes de seguro médico privados en dar respuesta al nuevo perfil epidemiológico que está surgiendo en Chile. Las presiones para contener los costos han dado como resultado que algunos de éstos se traspasen al sector público.

| Recomendaciones para mejorar la reglamentación de la atención de salud | |
|---|---|
| | **A corto plazo**<br>**(dentro de los próximos cinco años)** |
| Ampliación del uso de mecanismos de reglamentación y exigencia del cumplimiento | ● El gobierno podría utilizar en mayor medida mecanismos tributarios y de reglamentación para controlar el consumo de tabaco y de alcohol, incluidos los impuestos sobre los cigarrillos y el aumento de las restricciones a la venta y publicidad de cigarrillos y alcohol.<br><br>● El gobierno podría ampliar y hacer cumplir estrictamente las leyes relativas al uso generalizado de cinturones de seguridad en los automóviles y de cascos para los motociclistas y a la prohibición de conducir bajo la influencia del alcohol y las drogas. |

| Recomendaciones para mejorar la reglamentación de la atención de salud | |
|---|---|
| | **A corto plazo**<br>**(dentro de los próximos cinco años)** |
| Reglamentación del sector privado | • Podría desalentarse el traspaso de los costos al sector público a causa de la denegación de cobertura o de beneficios a personas que padecen de dolencias no transmisibles mediante la aprobación de las reformas propuestas en la nueva Ley de las ISAPRE y la eliminación de los actuales subsidios estatales a las ISAPRE. De la misma forma, una estructura de riesgo equitativo podría contemplarse en el sistema de las ISAPRE, por ejemplo, aquellas ISAPRE con membrecías de bajo riesgo e ingreso elevado subsidiarían a las que tienen una membrecía con alto riesgo y bajo ingreso. De esa manera se eliminaría el incentivo económico de discriminar entre afiliados potenciales y se controlarían los costos debidos a factores externos, como la estructura de riesgo individual de las membrecías de las ISAPRE. |
| | **A mediano plazo**<br>**(dentro de cinco a diez años)** |
| Ampliación del uso de mecanismos de reglamentación y exigencia del cumplimiento | • Se recomienda que el gobierno exija el cumplimiento más estricto de la legislación vigente sobre salud ocupacional.<br><br>• En cooperación con los SS, el Ministerio de Salud podría redoblar sus esfuerzos encaminados a educar e informar a los directivos y trabajadores acerca de los riesgos ocupacionales y las medidas de protección, y ayudar a las empresas pequeñas a establecer y poner en práctica programas de salud ocupacional.<br><br>• Podría revisarse la ley básica relativa a la salud ocupacional (Ley No 16.744) para hacerla extensiva a los trabajadores que actualmente no están protegidos. |

# CHAPTER I

## OVERVIEW OF THE CHILEAN HEALTH SYSTEM[1]

Chile's social development is impressive. While a GNP per capita of US$2,726 in 1992 places Chile among middle-income countries, its social indicators closely resemble those of an industrialized country. Public investment since the 1920's in health and nutrition, as well as basic education and potable water and sanitation, have had a significant impact in reducing the incidence of communicable diseases and malnutrition, playing a decisive role in overall health improvements.

To provide a context for the analysis of current and future demands posed by demographic and epidemiological changes in Chile and of alternative responses to them, this chapter describes the main characteristics of the Chilean health system. Recent policy and institutional reforms underway in the health sector are also briefly discussed for their relevance to addressing adult health problems.

### Who Provides Health Care in Chile?: A Public/Private Mix

Chile was a pioneer in Latin America in providing publicly-supported health programs.[2] In 1924, a general social insurance scheme that included sickness coverage for blue collar workers was organized; this arrangement was revised in 1938 to include preventive health services. By the 1940's, infant and child milk distribution programs for supplementary feeding had become well established. In 1952, the medical programs of diverse public institutions, including the social insurance medical program for blue collar workers, were consolidated under a unified health structure: the National Health Service (NHS). Up to the late 1970's, the NHS and SERMENA (a separate government-administered health insurance plan for white-collar workers and their dependents) covered approximately 85 percent of the population; about 10 percent of the population was covered by private providers working on a fee-for-service basis; and 5 percent by the armed forces medical program.

In the 1980's, the health care system was reorganized through a series of institutional and financial reforms. The reforms included: decentralizing the NHS regional service areas and re-grouping them into the National Health Service System (NHSS); transferring

---

1. This chapter draws heavily on various sections prepared by the author for inclusion in: World Bank. 1991. Staff Appraisal Report. Chile Technical Assistance and Hospital Rehabilitation Project. Report No. 10000-CH; and World Bank. 1992. Staff Appraisal Report. Chile Health Sector Reform Project. Report No. 10987-CH. These sections were prepared on the basis of information collected during missions to Chile over the 1990-93 period and from literature reviews, including a social development report prepared in 1990 by Karen Lashman and a 1989 assessment of social policies and programs by Tarsicio Castañeda. Additional information is from a background paper prepared by César Oyarzo and Rony Lenz on the financing of the Chilean health sector.

2. Jiménez de la Jara, J. 1993. Chile's Health Sector Reform. Paper submitted to the conference on Health Sector Reform in Developing Countries: Issues for the 1990's, organized by the Data for Decision Making Project, Department of Population and International Health, Harvard School of Public Health, September 1993.

responsibility, infrastructure and personnel for the delivery of primary health care to the municipalities; creation of a financial institution (FONASA) for administering health sector resources; establishing new mechanisms to finance hospitals and municipal health facilities according to the amount and type of services rendered; and establishing the legislative framework and financing mechanisms to support the development of prepaid private health insurance plans (ISAPREs).[3] The resulting institutional structure, which is characterized by a complex combination of public and private providers and financial agencies, is shown in Figure I-1.

**Figure I-1**

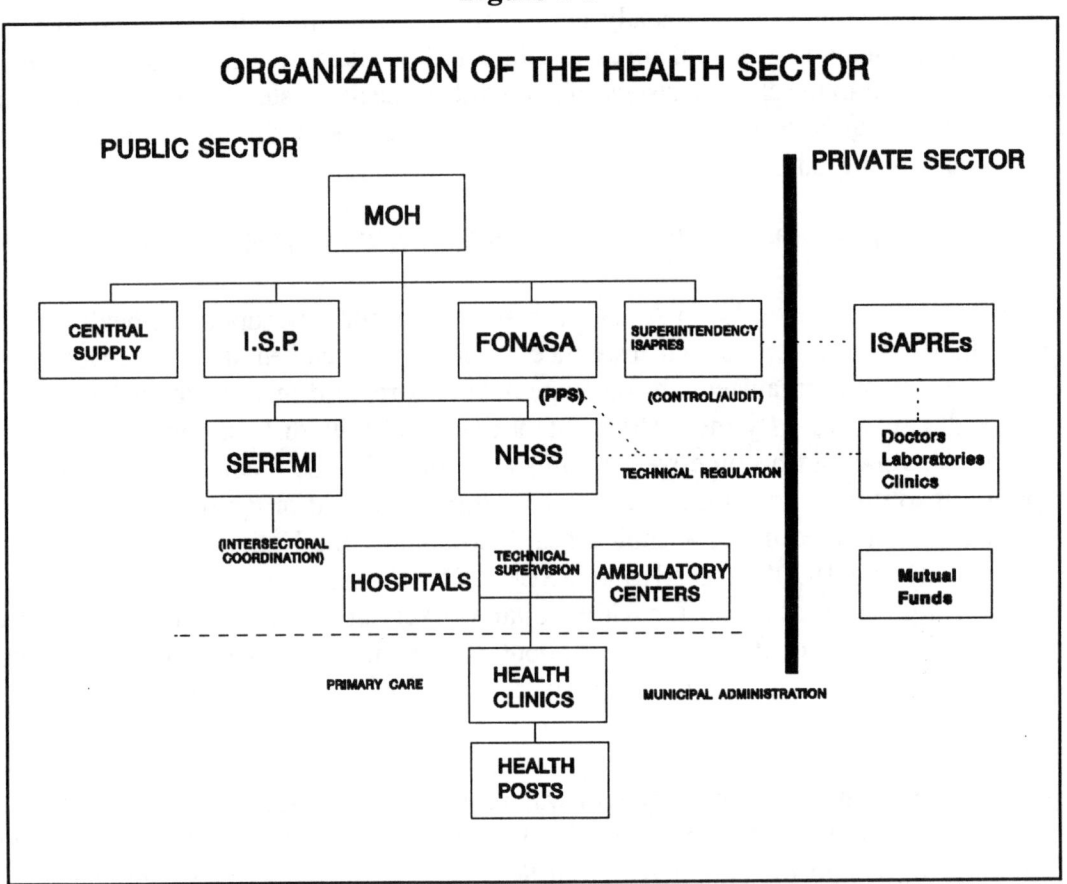

As detailed in Box I-1, formal public/private linkages in Chilean health sector are well established, offering patients choice in the selection of providers. Although there is a multiplicity of public and private health care providers in Chile today, the bulk of preventive and curative services is still offered by the NHSS through a vast network of ambulatory facilities and hospitals.

---

3.  Oyarzo, C. "Análisis Crítico de las Trasformaciones Financieras del Sector Salud en la Década de los 80 y Propuesta para una Reforma." In Jiménez de la Jara, J., ed. 1991. Chile: Sistema de Salud en Transición a la Democracia. Santiago: Editorial ATENA/OMS-OPS.

**Box I-1**

| Finance | Delivery | |
|---|---|---|
| | **Public** | **Private** |
| **Public** | ○ NHSS Hospitals<br>○ Municipal-Run Primary Care System | ○ Fonasa's Preferred Provider System (PPS)<br>○ Contracted-out services |
| **Private** | ○ Contracted-out services (e.g., impatient care for Isapre affiliates in special wards of public hospitals).<br>○ Co-payments in NHSS hospitals | ○ ISAPREs<br>○ Mutual Funds<br>○ Individual and Institutional Providers<br>○ PPS co-payments |

**Public/Private Mix in Chile's Health Sector**

## Publicly-financed and delivered health services

Publicly-financed and delivered health services are under the domain of the Ministry of Health (MOH), which is responsible for the formulation of policies, definition of national norms and standards, and planning and program monitoring. In performing these functions, the MOH coordinates and supervises the delivery and financing of health services through its Subsecretariat of Health, which oversees the operation of the NHSS, and four autonomous agencies: the National Health Fund (FONASA), the principal health care financing mechanism in the country; the Central Supply Facility (CSF), in charge of procurement and distribution of pharmaceuticals and other medical supplies to public health facilities, as well as milk and other products provided by the National Supplementary Feeding Program (PNAC); the Institute of Public Health (ISP), responsible for quality control of pharmaceuticals and food products; and the Superintendency of ISAPREs, created to regulate the private health insurance market.

NHSS provides most of the health services in the country. It is estimated that approximately 60 percent of the population receive health care solely in NHSS facilities (see Figure I-2). NHSS consists of 26 decentralized Health Service Areas (HSAs) and the Environmental Health Service in Santiago. The health services under the armed forces and public enterprises, covering approximately 6 percent of the population, are parallel public systems not included in the NHSS.

The HSAs are legally autonomous services distributed across the nation's 13 administrative regions and responsible for the operation of all public hospitals in their respective geographical areas, as well as for technical oversight of the primary care system managed by the municipalities. In spite of some discretionary control over personnel and financial matters, in practice the HSAs continue to act as implementors of decisions made at the MOH central level with regard to health services delivery and generally are not able to perform their monitoring and supervision responsibilities over the primary care facilities that were placed under municipal authority. Overall, HSAs have limited latitude to adjust MOH norms and standards for variations at the local level, and there generally are not enough trained staff to monitor and supervise activities at the service level.

FONASA is responsible for administering and distributing financial resources of the NHSS, including central government allocations for health and the mandatory 7 percent payroll deduction earmarked for health from all active and pensioned salaried workers who are not ISAPRE affiliates which is collected by the **Instituto de Normalización Previsional (INP)**.

**Figure I-2**

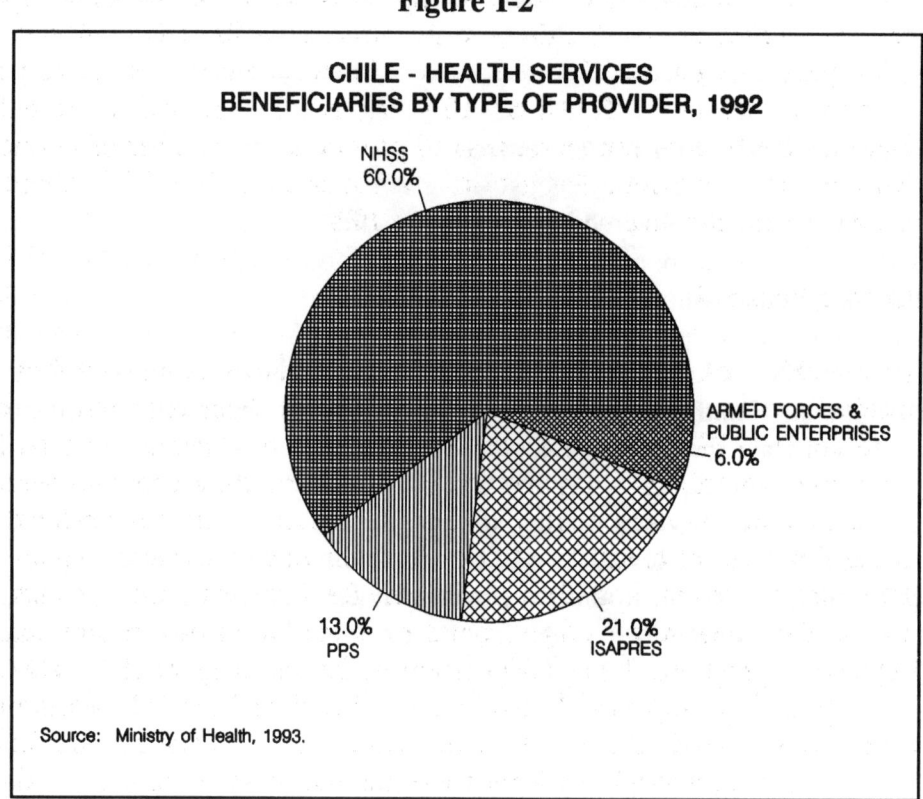

CHILE - HEALTH SERVICES
BENEFICIARIES BY TYPE OF PROVIDER, 1992

NHSS
60.0%

ARMED FORCES &
PUBLIC ENTERPRISES
6.0%

13.0%
PPS

21.0%
ISAPRES

Source: Ministry of Health, 1993.

**Publicly-financed, privately-provided health services**

All workers contributing to FONASA have the option to select private providers under the Preferred Provider System (PPS). The providers (physicians, laboratories, and clinics) receive reimbursement based on a fixed price system for specific ambulatory and inpatient medical services.  FONASA pays only a portion of the cost of the required ambulatory or inpatient service and the user pays the other part with a voucher purchased from FONASA.  The provider redeems the voucher for 100 percent of a pre-agreed price at one of FONASA's offices, or at selected commercial banks.  Under the PPS copayment system, users pay 60 percent of the cost of basic medical consultations and 50 percent of the cost of basic laboratory tests.  For more specialized consultations and diagnostic tests, the size of the copayments varies according to the relative prices of the services provided in relation to those for basic consultations and lab tests.  For inpatient services, FONASA reimburses only 50 percent of the cost of the services; the more expensive and specialized the service, the higher the copayment.

In 1992, approximately 12,140 physicians or 78 percent of all the physicians  in the country, included those who work in public facilities, provided services under the PPS.  Of these, 8 percent were in the basic services level (level 1), 22 percent in the secondary level (level 2), and 70 percent in the specialized level (level 3).  It should be pointed out, however, that the level at which a physician can register is not related to his/her speciality or years of experience, but rather is left entirely to the physician's discretion.  About 1,293 medical facilities operate under the PPS.  Of these, 35 percent are in level 1, 26 percent in level 2, and 39 percent in level 3.  In the last 10 years, as FONASA has not raised the prices for services and thus the level of reimbursement to providers, the number of physicians and medical facilities classified in level 3 has grown.  As indicated in Figure I-2, about 13 percent of the total population receive care under the PPS.

**How is health care financed?**

As shown in Figure I-3, four major NHSS revenue sources administered by FONASA are:  (1) **cotizaciones** or transfers generated by the mandatory 7 percent payroll deduction of workers who are not ISAPRE affiliates, accounting for close to 40 percent of total income; (2) central government contributions (**aporte fiscal**), which represent about 40 percent of revenues; (3) sale of vouchers to FONASA affiliates for selective services rendered under the PPS, representing 7 percent of revenues; (4) fees from the sale of services in public facilities, representing 9 percent; and (5) other income for 7 percent.  Copayments for hospital services in the public sector range from zero in the lowest two income categories (A and B) to 25 percent in the third (C) and 50 percent in the top category (D).  There are no copayments for primary care services offered in public health facilities.  In addition to these resources, capital investments in the health sector, particularly for primary care facilities and rural hospitals, are financed through the Ministry of the Interior-administered National Regional Development Fund (FNDR) and the Social Fund (SF) of the Office of the President.  Chapters VI and VIII discuss in detail recent health spending levels in Chile.

FONASA finances the delivery of public hospital services in part according to the number and type of services rendered, using a fee-for-service schedule called FAP (**Facturación por Atención Prestada Integral**).  FAP transfers, which are intended to cover all operating expenditures except salaries, follow a list of pre-established prices for more than 2,000 medical interventions. In addition to payments for services, FONASA provides a budget allocation to the HSAs to cover salaries, most of investments, and other fixed costs of public hospitals. There are no ceilings on the reimbursement a given hospital can receive from FONASA. Public hospitals obtain additional income from fees charged to ISAPRE and mutual funds (mutuales) affiliates for the use of hospital beds (excluding medical services related thereto) in special wards (**pensionados**) for which hospital authorities can set their own prices, and from service charges paid on a pre-established sliding scale by beneficiaries of the public health system that are classified by FONASA as non-indigent (income categories C and D).

The municipal-run primary health care network is financed on a facility-specific basis for the amount and type of services rendered, based on FAPEM (**Facturación por Atención Prestada en Establecimientos Municipalizados**), a detailed fee system. FAPEM includes 15 categories of primary care services, with precise levels of reimbursement per service delineated within each category. In practice, however, each municipality is subject to a monthly ceiling on the total amount of fees that could be reimbursed by FAPEM, regardless of the level or mix of services provided in its health facilities. Additional revenue to finance the primary health care network comes from municipal budgets. FAPEM transfers are expected to cover the costs of all goods and services, personnel, and maintenance expenditures incurred in the process of delivering health care services. Investment in infrastructure and equipment is a municipal responsibility. To this end, municipalities can apply for funds from the FNDR or the SF.

**Figure I-3**

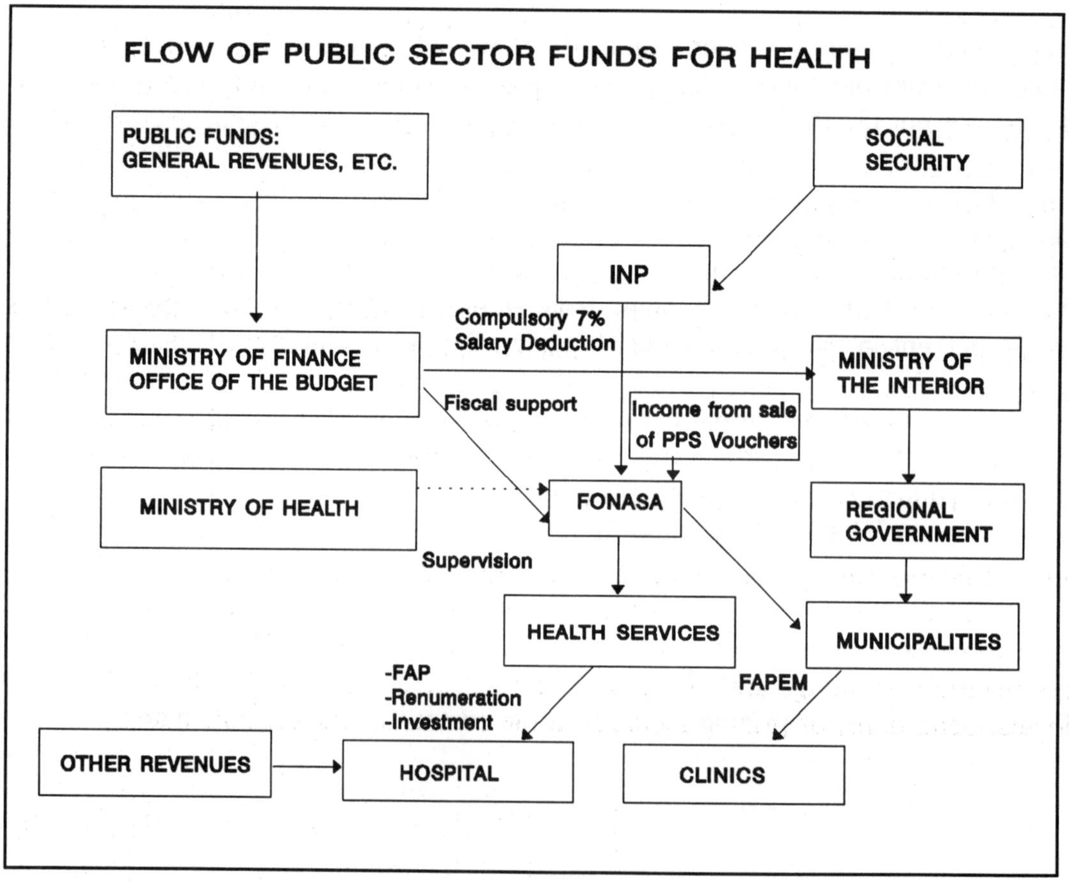

FLOW OF PUBLIC SECTOR FUNDS FOR HEALTH

**The rise of private health insurance schemes**

In addition to physician offices and inpatient facilities, health care is provided in the private sector through 35 prepaid health insurance schemes (ISAPREs), which cover about 21 percent of the population in 1992 (Figure I-2). Of these, 21 are "open", implying that they will enroll applicants meeting the eligibility criteria of individual ISAPREs. The remaining 14 are "closed", meaning that they only enroll employees from specific enterprises for which the ISAPRE was created.

The ISAPREs have grown rapidly since 1981 as the result of public policies that have encouraged private sector activity in the health field, including a government decree that allows the ISAPREs to collect directly the obligatory 7 percent salary deduction of persons willing to purchase private health care coverage. Additionally, public subsidies amounting to approximately US$51 million per year (about 5.3 percent of total public expenditures on health) are provided to the ISAPRE system, including tax rebates to employers who contribute an additional 2 percent of payroll to complement the compulsory 7 percent salary deduction used to pay ISAPRE premiums for low income employees or those with large families (US$20 million), and maternity leave payments (US$29 million), free distribution of vaccines (US$300,000) and food supplementation products (US$2.3 million) to ISAPRE members.

ISAPREs offer subscribers and their dependents both outpatient and inpatient care on a cost-sharing basis, via their own facilities or under contract with private or public providers. ISAPRE affiliates pay a monthly premium that varies according to the cost of the policy they choose to buy. In 1992, the average monthly premium per subscriber was approximately US$40, up from US$23 in 1981. These premiums are financed through assignment to the ISAPREs of the compulsory 7 percent salary deduction; the additional 2 percent of payroll to complement the 7 percent salary deduction; and out-of-pocket payments by affiliates varying between 10 to 40 percent of the cost of each service. Highly paid affiliates may pay nothing beyond their 7 percent salary deduction, while the payment by others depends on their salary level.

The number of affiliates (or primary beneficiaries) increased significantly in the last decade, from approximately 26,415 in 1981 to about 1.3 million in 1992. When family members of the affiliates are included, the number of beneficiaries increased from 62,000 in 1981 to over 3 million in 1992. More than 90 percent of ISAPRE beneficiaries belong to "open" ISAPREs. Simultaneously, the net profit of the ISAPRE system grew, rising by 28 percent in 1992 from about 6 percent in 1984.

Several factors have limited wider access to the ISAPREs. One of the most significant problems is the complexity of the contracts that are signed between affiliates and the individual ISAPREs. There are a multitude of different plans available, each with subtle differences regarding coverage and price. In addition, there are no standardized terminologies, definitions, or pricing methods in the contracts. As a result, many prospective affiliates do not understand the numerous stipulations of the contracts, finding it extremely difficult to choose the health plan that best suits their needs. This is exacerbated by the fact that the ISAPREs have imposed various restrictions regarding access to care in the form of exclusionary clauses denying coverage for certain medical services (e.g., those for some non-communicable conditions); waiting periods after enrolling before services are provided; and no coverage of pre-existing conditions.[4] The high cost of treating non-communicable conditions has been a disincentive for the ISAPREs to offer coverage for these illnesses. Coverage of the elderly, for whom the costs of care tend to be four or five times higher than of those in younger age groups, has also been limited (e.g., more than 70 percent of ISAPRE affiliates are less than 40 years of age and only 2 percent are 65 years of age or older).[5]

## Mutual funds for work-related injuries and illnesses

Since 1916, different Chilean laws have assigned responsibility to employers for work-related injuries and illnesses occurring to their workers.[6] Current legislation (Law No. 16.744 of 1968) mandates that all employers provide insurance against these risks, either through mutual funds (**mutuales**), INP/NHSS, or own arrangements (i.e., direct provision of services and disability benefits). Approximately 2.6 million workers from over 51,000 companies, representing about 60 percent of the economically active population are insured. Of these, about 71 percent are covered by 3 large mutual funds; the rest by INP/NHSS (16 percent), the armed forces (5.5 percent), public administration (5.1 percent), and own arrangements (2.3 percent).

The mutual funds, which were established as private, non-profit entities in the 1950's, provide medical services and administer short- and long-term disability payments. By law, the mutual funds utilize their own medical care infrastructure, including primary care centers, work-site clinics, and hospitals. Most medical services provided relate directly to the treatment of work-related injuries and their sequelae. The mutual funds also undertake various activities aimed at preventing injuries in the work place.

The average employer pays 1.85 percent of payroll to the mutual funds, with employers' contributions ranging from a minimum of 0.85 percent to a maximum of 3.4 percent. About 41 percent of the expenses of the mutual funds are for medical services, 24 percent for disability payments, 9 percent for preventive activities, and the remainder for

---

4. Sánchez, H. "Análisis del Subsistema Privado ISAPRE Período 1981-1990." In Jiménez de la Jara, J. 1991. Sistema de Salud en Transición a la Democracia. Santiago: Editorial ATENA/OMS-OPS.

5. See Ref. 4 and Sánchez, H. 1992. Proceso de Privatización en el Sector Salud de Chile. Mimeo. Report prepared for the Pan American Health Organization, Washington, D.C.

6. Jiménez de la Jara, J., and Gili, M. "Subsistema Mutuales de Seguridad." In Jiménez de la Jara, J., ed. 1991. Chile: Sistema de Salud en Transición a la Democracia. Santiago: Editorial ATENA/OMS-OPS.

other expenses (primarily reserves for future payments) and administration. Annual expenditures per affiliate of the mutual funds average US$50.

## How are Health Services Provided in the NHSS?

### A large network of primary health care centers, deteriorated hospitals

During the 1974-89 period, social policies were redefined as part of macroeconomic adjustment and structural reforms and state retrenchment.[7] Social expenditure fell by 16 percent in 1975-76 and 12.7 percent in 1983-87, and shifted from broad coverage to targeting towards vulnerable and poor groups. In the health sector, with the priority attached to the expansion of primary care, investments shifted away from hospitals in favor of primary care facilities. As a result, the number of primary care facilities increased substantially in urban and rural areas, extending the coverage of basic health and nutrition programs throughout the country, particularly for maternal and child health.

As it will be discussed in Chapter II, in Chile, the integration of health-related interventions (e.g., family planning, prenatal and well child controls, vaccination, health and nutrition education, and breastfeeding promotion) with the distribution of food products has served to deal with the twin problems of poor health and malnutrition among high risk groups, by attracting users to health facilities. Food supplementation for mothers and children carried out through PNAC since 1951 is part of the basic package of services that is offered in the primary health care network. Under PNAC, powdered milk is distributed free of charge to children 0-2 years of age and pregnant and lactating women; a milk-cereal mix for children 2-5 years of age is also provided. Children at risk of malnutrition receive a ration of rice in addition to the milk-cereal mix.

The primary care system that was transferred to the municipalities in the 1980's consists of four basic types of facilities: rural medical stations, rural health posts, rural health centers, and urban health centers. The rural medical stations, the lowest echelon, are buildings used as temporary sites for periodic visits by medical teams. Rural health posts, staffed with resident health auxiliaries, provide health promotion and protection services to catchment areas of approximately 1,000 persons. Rural health centers, located in communities of between 2,000 and 5,000 population, offer round-the-clock nursing and medical care for general health problems of limited complexity. Permanent professional and auxiliary staff operate these facilities. Urban health centers provide ambulatory care for general health problems. These facilities have fixed hours, generally providing care eight to nine hours daily, and the composition of their staff varies with the size of the locality. There

---

7.  For a complete discussion on this topic see: Marcel, M. and Solimano, A. 1993. Developmentalism, Socialism, and Free Market Reform. Three Decades of Income Distribution in Chile. Working Paper Series No. 1188. Washington, D.C.: Policy Research Department, The World Bank.

are 1,214 rural medical stations, 1,040 health posts, and 345 health centers distributed across the country.

Secondary and tertiary care is provided in hospitals and their outpatient departments (**consultorios adosados de especialidades**). While primary health care facilities were constructed in recent decades according to an MOH master plan, the current hospital network consists primarily of diverse hospitals inherited from religious or welfare institutions. Many of the hospitals are close to a century old; only a few additional hospitals have been built in the last two decades to complement the public sector network.

Public hospitals in Chile are classified under four categories, ranging from Type 4 rural hospitals with minimal technology to Type 1 with the maximum technology available in the public sector. The NHSS has 105 Type 4 facilities, which offer the first echelon of inpatient care. Type 3 hospitals, of which there are 25, are located in small towns and have only the four basic specialties (internal medicine, pediatrics, obstetrics-gynecology, and general surgery). Dispersed across the major cities are 30 Type 2 or general hospitals, which offer most medical and surgical specialties and have intermediate technology. Some of these facilities are specialized hospitals, such as the Pediatrics, Cancer, and Psychiatric Hospitals. Tertiary care is offered in 20 Type 1 facilities, which include all specialties and sub-specialties. Aside from outpatient departments of hospitals, there are no free-standing specialized centers for ambulatory care. Outpatient departments of hospitals are usually the only providers of specialized care for low-income groups.

In the private sector there are 1,069 ambulatory care centers for single or group medical practice and 190 hospitals (called **clínicas**), encompassing both general and specialized inpatient facilities. There are also 30 hospitals under the administration of universities, the armed forces or state enterprises that are not part of the NHSS.

**A skewed health personnel mix**

With seven medical schools, Chile graduates approximately 500 physicians per year. The total number of physicians in the country is close to 15,090, which is about 11 physician per 10,000 population. Of this total, 7,988 or 53 percent work in the HSAs, 1,270 or 8 percent in the primary care facilities run by the municipalities, and 5,832 or 39 percent exclusively in the private system. Although the physician/population ratio in Chile is below the ratio of OECD countries and some middle-income Latin American countries (Figure I-4), Chile has an adequate number of physicians. However, they are over-specialized as to type. Indeed, a serious issue of Chile's physician market is the low number of general practitioners (about 25 percent of total physicians) and the large and growing supply of specialists (about 75 percent of total physicians). One factor that may explain this imbalance is the rigidness and stagnation of the medical education curriculum as it continues to be more focused on disease treatment than on health promotion and prevention, and more oriented to hospital-based care than on ambulatory services.[8]  Another important issue is the geographic maldistribution of physicians, particularly those with specialized training, who are concentrated in the major urban areas.  The MOH-run rural scholarship program for young physicians who have agreed to serve between three and six years in rural areas has been an important vehicle to attract qualified young doctors to underserved areas.  This program finances additional training for enrolled physicians at the end of their assignment.  Since 1990, this program has placed over 1,000 physicians.  Nevertheless, there are still some 100 rural communities or municipalities that do not have a physician.

**Figure I-4**

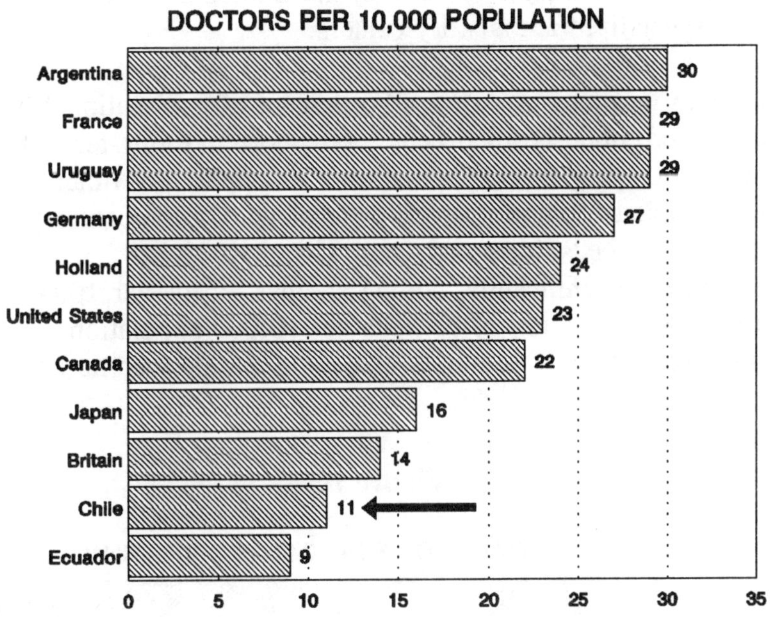

DOCTORS PER 10,000 POPULATION

| Country | Doctors per 10,000 |
|---|---|
| Argentina | 30 |
| France | 29 |
| Uruguay | 29 |
| Germany | 27 |
| Holland | 24 |
| United States | 23 |
| Canada | 22 |
| Japan | 16 |
| Britain | 14 |
| Chile | 11 |
| Ecuador | 9 |

Source:  World Bank, 1993.

The total number of nurses is about 3,573 in the NHSS, giving a ratio of nurse per 10,000 population of 4.4.  As the number of available nurses fell below the evolving needs of the primary care system, their functions were systematically delegated to auxiliary nurses.  The simultaneous growth of the ISAPREs has provided an alternative source of employment for the relatively few graduate nurses.  The number of dentists in the public health system is about 1,874; the dentist per 10,000 population ratio is 2.3.

---

8.   Giaconi, J., Valdivieso, V., and Guiraldes, E.  1994.  Algunas Ideas Para Contribuir A La Reforma Del Sector Salud En Chile.  Rev. Méd. Chile 122:346-350.

**Utilization of health care resources**

For the sector as a whole, the number of medical consultations averaged 2.5 per person per year in 1990, a figure less than half the corresponding figure for OECD countries. The NHSS reported 2.4 medical visits per beneficiary per year, and accounted for 75 percent of all outpatient visits in the country. By comparison, the ISAPREs had an average of 3.3 physician visits per beneficiary, showing a higher per capita use of services in this system. Mutual fund affiliates average 0.42 medical consultations and 0.56 rehabilitation sessions per year. Overall, emergency visits in outpatient departments of hospitals represent 30 percent of all consultations, indicating that although geographic coverage of health care in Chile is good, access is less adequate because of the limited hours of service in primary care facilities and lack of specialized ambulatory centers.

The public sector accounts for almost 75 percent of total national hospital bed capacity. The number of public hospital beds, both short-and long-term, has remained nearly stable at a ratio of 25 beds per 10,000 population. As opposed to other countries, Chile never went through a period of rapid hospital expansion. On the contrary, between 1981 and 1990, the number of public beds decreased from 33,692 to 32,818. It is only in the 1980's that the private sector grew significantly, adding another 8 beds per 10,000 population, to reach an overall total for the country of 33 beds per 10,000 population. This bed ratio is below the ratio observed in OECD countries and some middle-income Latin American countries (Figure I-5).

**Figure I-5**

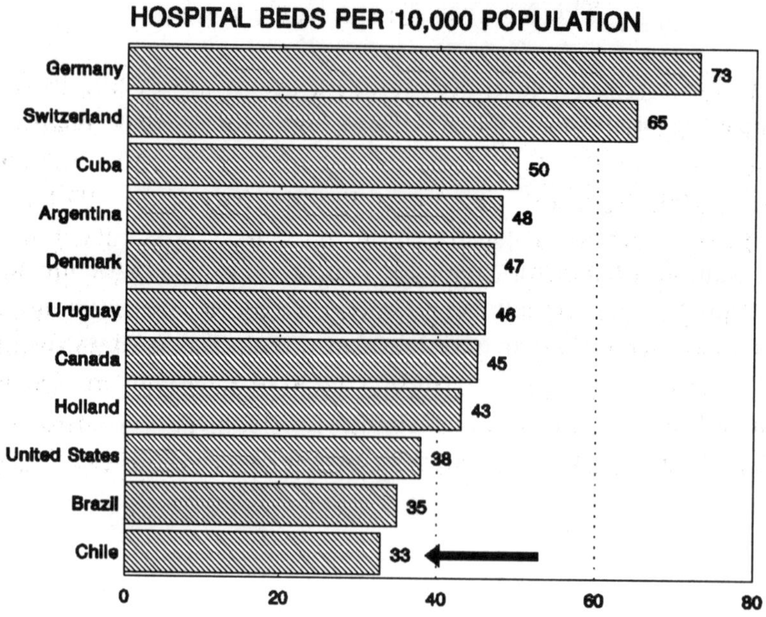

**HOSPITAL BEDS PER 10,000 POPULATION**

|  |  |
|---|---|
| Germany | 73 |
| Switzerland | 65 |
| Cuba | 50 |
| Argentina | 48 |
| Denmark | 47 |
| Uruguay | 46 |
| Canada | 45 |
| Holland | 43 |
| United States | 38 |
| Brazil | 35 |
| Chile | 33 |

Source: World Bank, 1993, and OECD, 1993.

In the early 1990's, the hospital occupancy rate in the public sector was estimated at about 75 percent, compared with a seventeen-country OECD average of 77.7 percent. The figure in Chile, however, may be misleading as it includes rural hospitals where a lower occupancy rate is expected given the need to maintain a minimum infrastructure in remote areas. Also, a number of available beds in the public sector are not operational because of the deteriorated condition of hospital wards, inoperative equipment, or lack of personnel. In the private sector, the hospital occupancy rate is estimated at about 64 percent, indicating an underutilized bed capacity.

In 1990, the average length of stay in public hospitals was estimated at 7-8 days, while private hospitals had an average length of stay of 4-5 days. These figures compare favorably with those in OECD countries such as Denmark (6.6), Ireland (6.9), the United States (7.3), and Norway (7.8). A study[9] on productivity in five public and private hospitals in Chile found that the case mix of the hospitals did not account for the variation in average length of stay. While the length of stay for obstetrical and gynecological care was similar, the length of stay for surgical care and internal medicine was lower in private hospitals. One of the reasons for this difference may be the lack of presurgical days in private hospitals compared to the public hospitals, where there were between 2 and 3 days. This probably reflects the fact that patients in the private sector arrive with their diagnosis already established. Once in the hospital, the intensity of care provided by the physician did not differ among the hospitals, although laboratory and x-ray tests were higher in the public hospitals studied. Again this may indicate the need to re-diagnose public sector patients once they enter the hospital. These findings may also reflect the limited specialized outpatient capacity in the public sector.

## The Reforms of the Early 1990's

In March 1990, a major political realignment occurred in Chile from a military to a democratically-elected civilian government. The promotion of social justice with macroeconomic stability and growth became the centerpiece of the Government's development agenda, yielding positive results in the first part of the 1990's. Chile's open economy, with robust private sector participation, grew by 6-8 percent; inflation declined significantly; and fiscal and balance of payments accounts registered a surplus. This notable performance was fueled in part by a strong growth in exports, mainly non copper products. Additionally, the Government adopted a tax reform to help finance improvements in the social sectors. As a result, without undermining fiscal equilibrium, the Government substantially increased public expenditures (about 12 percent in real terms in 1991-92) to enhance the quality of key social programs as a means to assure access of the less privileged

9. Rodriguez, J., and Jiménez, J., 1985. Comparative Analyses of Productivity in Public and Private Chilean Hospitals. Mimeo. Santiago: ILADES.

to basic needs, particularly health and education services. Between 1988 and 1992, the percentage of the population below the poverty line declined from 45 to 33-35 percent.[10]

With the support of international aid agencies, the Government began a national reform program to address critical problems in the public health system. In spite of efforts in the 1980's to decentralize the management of health service, revise health financing mechanisms and promote private sector participation, serious imbalances and inefficient resource use have continued to constrain health sector productivity and service quality. Major problems in the public health system include limited coordination and complementarity between primary care facilities and hospitals as reflected in the poor referral flow between levels of care; lack of specialized ambulatory facilities that contributes to inadequate backup for the primary care level and continued high dependence on emergency care at hospitals; deteriorated physical plant, medical equipment, and support services within the public hospital network; distortions introduced by the fee-for-service arrangements used for allocating resources, including incentives to physicians and hospitals to provide more services, regardless of their need or cost-effectiveness; weakness in the institutional and human resource capability of the MOH and its autonomous agencies; limited administrative and financial capacity in numerous municipalities for the provision of adequate primary care; and imperfections in the private health insurance market.

A major objective of the Government's reform program has been to achieve a balance in the public health care system, continuing its traditional focus on maternal and child health care while responding more effectively to the changing health needs of adults and the elderly. As will be discussed in detail in Chapter VIII, the thrust of the reforms for reorganizing the health care delivery system is two-fold: (a) to bridge the gap between primary and secondary care by establishing specialized outpatient services to support referrals from primary care levels, reduce the workload of hospitals, and serve a great number of patients in health facilities closer to their residence with less time and travel costs incurred by them; and (b) to rehabilitate and upgrade hospitals to improve their productivity in view of the deterioration of the public hospital network in the last two decades, particularly in Metropolitan Santiago.

The Government is also strengthening the organizational capacity of the MOH's central administration and of its executive agencies to implement and consolidate the decentralization of health services delivery. The implementation strategy consists of redefining the MOH mission to concentrate solely on policy-making, normative, and supervisory roles; introducing management tools to facilitate effective delegation of authority and to enhance supervision and performance evaluation of HSAs (e.g., annual service provision agreements between the MOH and the HSAs on the type and volume of services to be provided and on the level of payment); and strengthening and upgrading staff, financial resource allocation and transfer mechanisms, and information and communication systems.

---

10. MIDEPLAN. 1992. Población, Educación, Vivienda, Salud, Empleo y Pobreza. CASEN 1990. Santiago: Ministerio de Planificación y Cooperación.

In particular, to increase efficiency in the use of existing resources and provide incentives for cost-savings at the decentralized service delivery levels, the Government has decided to replace the FAP and the FAPEM resource allocation systems with a system of payment based on diagnosis (PADs) and a revised prospective fee schedule or PPP for hospitals and a fixed capitated rate system for primary care facilities, respectively. Additionally, the Government is financing the installation of a management information system in the MOH to facilitate the information flow within the different MOH departments and between the MOH and the HSAs. The establishment of this system is a prerequisite to the successful implementation of the policy and institutional reforms, especially for the new health financing schemes and the annual service provision agreements. The Government expects that savings from planned efficiency measures and wider cost recovery, including an increase in the sale of public hospital services to the ISAPREs, will help meet the country's changing health needs without significantly increasing public sector financing.

In order to eliminate some of the problems experienced with the ISAPREs, the Government created the Superintendency of ISAPREs in 1990. The Superintendency, acting as an arbitrator between the consumers and the ISAPREs, regulates the market in order to guarantee that all legal and contractual obligations are adhered to and provides information to the public to increase affiliates' knowledge and market transparency. This legislation also mandates that all affiliates subscribe to an ISAPRE for a year at minimum, prohibits the termination of contracts unilaterally, and obliges the ISAPREs to offer preventive services such as well child care until the age of 6. New legislation proposed by the Superintendency is under discussion to improve the availability of health care services for ISAPRE beneficiaries. This includes: extension of contracts to family members of an affiliate who dies; transferability of contracts from one employer to the next; definition of a minimum package of health benefits; restrictions on exclusions permitted for certain services; elimination of waiting periods for service coverage after enrollment; and regulation of coverage of pre-existing conditions.

## The Task Ahead

As noted above, an ambitious program is currently being implemented to reform the Chilean health system, including the urgent rehabilitation of public hospitals and additional investments for strengthening the delivery of specialized ambulatory care services to complement the well developed primary health care network. However, as demographic trends increase the absolute and relative importance of adult health problems, new efforts are required to meet this difficult challenge. As experience has shown in other countries,[11] in the medium and long term, further reductions in the social cost of illness and disease and improvements in the overall health status of the population will depend on vital disease prevention and health promotion and protection activities.

---

11. U.S. Department of Health and Human Services. 1991. Healthy People 2000: national health promotion and disease prevention objectives. Washington, D.C.: Government Printing Office (DHHS publication No. (PHS) 91-50213).

## Study Objectives and Methodology

This study examines the health transition in Chile.  Specifically, its primary objective was to analyze some demographic, epidemiological, financial, and institutional aspects of the transition and discuss alternative actions for addressing them.  The review includes data and information from Chile and other countries.  Most data contained in this report were provided in background papers commissioned to both Chilean and international consultants.  As such, the data obtained were not verified and no judgment was made about the reliability of the data systems.  For estimating epidemiologic and cost scenarios over the next thirty years, a computerized projection model was developed for this study.

In the following chapters, this study will first review the demographic and health patterns leading to the rise in importance of non-communicable diseases and injuries, their risk factors, and their likely future evolution.  Then the study will examine their implications for health care costs and intervention programs, as well as strategies for managing medical technology and containing the escalation of health care costs.

# CHAPTER II

## DEMOGRAPHIC AND HEALTH TRANSITION[1]

### The Aging of the Population

Any change in the composition of a population also produces changes in the epidemiological profile, which requires that health services be adapted to provide care according to changing needs and demands. The demographic components that determine the size, growth, and structure of the population are fertility, mortality, and migration. The theory of the demographic transition, based on the experience of developed countries, postulates the existence of predetermined stages of change in the dynamics of national populations. Accordingly, the demographic transition is the result of a succession of changes in the birth, mortality, and natural increase rates that generally accompany the modernization of a country.[2] The pace of these changes has been faster in developing countries, primarily owing to greater access to family planning services and to prevention and control of the causes of infant and childhood mortality.[3]

In the past three decades, the demographic profile of the Chilean population has been altered, from a profile characterized by high fertility and mortality rates to one with low fertility and declining mortality, coupled with low immigration. This has occurred primarily as a consequence of social and economic changes associated with the development of the country and the improved welfare of the population.

### Declining birth and death rates

Declines in fertility and increases in life expectancy have ushered Chile into the third stage of the demographic transition. While death rates began a rapid decline in the 1940's, birth rates remained high until the early 1960's (Figure II-1). The population growth rate reached its peak in 1965 at around 2.6 percent. During 1940-70, roughly one million people

---

1. This chapter was prepared on the basis of demographic and epidemiological data from the Chilean Ministry of Health, the National Institute of Statistics (INE), the Pan American Health Organization (PAHO/WHO), and the World Bank. Additional information came from a background paper on the elderly in Chile prepared by María C. Escobar.

2. The stages of the demographic transition are: first or pretransitional stage, high rates of fertility and mortality with low to moderate growth rates; second stage, mortality begins to decline, with no change in fertility, which produces high growth rates; third stage, declines in mortality and in fertility, causing a moderate decline in growth rates; and fourth stage, equilibrium, with low fertility and mortality and very low, zero or slightly negative growth.

3. U.S. Bureau of the Census, Current Population Reports, Series P95/92-2. 1992. Population and Health Transitions. Washington, D.C.: U.S. Government Printing Office.

per decade were added to the Chilean population, which grew from 5 to almost 9 million. The sharp decline in birth rates and the steady drop in death rates lowered the annual population growth rate to 1.7 percent. Total population in the country was estimated at 13 million in 1990 and is projected to rise to 14 million in 2000 and 17 million in 2015.

**Figure II - 1**

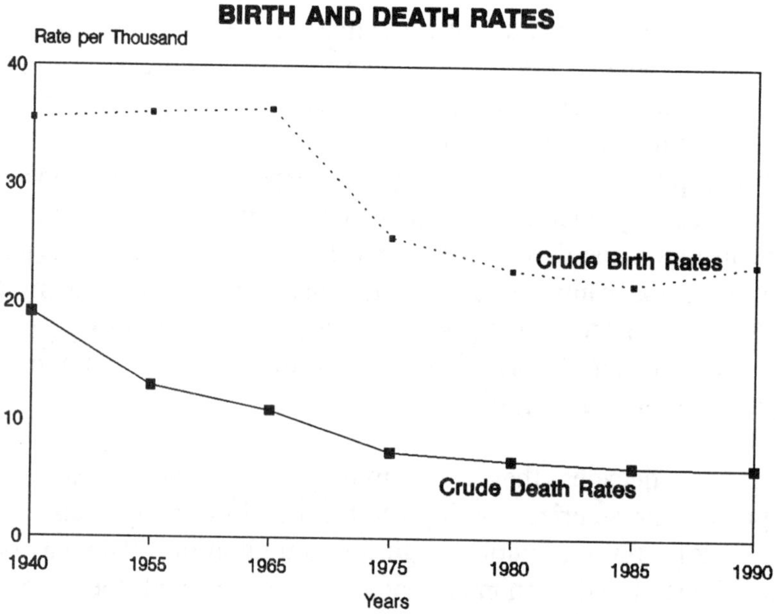

**BIRTH AND DEATH RATES**

Source: Chilean Ministry of Health.

## Rapid urbanization

The population transition in Chile has been geographic as well as demographic. Internal migration altered the spatial distribution of the population, which is characterized by an urban concentration in the metropolitan areas of Santiago (where close to 40 percent of the population lives), Valparaíso-Viña del Mar, and Concepción. The proportion of the population living in cities increased from 58 percent to 85 percent between 1950 and 1990.

## Fertility falls as life expectancy increases

Although life expectancy at birth increased by about 10 years in the past two decades to 72 years, largely as a result of successes in combating infant and childhood mortality and reducing the prevalence of infectious and parasitic diseases, the main determinant of the relative aging of the population has been declining fertility, which dropped almost 24 percent during the period (Figure II-2). While in 1970 the average woman had about 3.4 children in her lifetime, by 1990 the total fertility rate declined to 2.6 children compared with 1.9 in industrialized countries and a world average of 3.3. Total fertility is projected to drop to near the replacement level of 2.1 by 2000. The factors most evidently affecting low fertility in Chile are adoption of family planning, increasing participation of women in the labor force, and high female school enrollment ratios.

**Figure II - 2**

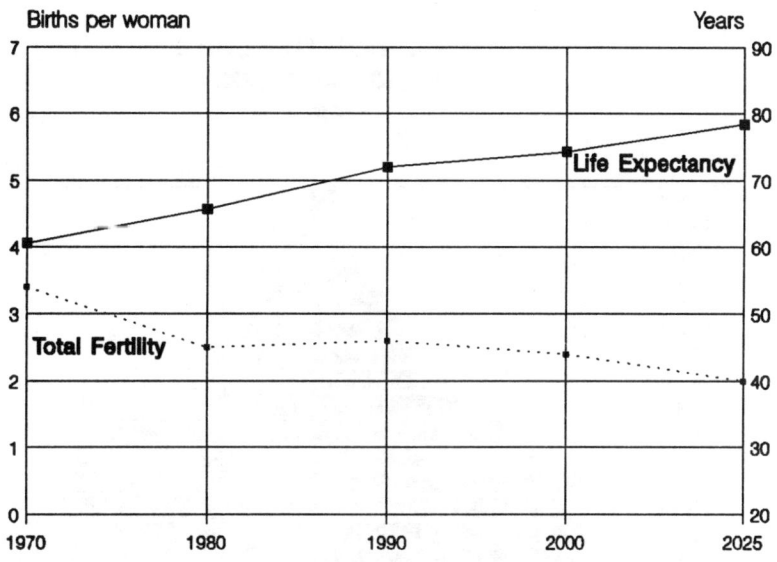

**TOTAL FERTILITY AND LIFE EXPECTANCY
1970 - 2025**

Source: INE, 1992, and World Bank, 1992.

## Changing population profile

The population age structure has been transformed as a result of declining fertility and mortality. As depicted in Figure II-3, the bottom third of the 1990 Chilean population pyramid was more rectangular than the relatively broad base that characterizes pre-demographic transition stages. The aging of the Chilean population, particularly since the 1970's, has meant not only an increase in older age groups, but more importantly, a major growth among young adult and middle aged groups. The median age has risen from 20 years in 1970 to 25 years in 1990, and will continue to do so in future decades. As a consequence of the decline in the size of successive birth cohorts due to the drop in fertility, the proportion of children (0-14 years) was reduced from almost 40 percent in 1970 to about 30 percent in 1990. The age group 15-59 years represented in 1990 roughly 64 percent of the total population (a relative increase of 18 percent from 1970), and the proportion of persons age 65 and older accounted for about 6 percent compared with 12 percent in developed countries.

By the year 2000, Chile is expected to have about 299,000 fewer children under the age of 15 than it did in 1985, and 313,000 more people aged 65 and up. Though life expectancy at birth rose for both males and females due to higher survival rates, women are living longer, outnumbering men in the older age groups (life expectancy stood at 68 years for men and 75 for women in 1990).

**Figure II-3**

**POPULATION FOR CHILE
BY AGE AND SEX
1990**

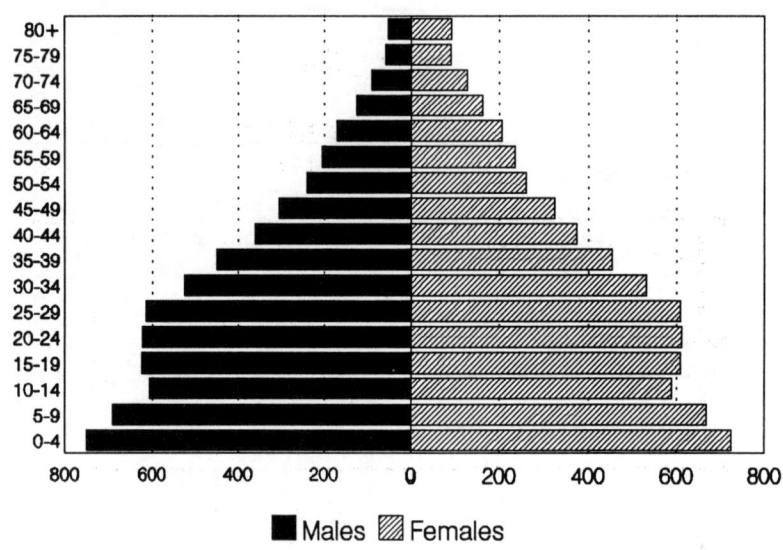

Source: INE, 1992.

## Impact on dependency ratios

As shown in Figure II-4, with the increase in the proportion of working age adults in the Chilean population, the age-dependency ratio (population groups under 15 and over 65 to population groups ages 15 through 64) has been gradually decreasing since 1980, standing at .57 in 1990 compared with .61 in the Americas and .52 in Europe. It is projected to continue to drop well into 2010. Not before 2025 is the age-dependency ratio expected to register an increase as the numbers of elderly begin to offset reduced numbers of children. A lower age-dependency ratio implies not only proportionally more workers for the economy, including an increase in the proportion of women in the labor force, but a potential reduction in public resources needed for young dependents.

As the number of elderly increases in Chile in the future, however, the potential economic benefit of reduced numbers of children may be offset by a greater relative claim on health resources placed by the elderly. For example, in the United States, in 1987 those 65 years or over comprised 12 percent of the population but consumed 36 percent of the total personal care, up from 30 percent in 1977; per capita spending for personal health care for the aged was US$5,360, while for the non-aged amounted to only US$1,286.[4] From 1985 to 2025, the proportion of elderly in Chile will increase by 50 percent, but the absolute number of elderly will rise by 97 percent. The old-age dependency ratio (population above age 65 as a percentage of the working population) will grow steadily from a modest 8 percent to 19 percent in 2025, about the same as in today's industrialized countries. Equally significant, the medically vulnerable age groups (those below age 5 and over age 50, which are prone to illness) will increase from 37 percent in 1990, 40 percent in 2000, to 60 percent of the working age population in 2025.

**Figure II-4**

**SUPPORT RATIO**
**1950 -2025**

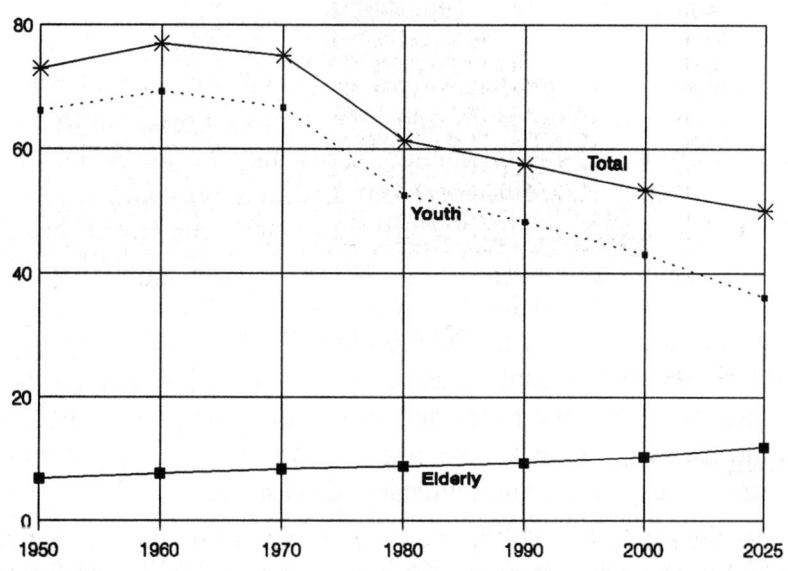

Source: INE, 1992 and World Bank, 1992.

---

4. Waldo, D., Sonnefeld, S.T., McKusick, D.R., and Arnett, R.H. Health expenditures by age group, 1977 and 1987. 1989. Health Care Financing Review/Summer 10(4):111-120.

## The Shifting Disease Profile

### A framework for the analysis of the health transition

The term epidemiologic transition, a commonly used term in the literature, refers to the demographic and socioeconomic changes that contribute to long-term shifts in health patterns.[5] These shifts refer mainly to changes in the relative importance of different diseases. To more fully comprehend this phenomenon, the term health transition has been proposed to explain all those changes in the levels and causes of illness and death which are now occurring in developing countries and that have previously taken place in developed regions.[6] According to this interpretation, the health transition is the net result of three components: (a) a demographic component; (b) a risk factor component; and (c) a therapeutic component. The demographic component is the main agent of the health transition and is inexorable as populations become older and live longer, and the number of adults and elderly increases. The risk factor component, which influences the demographic component, refers to changes in the exposure to and magnitude of different risk factors (e.g., urbanization, industrialization, and changing lifestyles), as well as risk-averting factors (e.g., vaccinations and environmental sanitation), associated with the development process. The therapeutic component, which refers to the changes in the access to, use of, and effectiveness of health services, reduces disability and mortality.

Indeed, largely as a function of changes in the age structure of the population, the absolute number of sick and dying adults and elderly has increased in the developing world. Changes in the exposure to and the magnitude of risk factors, as well as risk-averting interventions, have altered age-specific morbidity and mortality rates. Health care improvements have caused changes in absolute and relative rates of ill health and death. The demographic and risk factor components have determined that in relative terms, non-communicable diseases have gradually displaced communicable diseases as the primary causes of illnesses and death (i.e., disease and death rates are declining faster among children than adults and rates of communicable diseases are declining faster than those for non-communicable diseases). The risk factor and therapeutic components have caused relative increases in certain causes of adult and elderly ill health (e.g., non-communicable diseases) compared with other causes (e.g., communicable diseases).

Overall, in most developing countries today, in spite of the sharp reduction in morbidity and mortality due to communicable diseases, the health transition is characterized

---

5.  Omran, A.R. 1971. The Epidemiologic Transition. A Theory of the Epidemiology of Population Change. The Milbank Memorial Fund Qtly. 49:509-538.

6.  Feachem, R.G.A., Kjellstrom, T., Murray, C.J.L., Over, M., and Phillips, M.A. 1992. The Health of Adults in the Developing World. New York: Oxford University Press for the World Bank.

by the coexistence of communicable and non-communicable diseases and injuries.[7] In some countries, this disease pattern has led to an "epidemiological polarization", whereby the poor present higher rates of different types of diseases as a result of higher exposure to risk factors and limited access to effective medical treatment.[8]

As discussed in detail below, Chile has been no exception to the above trends and challenges. Communicable diseases, malnutrition, and maternal complications are no longer the leading health problems although they are still present. Rather, non-communicable diseases and injuries are on the rise in both relative and absolute terms as the population has continued to age.

## Mortality declines as communicable diseases among the young are reduced

The health status of the Chilean population greatly improved in the past three decades. Age-specific mortality declined among all age groups. The decline was greatest in the population group under 15 years as a consequence of significant reductions in the prevalence of infectious and parasitic diseases. Indeed, until the early 1960's, Chile had one of the highest infant and pre-school mortality rates in the Americas. After that period, child deaths from diarrhea, acute respiratory infections, and malnutrition decreased dramatically, with infant mortality rates falling from 109/1,000 in 1960 to 17/1,000 in 1990, well below the average rate for Latin America of 55/1,000 and comparing favorably with most developed countries (Figure II-5). Pre-school mortality dropped to a rate of less than 1 per 1,000 children aged 1-4 years in 1990. Malnutrition (measured by weight-for-age) was also reduced significantly among children under the age of 6 years, from 15.9 percent in 1976 to 6.9 percent in 1990. The prevalence of moderate and severe malnutrition is among the lowest in the developing world, affecting less than 1 percent of children under 6 years of age.

---

7.   Bobadilla, J.L., Frenk, J., Frejka, T., Lozano, R., and Stern, C. The Epidemiological Transition and Health Priorities. In Dean T. Jamison, W. Henry Mosley, Anthony R. Measham, and José-Luis Bobadilla, eds. 1993. Disease Control Priorities in Developing Countries. New York: Oxford University Press.

8.   Frenk, J., Bobadilla, J. L., Sepulveda, J., and Lopez Cervantes, M. 1989. Health transition in middle-income countries: new challenges for health care. Health Policy and Planning 4(1): 29-39.

**Figure II-5**

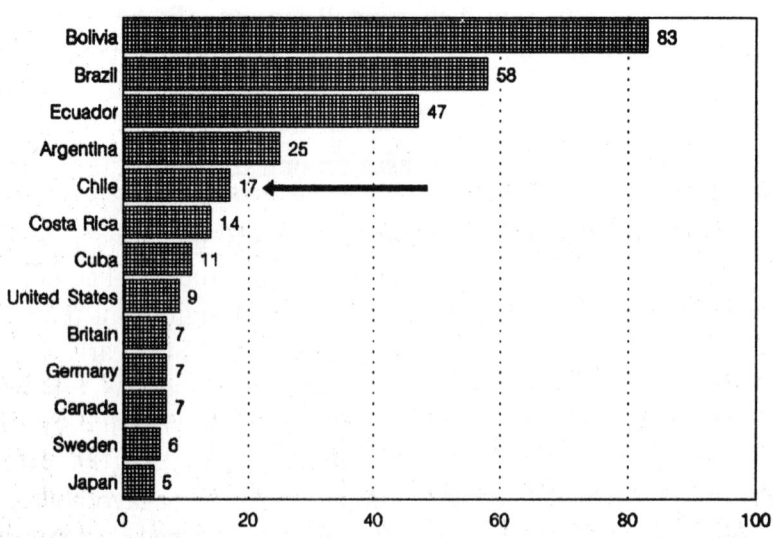

INFANT MORTALITY RATES IN SELECTED
LATIN AMERICAN AND OECD COUNTRIES
1991

Source: World Bank, 1993 and PAHO/WHO, 1993.

Maternal mortality dropped sharply from 30/10,000 live births in 1960 to about 4/10,000 in 1990, compared to 3.9 in Cuba, 1.8 in Costa Rica, 1.5 in Western Europe, and 0.7 in the United States. Maternal nutrition improved as reflected in the reduction of low birth weight newborns (under 2.5 kgs.) from 11.6 to 6.4 percent in the 1970-90 period.

As infant and child health improved, the proportional contribution of younger age groups to overall mortality dropped (Table II-1). While in 1960 infant deaths accounted for 36 percent of all deaths in the country, this proportion declined to 6 percent in 1990. Concurrently, with the greatly lengthened life expectancy at birth and the increased average age of the population, many preventable deaths are now occurring at more advanced ages. As a result, the relative importance of deaths among the age group 15 years and older increased from 52 percent in 1960 to 91 percent in 1990 (a 75 percent increase).

### Table II-1
### Percent of Deaths by Age Group
### 1960-1990

|  | 1960 | 1970 | 1980 | 1990 | % Change 1960-1990 |
|---|---|---|---|---|---|
| - 1 year | 35.9 | 25.0 | 11.0 | 6.2 | -82.1 |
| 1 - 4 | 9.1 | 4.4 | 1.7 | 1.2 | -86.8 |
| 5 - 14 | 2.8 | 2.4 | 1.8 | 1.0 | -64.3 |
| 15 - 44 | 13.1 | 13.2 | 13.0 | 11.7 | -10.7 |
| 45 - 64 | 16.6 | 20.4 | 22.7 | 22.7 | +26.9 |
| 65 and older | 22.5 | 34.6 | 49.8 | 57.2 | +60.1 |
| Total | 100 | 100 | 100 | 100 |  |

Source: PAHO/WHO 1990, and INE, 1992.

These advances, which largely attest to the effectiveness of public health programs and essential clinical services that have been maintained and perfected by successive governments since the 1920's,[9] resulted from an interplay of a number of factors, among them high coverage of vaccination programs (in 1990, 98 percent for polio, 98 percent for third DPT dose, and 97 percent for BCG for newborns); increased access of pregnant women to prenatal care; greater number of births attended by health professionals (99 percent in 1990); widespread access to family planning services, regular checkups for close to 80 percent of all infants under one year of age; and provision of milk and other supplementary foods to both pregnant and lactating women and children offered under the PNAC together with promotional and health care programs. Large-scale investments to improve housing and sanitary conditions and expand access to basic education also played a role since the Chilean population is in general better housed and educated and the labor force is richer in human capital than that of other Latin American countries.[10]

### Increasing mortality due to non-communicable conditions and injuries

The increased average age of the Chilean population, rapid urbanization and industrialization, as well as significant changes in lifestyles, have contributed to the emergence of a new set of health problems. As a result, the mortality profile and the disease burden are now characterized by the prevalence of non-communicable diseases and injuries.

Although most disease-specific mortality rates declined in the past 30 years, the total number of deaths due to non-communicable conditions and injuries increased as a

---

9. Monckeberg, F. Mimeo. Integrating National Food, Nutrition, and Health Policy. The Chilean Experience. Institute of Nutrition and Food Technology. University of Chile.

10. Meller, P. Adjustment and Equity in Chile. 1992. Paris: OECD.

consequence of the shifting population age structure which has produced a progressively larger number of adults and elderly persons susceptible to non-communicable diseases and disability. With the sharp decline in the relative importance of infectious and parasitic diseases as major causes of death (from 12 percent in 1968 to only 3 percent in 1990), the relative importance of non-communicable conditions and injuries has grown steadily. At present the situation in Chile is very similar to that found in the more industrialized Latin American and OECD countries, where non-communicable diseases and injuries account for between 55 and 80 percent of all deaths.

## Implications of These Trends

The changes in the demographic profile have profound implications for Chilean society as a whole. As the population continues to evolve inevitably toward an older age structure, the relative importance of non-communicable diseases and injuries as leading causes of morbidity and mortality will grow relative to acute infectious diseases, increasing the demand for high-cost health services. The magnitude of the challenge is clearly reflected in the rising absolute number of persons affected by these conditions, in spite of decreasing age-adjusted death rates for most causes. In general, the demographic and epidemiological trends analyzed above mean that the capacity of the health care delivery system will be severely tested in the decades ahead as it seeks to adapt to this situation by developing new programs to reduce the exposure to risk factors associated with the onset of non-communicable diseases and injuries and increase access to and use of effective health services, particularly among the poor, while maintaining essential programs for the control of communicable diseases.

## A Framework for Devising Responses to the Health Transition

In devising appropriate responses to the health transition, it is important to clarify issues concerning policy aims (e.g., efficiency and equity objectives) and the most efficient methods for achieving them (e.g., private production of services, regulation of the market place).[11] The respective roles of the public and private sectors, therefore, should be determined on the basis of which methods may best achieve agreed upon aims. Experience in developed countries suggests that given the pervasiveness of market imperfections in the health sector (e.g., imperfect consumer information about technically complex medical services with uncertain effectiveness; gaps in private insurance coverage for preexisting conditions and for the elderly[12]), regulatory policies enacted and enforced by governments must be an integral part of a response strategy. Governments play a fundamental role in

---

11. Barr, N. "The Role of Government in a Market Economy." In Barr, N., ed. 1994. Labor Markets and Social Policy in Central and Eastern Europe. The Transition and Beyond. New York: Oxford University Press. Published for the World Bank and the London School of Economics and Political Science.

12. Arrow, K. J. 1963. Uncertainty And The Welfare Economics of Medical Care. The American Economic Review Vol. LIII (5):941-973.

fomenting health promotion and protection and disease prevention activities, particularly for the poor; ensuring the quality of goods and services; establishing a legal framework to facilitate private sector activity; and containing the escalation of health care expenditures. On the other hand, to counter government failures in health activities (e.g., public health services are disproportionately utilized by middle-income groups, who have a larger political voice than the poor;[13] creation of monopolies through regulation of the medical labor market), the introduction of market mechanisms associated with direct charges should be actively supported.

---

13. Petrei, A. H. 1987. El gasto público social y sus efectos distributivos. Rio de Janeiro: ENCIEL.

# CHAPTER III

# *THE BURDEN OF DISEASE IN CHILE*[1]

The magnitude of the non-communicable disease and injury problem in Chile is reviewed in this chapter and in Annex A on the basis of mortality data, which is still the vital event that is recorded most extensively and reliably in the country, health services utilization data, and estimates of disability-adjusted life years (DALYs) for various conditions. The conditions are: cardiovascular disease, cancer, injuries, chronic obstructive pulmonary disease, diabetes, and mental illness; other non-communicable diseases such as liver cirrhosis, occupational diseases, and emerging nutrition-related problems associated with aging, such as osteoporosis, are reviewed as well. AIDS, though an infectious disease, is also considered because it shares certain characteristics with many non-communicable illnesses such as a long latency period and affects predominantly the adult population.

## Selected Mortality Indicators

Together the above conditions are the leading causes of mortality and morbidity among adults and the elderly in Chile today, particularly among low socioeconomic groups. As summarized in Table III-1, they accounted for approximately 66 percent of all deaths in 1990, and consumed a large number of hospital resources. Specific trends in mortality and service utilization for each major illness group, as well as comparisons with other countries, are discussed in Annex A.

---

1. This chapter and Annex A were prepared on the basis of information from background papers by: Ernesto Medina (Cardiovascular Disease), Luis Martinez (Cancer), Erica Taucher (Injuries), Sergio Bello (Chronic Obstructive Pulmonary Disease), Cecilia Albala (Diabetes), Alfredo Penjam (Mental Illness), Eduardo Medina (Alcohol and Drug Use), María Inés Pino (Occupational Diseases), and Jaime Rozovski and Cecilia Albala (Nutrition). Data for AIDS are from the Chilean MOH. The section on DALYs was prepared on the basis of estimations done by H. Dennis Tolley.

## Table III-1
## Leading Non-Communicable Diseases and Injuries in Chile[a]

| Cause | Number of deaths | % of total deaths in the country | Age-adjusted death rate | Number of hospital discharges[b] |
|---|---|---|---|---|
| Cardiovascular disease (CVD) | 21,568 | 27 | 155.8/100,000 | 65,593 |
| Cancer | 14,153 | 18 | 102.6/100,000 | 30,645 |
| Injuries | 9,587 | 12 | 70.2/100,000 | 133,281 |
| Chronic obstructive pulmonary disease (COPD) | 1,000[c] | 1.3 | 19.4/100,000[c] | 6,492[c] |
| Non-insulin dependent diabetes mellitus (NIDDM) | 1,300[c] | 1.7 | 14.6/100,000[c] | 10,786[c] |
| Mental illness | 1,108[c] | 1.4 | 11.7/100,000[c] | 25,469[c] |
| Cirrhosis of the liver | 3,749[c] | 4.8 | 39.8/100,000[c] | 5,962[c] |

[a] Data for 1990 unless otherwise indicated.
[b] Figures are for 1989.
[c] Figures are only for population 15 years and older.
Source: MOH data.

## Risk of adult mortality due to non-communicable diseases and injuries

An indicator used to measure the burden of adult mortality is the probability of death from age 15 to 60 (the demographic term 45Q15) if current mortality rates apply. In Chile today about 20 percent of adult males and 10 percent of adult women die before reaching their 60th birthday.[2] This is much higher than in developed countries such as Japan, the Netherlands, Sweden, and Switzerland with male 45Q15 between 11 and 13 percent and female 45Q15 between 5 and 8 percent.[3] Among all causes, non-communicable diseases are the largest contributors of premature mortality in Chile, accounting for about 12 percent and 8.3 percent male and female 45Q15, respectively. Injuries are also a large cause of adult deaths, with male 45Q15 of about 6 percent and female 45Q15 of 1.1. Communicable and reproductive causes account for about 2 percent of adult males and 1 percent of adult females premature deaths.

---

2. Feachem, R.G.A., Kjellstrom, T., Murray, C.J.L., Over, M., and Phillips, M.A. 1992. Health of Adults in the Developing World. New York: Oxford University Press for the World Bank.

3. Murray, C.J.L., and Feachem, R.G.A. 1990. Adult Mortality in Developing Countries. Transactions of the Royal Society of Tropical Medicine and Hygiene 84:1-2.

## Potential years of life lost

The relative importance of different health problems in Chile is also appreciated when years of potential life lost (YPLL), an indicator which measures the effect of a particular cause of death on life expectancy, is used instead of mortality rates. YPLL measures premature mortality before age 65. Given that the causes that kill at early ages acquire greater relative importance, injuries rank first, accounting for about 32 percent of potential years of life lost from defined death causes. Cardiovascular disease and cancer, concentrated in the more advanced ages near 65 years, have lower YPLL proportions. When grouped together, injuries, cardiovascular disease, and cancer account for a total of 408,962 years of life lost prematurely as a result of 18,564 deaths, representing about 50 percent of total years of potential life lost due to defined causes before the age of 65. The percent of all YPLL from these three conditions in Chile during the 1980's was as high or higher than that in other Latin American countries of similar level of development.[4]

## Quantifying the Global Burden of Disease through Disability-Adjusted Life Years

To fully comprehend the burden of major non-communicable conditions and injuries afflicting Chilean adults and elderly, this study attempted to measure the burden of various of these conditions through DALYs following the methodology presented in Annex B developed in conjunction with the World Bank's 1993 World Development Report.[5]

While death is the ultimate expression of loss, the full burden to society of illness also includes the pain and disability which individuals suffer prior to death and which detracts from their enjoyment of a fully healthy life. The global burden of disease, therefore, is composed of losses due to premature death as well as the loss of healthy life resulting from disability. This global burden can be measured and compared across a variety of ailments through the use of DALYs. DALYs lost due to mortality are calculated by summing the discounted value of years lost to premature death across all causes and age groups. DALYs lost due to disability are based on the incidence and duration of various types of disability

---

4.  PAHO/WHO. 1990. Health Conditions in the Americas. Vol.I. Washington, D.C.:PAHO/WHO.

5.  World Bank. 1993. World Development Report. Investing in Health. New York: Oxford University Press for the World Bank.

    Murray, C. 1993. Quantifying the Burden of Disease: The Technical Basis for Disability Adjusted Life Years. Health Transition Working Paper Series No. 93.03. Harvard University.

    Murray, C., and Lopez, A. 1993. Quantifying the Burden of Disease: Data, Methods, and Results. Health Transition Working Paper Series No. 93.05. Harvard University.

    Murray, C., Lopez, A., and Jamison, D. 1993. Global Burden of Disease in 1990: Summary Results, Sensitivity Analysis and Future Directions. Health Transition Working Paper Series No. 93.06. Harvard University.

multiplied by a severity weight that estimates the severity of the disability in comparison with loss of life. Total DALYs result from the sum of DALYs lost due to mortality and to disability, adjusted by a discount rate of 3 percent (so that future years of healthy life are valued at progressively lower levels) and by age group weightings (so that years of life lost at different ages are given different relative values). The effect of these adjustments is that the value of each year of life rises steeply from zero at birth to a peak at age 25 and then declines steadily with increasing age.

Total DALYs for Chile for 1990[6] are presented by category of disease, type of loss and sex in Table III-2, by age group in Table III-3, and by major cause of death or disability in Table III-4.

Table III-2 shows that across most categories of disease, DALYs lost due to premature death are higher for men than women. The difference is most striking for injuries, where the number of DALYs lost by men due to premature death is five times the number lost by women. About 42 percent of DALYs lost for males 15 years of age and older are due to premature death and about 58 percent to disability. For females, the proportion due to premature death is lower at 38 percent. A major reason for the difference is that women in Chile live longer than men and consequently experience less loss due to premature death. Men also experience higher losses due to disability than women with the exception of a higher number for women due to communicable diseases.

---

6. Since an indirect method was utilized for estimating DALYs for Chile due to the incompleteness of the Chilean data (e.g., lack of information on disability), these estimates should be seen as preliminary.

**Table III-2**
**Burden of Disease Among Chilean Adults and Elderly**
**By Sex, Leading Cause and Type of Loss, 1990**
**(in thousands of DALYs[a])**

| Sex and Outcome | Disease Category | | | |
|---|---|---|---|---|
| | Communicable[b] | Non-communicable[c] | Injuries[d] | Other[e] |
| Male | | | | |
| Premature death | 32 | 162 | 135 | 99 |
| Disability | 6 | 62 | 121 | 433 |
| Female | | | | |
| Premature death | 13 | 115 | 26 | 118 |
| Disability | 11 | 48 | 74 | 320 |

Notes:
[a]  Disability-adjusted life year.
[b]  Includes AIDS, hepatitis/typhoid fever (070, 002 under the International Classification of Disease (ICD) 9 code), and other infectious diseases (except 002 and 070 under the ICD9 code).
[c]  Includes lung cancer (162/ICD9) and other cancers (cervical 180/ICD9, esophagus 150/ICD9, and stomach 151/ICD9), diabetes (250/ICD9), cirrhosis (571/ICD9), chronic obstructive pulmonary disease (491-496/ICD9), coronary infarction (410-414/ICD9), other coronary (440-447/ICD9), hypertensive heart disease (401-404/ICD9), and stroke (430-438/ICD9).
[d]  Includes trauma (E800-E999, excluding E804-E820/ICD9) and injuries from traffic accidents (E804-E820/ICD9).
[e]  Includes: other cancer (140-239, except 150, 151, 162, 180/ICD9), all endocrine and nutritional (240-280/ICD9, except for diabetes), all mental disorders (290-319/ICD9), respiratory system (460-519/ICD9, except 491-496), and digestive system (520-579/ICD9, except cirrhosis).
Source:  World Bank calculations.

The increasing significance with age of DALYs lost to disability is seen in Table III-3, which shows the burden of disability experienced by middle-aged and elderly women and by elderly men.  Overall, DALYS lost for men from all causes are about 45 percent higher than DALYs lost for women.

**Table III-3**
**Burden of Disease Among Chilean Adults and Elderly**
**By Age Group and Sex, 1990**
**(in thousands of DALYs)**

| Age group | Males | | | Females | | |
|---|---|---|---|---|---|---|
| | Mortality | Disability | Total | Mortality | Disability | Total |
| 15-44 | 184 | 229 | 433 | 84 | 165 | 249 |
| 45-59 | 112 | 145 | 257 | 76 | 131 | 207 |
| 60+ | 132 | 248 | 380 | 112 | 157 | 269 |
| Total | 428 | 622 | 1050 | 272 | 453 | 725 |

Source:  World Bank calculations.

Table III-4 shows the distribution of DALYs lost due to individual diseases and types of injury and provides one measure of the overall burden to society of specific causes of death and disability. Trauma due to injuries other than traffic-related is the largest single cause of DALYs lost for both men and women, accounting for about 20 percent and 12 percent, respectively, of total loss. Cirrhosis is the second leading cause of DALYs lost for men, accounting for 5.4 percent of total loss. For women, other cancers are the second leading cause of DALYs lost, accounting for 6.2 percent of total loss. For men, the third leading cause of DALYs lost is injury from traffic accidents, accounting for 4.5 percent each of DALYs lost, followed by coronary infarction (4.4 percent). For women, stroke occupies the third place accounting for 5.1 percent of total DALYs lost, followed by coronary infarction (4.0 percent) and other infectious diseases (2.9 percent). When 1990 disease burden is expressed in relation to population, Table III-4 shows that Chile loses 329 DALYs per 1,000 male adult and elderly population, and 225 DALYs per 1,000 female adult and elderly population. The ratio of male/female DALYs lost is 1.46.

**Table III-4**
**Distribution of DALYs Lost Among Chilean Adults and Elderly**
**By Major Cause and Sex, 1990**

| Cause | Males | | Females | |
|---|---|---|---|---|
| Communicable Diseases[a] | (thousands) | % | (thousands) | % |
| AIDS | 18 | 1.7 | 2 | 0.3 |
| Other Infectious Diseases | 19 | 1.8 | 21 | 2.9 |
| Non-Communicable Diseases[b] | | | | |
| Lung Cancer | 13 | 1.2 | 5 | 0.7 |
| Other Cancers | 34 | 3.2 | 45 | 6.2 |
| Diabetes | 8 | 0.8 | 8 | 1.1 |
| Cirrhosis | 57 | 5.4 | 19 | 2.6 |
| Chronic Obst. Pulmonary | 16 | 1.5 | 10 | 1.4 |
| Coronary Infarction | 46 | 4.4 | 29 | 4.0 |
| Other Coronary | 4 | 0.4 | 4 | 0.6 |
| Hypertensive Heart | 5 | 0.5 | 6 | 0.8 |
| Stroke | 42 | 4.0 | 37 | 5.1 |
| Injuries[c] | | | | |
| Trauma | 209 | 19.9 | 87 | 11.9 |
| Injuries from traffic accidents | 47 | 4.5 | 13 | 1.8 |
| Other[d] | <u>532</u> | <u>50.6</u> | <u>439</u> | <u>60.6</u> |
| Total | 1,050 | 100.0 | 725 | 100.0 |
| DALYs per 1,000 adult and elderly population | 329 | | 225 | |
| Ratio of male/female DALYs lost | 1.46 | | | |

| | |
|---|---|
| a | Includes AIDS, hepatitis/typhoid fever (070, 002 under the International Classification of Disease (ICD) 9 code), and other infectious diseases (except 002 and 070 under the ICD9 code). |
| b | Includes lung cancer (162/ICD9) and other cancers (cervical 180/ICD9, esophagus 150/ICD9, and stomach 151/ICD9), diabetes (250/ICD9), cirrhosis (571/ICD9), chronic obstructive pulmonary disease (491-496/ICD9), coronary infarction (410-414/ICD9), other coronary (440-447/ICD9), hypertensive heart disease (401-404/ICD9), and stroke (430-438/ICD9). |
| c | Includes trauma (E800-E999, excluding E804-E820/ICD9) and injuries from traffic accidents (E804-E820/ICD9). |
| d | Includes: other cancer (140-239, except 150, 151, 162, 180/ICD9), all endocrine and nutritional (240-280/ICD9, except for diabetes), all mental disorders (290-319/ICD9), respiratory system (460-519/ICD9, except 491-496), and digestive system (520-579/ICD9, except cirrhosis). |

Source: World Bank calculations.

# CHAPTER IV

## *THE RISK FACTORS*[1]

This chapter focuses on the main population risk factors for non-communicable diseases and injuries, which are assuming priority in Chile's mortality and morbidity profile. Lifestyle factors such as the consumption of tobacco, alcohol and drugs, poor nutritional habits, and insufficient physical activity, coupled with population aging, are associated with the rising incidence of non-communicable diseases, nonintentional injuries, violence, and mental disorders. Hypertension and occupational and environmental hazards also pose important risks. Moreover, the synergistic effects of multiple risk factors greatly increase the probability of developing non-communicable conditions.

The historical evolution and geographical distribution of non-communicable disease risk factors in Chile are only partially understood, with limited information available for some of the risks. Today's mortality and morbidity profile, however, is not the result of recent exposure to some of these risks. Rather, it is the consequence of long and continuous exposure to several risks, acting alone or possibly in combination, over the lifetime of an individual. Usually, non-communicable conditions have long incubation periods, with symptoms appearing only after an interval of 5 to 30 years. Consequently, the prevalence of key risk factors observed in Chile today will shape the non-communicable illness profile of the population well into the next century.

### Major Individual Risk Factors

#### Smoking

Tobacco use is a major public health problem in Chile owing to its high prevalence and the high frequency of smoking-related diseases among the population, which are leading causes of death. Given the long incubation periods before the onset of these diseases (20-40 years), smoking will continue to be a major contributor to illness and mortality in future decades. By the same token, the effects of smoking intervention programs conducted now will only translate into reductions in morbidity and mortality after a similarly long period.

National data on tobacco use were obtained from the Ministry of Planning's (**MIDEPLAN**) 1990 CASEN Survey, which focused, among other variables, on cigarette consumption. The survey yielded data by region, socioeconomic level, sex, and age. CASEN data indicate there are approximately 2.9 million smokers in Chile aged 15 years and older. The habit is more frequent among men (38 percent) than women (25 percent) in all regions of the country. Two-thirds of smokers use tobacco daily, and of these, about 30

---

1. This chapter was prepared on the basis of information from background papers by: Cecilia Sepúlveda (Smoking), Eduardo Medina (Alcohol and Drug Use), Ernesto Medina (Cardiovascular Disease), Jaime Rozovski and Cecilia Albala (Nutrition), and María Inés Pino (Occupational Diseases). Information for environmental contamination is from the World Bank.

percent smoke more than 10 cigarettes a day (Figure IV-1). The number of cigarettes smoked daily is higher for men, and the gap between the sexes widens with the number of cigarettes smoked per day. The Santiago Metropolitan Region has the highest proportion of smokers of both sexes, and the proportion of smokers in cities (33 percent) is higher than in rural locations (27 percent).

**Figure IV-1**

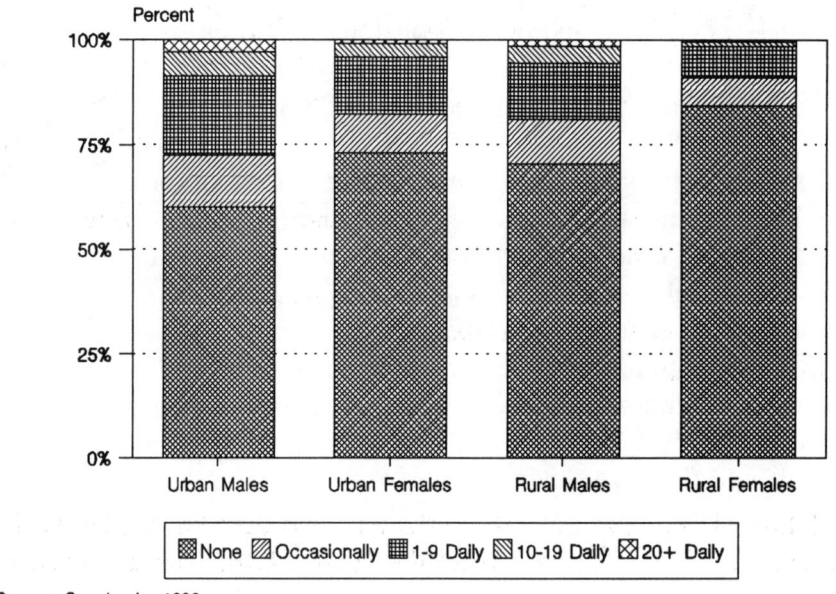

**PREVALENCE OF SMOKING BY QUANTITY, SEX, AND REGION, 1990**

Source: Sepulveda, 1992.

Tobacco use was found to be most prevalent between the ages of 20 and 64 years in both sexes. The highest prevalence in both sexes was between the ages of 20 and 49 (Figure IV-2). The prevalence of smoking was lower for women in all age groups. A slightly higher proportion of smokers was found in the highest (33 percent) than in the lowest (30 percent) income groups, but a marked difference exists in the onset of smoking before age 20 according to level of income (14 percent in the lowest income quintile vs. 21 percent in the highest income quintile).

**Figure IV-2**

**PREVALENCE OF SMOKING BY AGE\* AND
BY SEX, 1990**

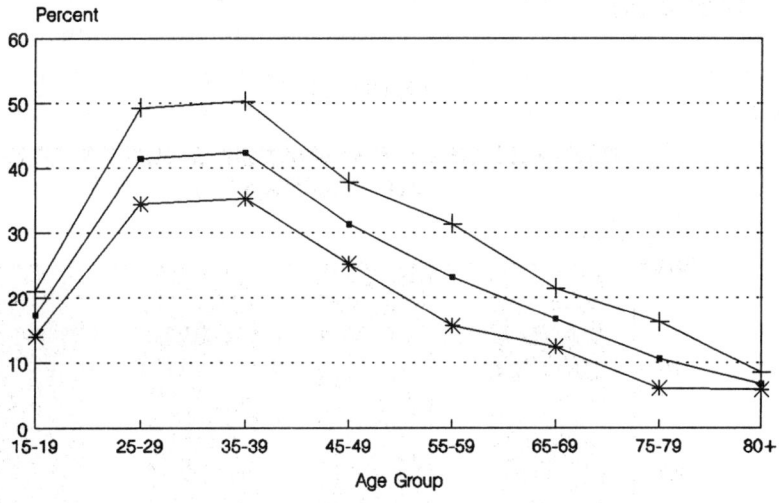

\* Includes Both Occasional and Daily Smokers

Source: Sepulveda, 1992.

The evolution of smoking in Chile in the past two decades can be partially gleaned by comparing data from a 1971 study[2] and from the 1990 CASEN survey, since both surveys utilized representative samples for Santiago. Among men, the prevalence of smoking decreased from 47 to 43 percent. In females, the prevalence increased from 26 to 30 percent. The percentage of heavy smokers declined greatly in both sexes in this period, and the proportion of those who smoked fewer than 10 cigarettes a day increased.

Nevertheless, it is estimated that smoking accounts for approximately 6,000 to 9,000 of deaths among persons above the age of 15 years or 10 to 12 percent of all deaths. This is comparable to findings in the United States that smoking accounts for 17 percent of all deaths.[3] The great damage done by cigarettes is reflected in increasing mortality, morbidity, and disability due to smoking-related diseases. These include cancers of the buccal cavity, larynx, trachea, bronchi, lungs, esophagus, pancreas, kidneys, and gallbladder (Figure IV-3). Except for esophageal and buccal cancers, mortality rates for malignant tumors are generally on the rise in both sexes, particularly for persons aged 35 years and

2.  Joly, D. J. 1977. Encuesta Sobre las Características del Hábito de Fumar en América Latina. Publicación Científica No. 337. Washington, D. C.: Organización Panamericana de la Salud.

3.  McGinnis, J.M, and Foege, W.H. 1993. Actual causes of death in the United States. JAMA 270(18):2207-2212.

older. It is estimated that smoking is responsible for 20 percent of all cancer deaths in Chile, as compared with 30 percent in the United States. In addition, smoking is closely associated with cerebrovascular disease, hypertensive disease, ischemic heart disease, and chronic obstructive pulmonary disease. Although the tendency among age-adjusted death rates for cardiovascular diseases is downward, the absolute number of deaths has continued to grow because of the population's aging. Also, the number of deaths for chronic obstructive pulmonary disease is on the rise. Further evidence of the burden imposed on the Chilean society by smoking-related diseases is gleaned from hospital discharge data, which show an increasing trend for most of these diseases among adults and the elderly in the last 20 years.

## Figure IV-3

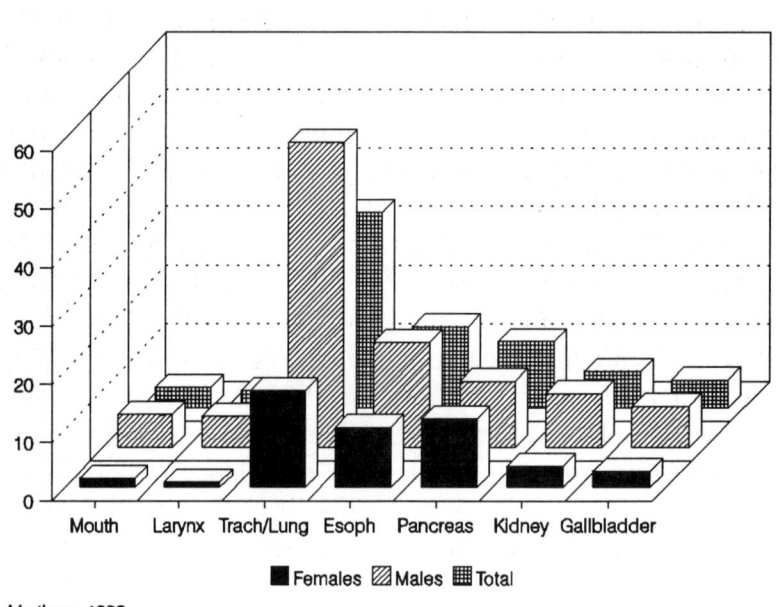

**AGE-ADJUSTED MORTALITY RATES FOR SMOKING-RELATED CANCER SITES, 1990**

Source: Martinez, 1992.

Measurements of the economic impact of smoking in Chile have focused on direct costs of medical expenditures, including hospitalizations and consultations, and the indirect cost of loss of income.[4] In 1987, the direct economic cost of smoking was estimated to be between US$2.5 and US$4 million. A full 63 percent of these costs correspond to care received in the private sector, and 27 percent is for care in the public sector. The economic cost associated with premature death was estimated to be between US$3.6 million and

---

4.    Ceron, I. and Videla, M. 1989. Evaluación del Costo del Tabaquismo en Chile 1987. Mimeo.

US$4.5 million. In addition, absence from work due to smoking-related conditions was estimated to cost between US$320 thousand and US$500 thousand.

## Alcohol abuse

Alcohol abuse is a long-standing problem in Chile, causing direct and indirect health effects, abnormal social behavior, and alteration of family and working life. More specifically, alcohol abuse is a leading contributor to the onset of mental disorders, birth defects, chronic liver disease, digestive diseases, cancer, and mortality due to motor vehicle injuries. In addition, a recent study[5] found not only that alcoholics consume low amounts of calcium, but that alcohol consumption diminishes the ability of the body to absorb calcium and thus may be a risk factor for osteoporosis. Several studies on alcohol intake indicate that 70 percent of the adult population drink frequently. Of these, 55 percent are moderate drinkers (up to 100 ml of ethanol/day, with no more than one intoxication/month), 10 percent excessive drinkers (more than 100 ml of ethanol/day, with more than one intoxication/month), and 5 percent alcoholics (alcohol dependent, intake of more than 100 ml/day). Abnormal drinking, including excessive drinkers and alcoholics, is directly associated with being male and inversely with socioeconomic status (Figure IV-4). Although the prevalence of abnormal drinking in adults has remained constant for the last 30 years, the initiation of drinking is occurring at an earlier age than in the past. Increased production levels and low price of wine in the past decades may have contributed to increase the availability and consumption of alcohol among the Chilean population.[6] The most recently available data on per capita alcohol consumption in Latin America and the Caribbean demonstrate that Chile has the fifth highest average liter consumption per person per year (6.72) after Argentina (12.59 liters), Martinique (11.61 liters), Guadeloupe (10.51 liters), and Barbados (7.44 liters).

5. López, R., Pumarino, C., Bustamante, V., et al. 1991. Estudio nutricional en alcoholicos con particular referencia a cálcio y fósforo. Rev. Med. Chile 119:652-658.

6. López, A. C. 1984. Aspectos Económicos del Alcoholismo. Segunda Parte. Mortalidad por Cirrosis Hepatica, Producción y Precio del Vino en Chile: 1950-1982. Mimeo. Departamento de Economía, Universidad de Chile.

**Figure IV-4**

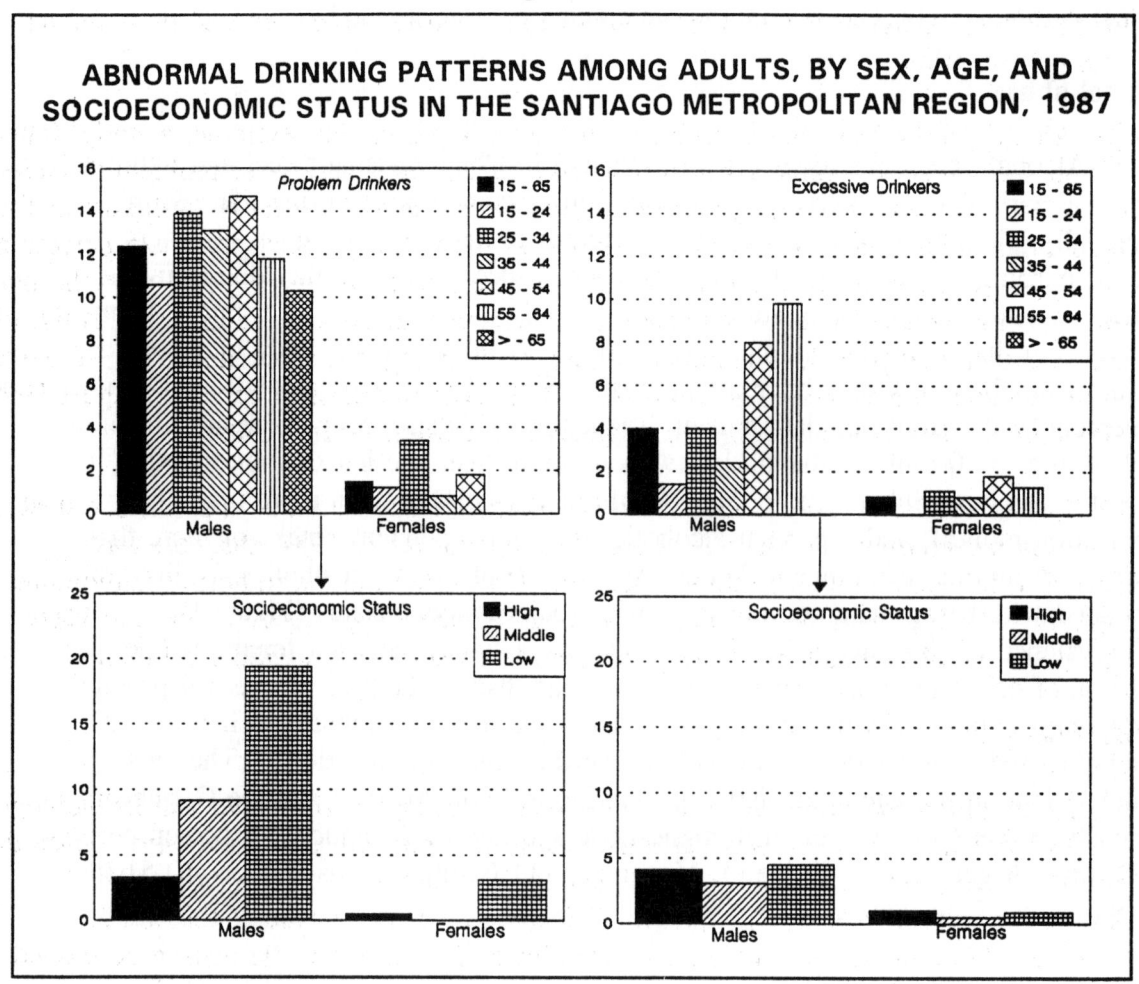

ABNORMAL DRINKING PATTERNS AMONG ADULTS, BY SEX, AGE, AND
SOCIOECONOMIC STATUS IN THE SANTIAGO METROPOLITAN REGION, 1987

Source:  Berrios, X, et al, 1990.

In 1989, it was estimated that 7 percent of ambulatory care visits for mental health-
related diagnoses among adults were due to alcoholism.  The impact on the use of inpatient
services is difficult to evaluate since in many instances, alcoholism is given as a secondary
diagnosis or cause for discharge.  If only the primary diagnosis is considered, alcoholism
accounted for about 7 percent of hospital discharges; if alcoholism-related pathologies are
taken into account, this figure increases to 38 percent.[7]  A similar situation occurs with
causes of death:  although alcohol was the primary cause of death in only 3 percent of the
deaths, this proportion reached 42 percent when other diagnoses associated with alcohol
abuse were considered.  In the United States, alcohol abuse was responsible for

---

7.  These include, among others, tuberculosis, psychosis, neurosis, epilepsy, pneumonia, bronchitis, gastric ulcers,
cirrhosis of the liver, digestive hemorrhages, pancreatitis, injuries and violence.

approximately 5 percent of all deaths.[8] Since alcohol intoxication is a major avoidable risk factor for injury, a significant number of fatal traffic injuries can be reduced by reducing alcohol consumption.

Alcohol abuse also causes problems at the work place. For example, a study[9] found that about 30 percent of employed men in a large copper enterprise were problem drinkers. It is also estimated that the average absentia from work due to drinking is 20 days/year for each abnormal drinker and that drinking diminishes individual productivity by 25 percent and that of the co-workers by 10 percent. In 1989, police arrests for intoxication in public places and for driving while intoxicated represented 23.4 percent and 0.4 percent, respectively, of all the arrests in that period. In terms of disability, drinking was associated with 3-6 percent of all retirements due to medical reasons (total and partial retirement) between August 1990 and December 1991 as reported by the privately-run pension funds (AFPs).

The economic cost of alcohol abuse is important since it results in premature deaths, reduction in productivity, and increased social expenditures. In 1981, this cost was calculated to be about US$ 1.8 billion, including US$ 116.5 million in hospitalization and consultations.[10] The magnitude of this amount can be better appreciated if one considers that the total social expenditure of the government for that year was US$ 1.5 billion.

**Drug abuse**

Although by the early 1960's the occasional consumption of opiates and hallucinogens was known in Chile, their use was not important from a public health standpoint. Since that period, there has been a slow but gradual increase in drug use, involving primarily adolescents and young adults belonging to all income groups. In spite of this trend, however, available information indicate a much lower drug use in Chile than in developed countries. As with alcohol abuse, drug use is linked to abnormal social behaviors and problems such as delinquency and school failure. It also contributes to the onset of mental disorders and, more recently, to the spread of the AIDS epidemic.

Information on the prevalence of drug use has to be analyzed carefully, since definitive criteria of evaluation have not been adopted in the country and diverse methodologies have been used in different studies. Marijuana is estimated to be used at least once a week by 5 percent of adolescents and young adults aged 12 to 19 years, although it is estimated that 50 percent of persons in these age brackets in Chile have smoked it at least once. Stimulants (amphetamines, anorectic drugs) are estimated to be used at least once

---

8.   Ref. 3.

9.   Vega, M.S. and Medina, E. 1983. Beber abnormal en trabajadores de una empresa de la gran minería del cobre. Rev. Med. Chile 111:193-200.

10.   López, A. C. 1984. Aspectos Económicos del Alcoholismo. Primera Parte. El Costo Económico del Alcoholismo en Chile: 1981. Mimeo. Departamento de Economía, Universidad de Chile.

a month without medical prescription by 3-5 percent of persons aged 12 to 19 years. Cocaine is estimated to be consumed at least once a month by 3-5 percent of adolescents and young adults. In recent years, there has been an increase in the availability of cocaine sulfate or base paste, which is smoked instead of inhaled. Inhalable substances, including industrial solvents and various glues, are estimated to be used as recreational drugs at least once a month to produce a "high" by 3-8 percent of children and adolescents aged 8 to 15 years in marginal social conditions. These substances are frequently used in industrial and construction activities, making them widely available. Although psychopharmacological drugs (anti-anxiety drugs) are not estimated to be abused to an important extent, pharmaceutical sales data appear to suggest otherwise, since they are widely and freely consumed with and without therapeutic objectives, including those drugs that are considered controlled substances and classified as psychotropic. An association has been found in Chile between tobacco and alcohol consumption and drug abuse. Smokers are 5-6 times more vulnerable to drug abuse. Also, in a group of adolescents arrested for drug abuse, 51 percent of the fathers and 9 percent of the mothers were problem drinkers.

In cases where treatment is requested, it is usually solicited by family members of the affected individual. Public psychiatric facilities also provide services for cases referred by the judicial system since by law they have to perform an expert analysis of each case. Expert analysis of drug abuse cases represents approximately 3 percent of the total ambulatory visits in public psychiatric facilities. A more serious condition is observed in the northern regions of the country that border the coca-producing countries of Peru and Bolivia as a consequence of increased consumption of cocaine base paste. Discharges associated with drug addiction in the psychiatric services of Arica and Iquique increased from 5 percent in 1988 to about 15 percent in 1990. According to police estimates, about 15 percent of the adult urban population in these regions consumed cocaine base in 1990, up from 3 percent in 1988. This rapid increase has not been seen in other regions of the country.

**Hypertension**

Hypertension is a major risk factor for cardiovascular disease. Population-based studies in Chile have found that the prevalence of hypertension among the adult population ranges between 10 and 16 percent. The variation is due to the cut-off point selected, either 90mm or 95mm for diastolic pressure, and to the starting age of adulthood chosen (15 or 20 years). The above figures imply that between 800,000 and 1.4 million Chileans are hypertensive. There are no important differences in prevalence as it relates to urban and rural areas and by sex. However, prevalence increases significantly with age (Figure IV-5). Information for the whole country extrapolated from the results of a sample study in Santiago shows that 85 percent of hypertensives are 45 years of age or older.

Studies conducted elsewhere have found a correlation between salt intake and elevated blood pressure, however, the relationship between these variables is unknown in Chile. Alcohol intake also increases blood pressure. Beside reductions in salt and alcohol intake among the population, the most promising preventive strategy is the identification and treatment of hypertensives. Since the existing screening program for the general hypertensive population needs to be strengthened, a preventive strategy could target persons above the age of 45 years to maximize impact. The undertaking of such an effort is of great importance given that CVD is the leading cause of death in the country. As shown elsewhere, sustained blood pressure control can help reduce new cases of morbidity and mortality due to coronary heart disease, hypertensive heart disease, and stroke.

**Figure IV-5**

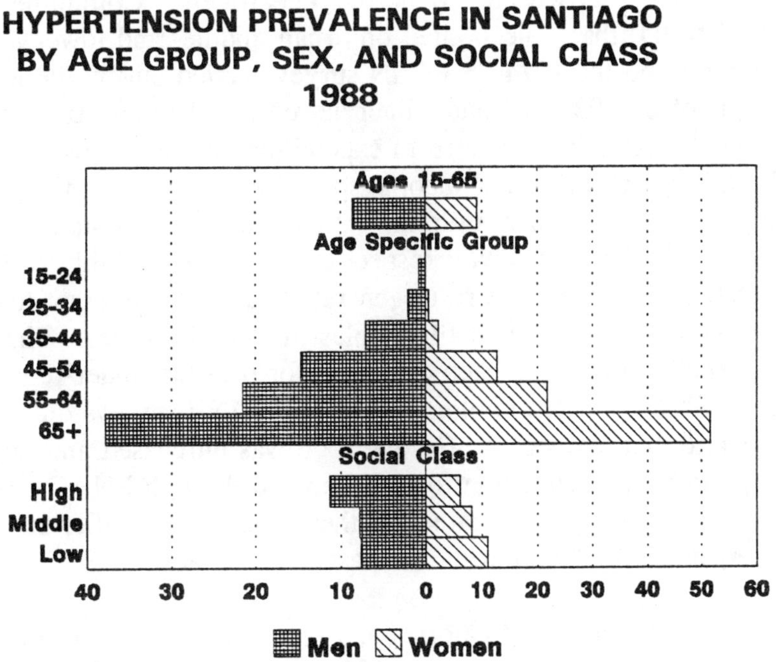

**HYPERTENSION PREVALENCE IN SANTIAGO BY AGE GROUP, SEX, AND SOCIAL CLASS 1988**

Source: Berrios, X. and Jadue, L., 1991.

## Sedentary life

Different studies in developed countries have provided evidence that regular physical exercise can help prevent and manage a variety of non-communicable health conditions, such as coronary heart disease, stroke, hypertension, diabetes, osteoporosis, obesity, colon cancer, and mental health disorders.[11] Longer life span for the population as a whole and increased functional independence among the elderly are additional benefits associated with regular physical exercise. Leisure-time exercise, however, is not a long-held tradition in Chile.

---

11. U. S. Department of Health and Human Services. 1991. Healthy People 2000: national health promotion and disease prevention objectives. Washington, D.C.: Government Printing Office (DHHS Publication no. (PHS) 91-50213).

As found in a study conducted on a representative sample of Santiago, less than 25 percent of men and 13 percent of women exercise regularly or perform exercises for periods of 20 minutes or longer 2 or more days per week. Physical inactivity increases with age in both sexes.

**Nutrition-Related Factors**

**Nutrition patterns**

There have been two major national surveys in Chile where actual food intake was estimated: the 1960 survey carried out by the Interdepartmental Committee on Nutrition for National Defense (ICNND) that concentrated on urban middle- and lower-income groups throughout the country, and the 1974-75 ECEN survey carried out by the MOH based on a representative sample of 24,492 individuals interviewed in urban and rural regions. Food intake has also been estimated indirectly from expenditure surveys carried out by the INE in 1969, 1978, and 1988, which measured income spent by families on food. In addition to these national surveys there are others utilizing smaller, non-representative samples. All these surveys present some problems with respect to the generalizability of their results. Although the ICNND survey results were in general reliable, the attempt to cover most regions of the country produced very small samples in some localities. The ECEN survey, which was not analyzed entirely, has been criticized for possible under-reporting and under-representation of the Santiago Metropolitan Region. The INE surveys did not take into consideration any waste that may occur after the food was purchased and not always included food that was not purchased, such as the food distributed through PNAC. In spite of these methodological concerns, the results obtained in these and other smaller surveys present a general food intake pattern in Chile during the past three decades.

Table IV-1 shows the intake of calories and proteins in Chile since 1960, combining data from the above surveys and other studies. The average intake of protein and calories in Chile has decreased since 1960. The average caloric contribution of macronutrients in the Chilean diet consists of 10-13 percent protein, 17-20 percent fat, and 70 percent carbohydrates, without any major changes since 1960. The proportion of complex carbohydrates to total carbohydrates ranges between 65 percent and 75 percent. The average contribution of fat to the diet is low, and the ratio of unsaturated: monounsaturated:saturated fatty acids equals 1:1:1. Vitamin and mineral intake is on average adequate but with substantial differences among socioeconomic groups.

### Table IV-1
### Average Calorie and Protein (g) Intake in Chile, 1960-1988

|  | 1960[a] | 1964[b]2 | 1969[c] | 1974[d] | 1978[c] | 1988[c] |
|---|---|---|---|---|---|---|
| Calories | 2512 | 2760 | 2587 | 2303 | 2328 | 2133 |
| Proteins | 73 | 91 | 74 | - | 71 | 58 |

[a] ICNND, including kitchen garden, 1960. [b]Arteaga et al., 1964, (probably slightly higher than the average). [c] INE. [d] 1974-75 ECEN survey.
Source: Rozovski, J., and Albala, C., 1992.

Estimates of food consumption based on the three INE surveys indicate that calorie intake fell since 1969 in all social groups; the decrease being most pronounced in low income groups (Table IV-2). The average drop in calorie consumption from 1969 to 1988 was 17.5 percent. The drop in calorie intake among higher income groups is attributed to concerns about excessive intake of saturated fats and cholesterol. Based on the results of the INE surveys, several studies have concluded that 50 percent of the Chilean population (close to 60 percent in Santiago) have a caloric intake below basic requirements.

### Table IV-2
### Daily Calorie and Protein Intake Per Person,[a,b] by Social Group

| | Calorie Intake | | | Protein Intake | | |
|---|---|---|---|---|---|---|
| Quintile | 1969[a] | 1978[a,b] | 1988[a,b] | 1969 | 1978 | 1988 |
| I | 1,925 | 1,626 | 1,425 | 54 | 47 | 39 |
| II | 2,113 | 1,875 | 1,805 | 62 | 51 | 47 |
| III | 2,422 | 2,176 | 2,112 | 68 | 64 | 57 |
| IV | 2,830 | 2,504 | 2,259 | 84 | 77 | 60 |
| V | 3,160 | 3,186 | 2,805 | 100 | 106 | 81 |
| All | 2,587 | 2,328 | 2,133 | 74 | 71 | 58 |

[a] Values for 1969 cover the entire country. Those for 1978 and 1988 cover the Greater Santiago region. [b]The values for 1978 and 1988 include food distributed by PNAC. Those for 1988 also include food distributed by the School Lunch Program. Quintile I: Poorest, and Quintile V: Wealthiest. The present recommendations for calories of the FAO and the U.S. National Academy of Sciences range from 2,150 to 3,050 calories, varying with sex and level of physical activity. For protein the recommendation is around 56 g.
Source: Cabezas, K., 1991.

Protein consumption also decreased between 1969 and 1988 by about 22 percent for the population as a whole. While the consumption of animal protein decreased among the poorer income groups, it remained essentially the same among people in the third, fourth, and fifth income quintiles. The highest consumption of animal protein was observed in the fifth income quintile, where half of the protein consumed is of animal origin. In 1989, a study found consumption of animal protein as a percent of total protein at 66 percent in obese women of high socioeconomic level.[12]

**Table IV-3**
**Proportion of Animal Protein in**
**the Total Intake of Protein, by Social Group**

| Quintile | 1969 | 1978 | 1988 |
|---|---|---|---|
| I | 35.0% | 27.3% | 20.0% |
| II | 37.4% | 32.3% | 30.6% |
| III | 36.0% | 38.6% | 37.2% |
| IV | 39.6% | 43.2% | 43.8% |
| V | 47.1% | 50.6% | 49.4% |
| All | 40.4% | 41.4% | 38.5% |

Source: Cabezas, K., 1991.

Vis-a-vis dietary recommendations to lower the risk of non-communicable diseases, the average Chilean diet is a relatively healthy one from the point of view of fat content. Furthermore, while a large segment of the population consumes a diet low in calories, certain groups of higher socioeconomic status show an excessive caloric intake. The wealthier 60 percent of the population consumes a diet quantitatively and qualitatively different from the poorer 40 percent. The relatively higher prevalence of obesity in poor groups compared to wealthier ones (see next section) suggest a patterns of consumption or intra-household distribution of food that is not reflected in the average values given in the studies available.

Calcium intake by Chileans is about 700 mg/day, below the current recommendations of 1,200 mg/day and 800 mg/day for adolescents and adults, respectively. Particularly disturbing is the low calcium intake by adolescents, especially among low income groups. The early years of life are those in which calcium needs are increased due to the rapid formation of the bone. The attainment of a high bone mass at skeletal maturity (around age 25) is the best protection against age-related loss of bone mass and the development of osteoporosis. Calcium intake throughout life and especially during the early years is critical to maintain proper mineral balance at later ages. The high consumption of alcoholic beverages in Chile may further aggravate the problem. A recent study[13] showed that alcoholics consume low amounts of calcium which correlates to some extent with the decrease in caloric intake from non-alcohol items. The damage inflicted by alcohol to the intestinal mucosa (which in turn diminishes calcium absorption) may further exacerbate the problem.

---

12. Albala, C., Villarroel, P. M., Olivares, S., et al. 1989. Mujeres Obesas De Alto y Bajo Nivel Socioeconomico: Composición de la dieta y niveles séricos de lipoproteinas. Rev. Med. Chile 117:3-9.

13. López, R. D. G., Pumarino, C. H., Bustamante, V. E., et al. 1991. Estudio nutricional en alcoholicos con particular referencia a cálcio y fósforo. Rev. Med. Chile 119:652-658.

## Obesity.

The last decades have witnessed a dramatic increase in developed countries in the prevalence of obesity, a nutritional problem with serious health consequences. The importance of this condition has also grown substantially in developing countries. Although the causal relationship between obesity and disease has not been clearly established, it is well accepted that obesity is a major risk factor in mortality, particularly mortality from coronary heart disease.[14] An association has also been found between obesity and hypertension, diabetes, altered serum lipid profile, ischemic heart disease, certain types of cancer, and pulmonary disease. Stones in the biliary tract are a main risk factor in gallbladder cancer and are twice as common among the obese. Its treatment is difficult and usually unsatisfactory. All this makes obesity a major public health problem which, if prevented, would have a positive multiplier effect on the improvement of the health of adults and the elderly.

The prevalence of obesity ( >120 percent of weight/height index) in Chile can be gleaned from the results of studies undertaken in the past decade. Due to differences in indicators and cut-off points utilized, it is difficult to make direct comparisons between these studies. In addition, the results of the studies are not generalizable for the country as a whole since most of them were conducted in Santiago. In all the studies analyzed, obesity was found to be more prevalent in women than in men. Prevalence increased with age and was higher in women of lower socioeconomic level. These findings are consistent with those in other countries.

A study[15] performed in the mid-1980's based on an adult population sample drawn from users of an out-patient center in the Santiago Metropolitan Region found that 28 percent of women and nearly 5 percent of men were obese. The overall prevalence for both sexes combined was 21 percent, with a significant statistical difference between persons above and below 45 years of age for both sexes. Another study[16] of adults of different socioeconomic levels in Santiago conducted in the mid-1980's found that the prevalence of obesity was 31 percent and 20 percent for women and men, respectively. Prevalence was higher in females of lower socioeconomic levels but not in men (Figure IV-6).

---

14. World Health Organization. 1990. Diet, Nutrition and the Prevention of Chronic Diseases. Report of a WHO Study Group. WHO Technical Report Series 797. WHO: Geneva.

15. Paez, G., Buguna, C., and Flaskamp, R. 1986. Evaluación del estado nutritivo en un policlínico de medicina de adultos. Análisis sobre obesidad y sexo. Proceedings of the VI Jornadas Chilenas de Salud Pública. No. 117:319.

16. Bove, I. 1985. Prevalencia de obesidad de 4241 adultos pertenecientes a diferente nivel socioeconomico de Santiago. Tesis para obtener el Grado de Magister en Nutrición Humana. Instituto de Nutrición y Tecnología de Alimentos.

**Figure IV-6**

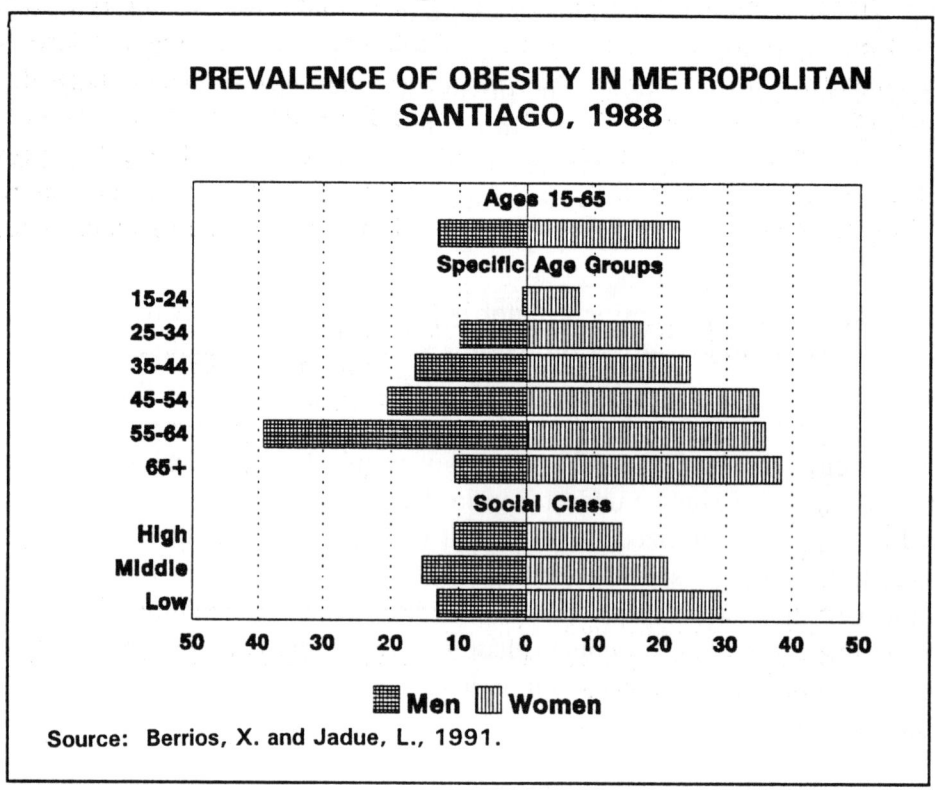

**PREVALENCE OF OBESITY IN METROPOLITAN SANTIAGO, 1988**

Source: Berrios, X. and Jadue, L., 1991.

Another way to assess obesity based on the relationship between body weight and height is the use of the Quetelet Index, also known as Body Mass Index (BMI). The BMI, which correlates well with body fat, is calculated by dividing body weight in kilograms by the square of height in meters. When the subjects in the latter study were evaluated based on BMI above 30 kg/m$^2$ for men and 28 kg/m$^2$ for women, the sex and socioeconomic differences persisted. Although the prevalence of obesity based on BMI is lower than when based on weight/height index, women still had a higher prevalence than men and among women, there was an inverse relationship between socioeconomic level and prevalence of obesity. Other study[17] has also shown this relationship (Figure IV-6). A substantial increase in prevalence with age was also noted in women. Based on these figures, the prevalence of obesity in females in this population is comparable to the prevalence of this condition in women from the United States and other developed countries. When the degree of obesity was assessed, women had a higher degree than men, but only a small proportion in both groups was above 50 percent overweight.

17. Berrios, X., Jadue, L., Zenteno, J., et al. 1990. Prevalencia de factores de riesgo de enfermedades crónicas. Estudio en la población general de la Región Metropolitana. Rev. Med. Chile 118:597-604.

Several studies[18] have looked at the prevalence of obesity in adolescents in Chile. Table IV-4 summarizes their findings. The relatively high prevalence of adolescent obesity in Chile, specially in women, is disturbing given the high risk of this condition for the development of diabetes, high-risk pregnancy, and other conditions. In addition, there is a strong familial association with obesity. When both parents are overweight, approximately 80 percent of the children born to those parents are also overweight, which suggests a perpetuation of the problem through generations. Childhood obesity also increases the likelihood of obesity in adult life. It strongly points to the necessity of targeting prevention programs to the younger groups in the country. Once this condition is present, its treatment is extremely difficult, and even when successful, it exhibits a high rate of recurrence.

**Table IV-4**
**Prevalence of Obesity (%) in Adolescents**

|       | 1982[a] Santiago | 1986[a] Chillan | 1986-87 Santiago | 1987 |
|-------|------------------|-----------------|------------------|------|
| All   |                  |                 |                  | 19.4 |
| Men   | 4.7              | --              | 10.5             | 4.9  |
| Women | 28.0             | 13.3            | 32.4             | 30.4 |
| Age   |                  | 15-18           | 16-18            | 15-18 |
| N     | 351              | 1147            | 4509             |      |

[a] Low and middle socioeconomic level.
Source: Rozovski, J., and Albala, C., 1992, on the basis of various studies in Chile.

## Cholesterol

Multiple epidemiological studies have demonstrated the role of serum cholesterol in the pathogenesis of coronary heart disease (CHD). Population groups with high incidence of CHD show high serum cholesterol levels (above 200 mg/dl). The opposite is also true: in population groups where serum cholesterol is low, there is a lower incidence of CHD. Many studies have also shown that a reduction in blood cholesterol levels in an individual significantly reduces the risk of contracting CHD.

Furthermore, studies have indicated that the type of diet has a strong influence on serum cholesterol levels: the number of dietary calories and the quantity and quality of dietary fats, protein, and carbohydrates can alter cholesterol levels. Those individuals consuming high amounts of saturated fats, animal proteins, and simple carbohydrates show higher cholesterol levels than individuals consuming less of these macro nutrients.

---

18. Burrows, R., Diaz, L., and Muzzo, S. 1982. Estado Nutritivo en adolescentes de clase media y baja. Rev. Chilena de Nutrición 10:129; Mardones, M. A, Atalah, E. 1987. Prevalencia y factores condicionantes de la obesidad en adolescentes de sexo femenino. Rev. Chilena Pediátrica 58:311-316; Ivanovic, D., Olivares, M., and Ivanovic, R. Estado nutricional de escolares según sexo y edad. Región Metropolitana, Chile 1986-1987. Rev. Med. Chile 118:916-924; and Araya, H., Ayala, B., Dominguez, C., et al. 1979. Diagnóstico de políticas y programas de alimentación y nutrición en Chile. Informe Técnico Docente 98/79. Instituto de Nutrición y Tecnología de Alimentos, Universidad de Chile.

The relationship between diet and cholesterol levels has been studied in Chile by different investigators. Most studies were conducted in Santiago, and they usually comprised small, non-representative samples of individuals of different socioeconomic levels and ages. In only a few studies was the composition of the diet studied. Although the quality of the results of these studies varies, there is a certain consistency among them that allows some conclusions to be drawn. In the early 1980's, while a study[19] of professional males in Concepción found values of serum cholesterol above 200 mg/dl in 24 percent of the subjects, a study[20] in Santiago found that 52 percent of professional males 40 years of age and older had serum cholesterol values above 220 mg/dl. A 1984 survey of outpatients from two large hospitals in Santiago,[21] which served a low income population, found a median serum cholesterol level of 185 mg/dl. In 1987-1988, a survey[22] of a representative sample of men and women over 15 years of age in Santiago found that about 32 percent of men and 33 percent of women had cholesterol levels above 200 mg/dl. In addition, a significant increase in cholesterol values was found with income and age.

The average levels of serum cholesterol observed in Chile are less than those found in the United States and other developed countries. Chilean average levels are close to those recommended internationally. However, as shown in Table IV-5, Chileans in higher socioeconomic levels show higher levels of cholesterol than those in lower strata. It is conceivable that the role played by serum lipoproteins as a risk factor for coronary heart disease in the middle to lower income levels in Chile is less than in industrialized countries. The reason may be the type of diet consumed by this population, with the average share of fat as a proportion of total calories of less than 30 percent, an adequate relationship between saturated, monounsaturated and polyunsaturated fats, protein consumption of 15-25 percent of total calories, and carbohydrate consumption at 55-65 percent, with predominance of complex carbohydrates. Conversely, persons of higher income levels tend to consume a diet higher in saturated fats and animal proteins and demonstrate higher level of serum lipoproteins. In the last three decades there has been a trend in higher income groups toward an increase in blood lipid levels.

19. Chamorro, G., Costa, E., Valenzuela, G., et al. 1980. Riesgo cardiovascular en dos poblaciones laborales Chilenas. Rev. Med. Chile 108:697-699.

20. Chamorro, G., Arteaga, A., Casanegra, P., et al. 1983. Factores de riesgo de enfermedad cardiovascular ateroesclerótica y prueba de esfuerzo en hombres de nivel profesional en Santiago. Rev. Med. Chile 111:1009-1017.

21. Gomez, R., Sandoval, S., Getavagno, A. 1984. Valores de referencia para población adulta en química clínica. Boletín del Instituto de Salud Pública de Chile 25:236-240.

22. Ref. 17.

**Table IV-5**
**Serum Lipoprotein and Diet (average) by**
**Socioeconomic Level (SEL)**

|  | High SEL1 | | Low SEL | |
|---|---|---|---|---|
|  | Males | Females | Males | Females |
| Cholesterol (mg/dl) | 211 | 226 | 185 | 179 |
| % HDL Cholesterol (mg/dl) | -- | 43.8 | 46.2 | 50.7 |
| Triglycerides (mg/dl) | 52.9 | 148.7 | 109 | 104.9 |
| Total Calories | 2475 | 2420 | 2168 | 2340 |
| % Calories from fat | 30.6 | 31 | 23 | 22 |

Source: Rozovski, J. and Albala, C., 1992, on the basis of various Chilean studies.

## Community-Wide Risk Factors

### Air pollution

Air pollution in Chile is associated with the rapid economic growth and continued urbanization of recent decades. The only information available about this risk factor is from Santiago, one of the most polluted cities in Latin America. Air pollution measurements have been taken in Santiago since 1978. In 1989, the levels of air pollution found in different measurement stations throughout the city frequently exceeded the yearly maximum permissible concentration of suspended particles of 60-90 ug/m3 under World Health Organization standards, varying from 177 in La Granja to 313 ug/m3 in Pudahuel. The same occurred with carbon monoxide, which exceeded the accepted standards between 12 days in Northern Santiago and 80 days in Eastern Santiago. Due to a thermal inversion (an increase in temperature with altitude), carbon monoxide levels tend to be very high during fall and winter. In 1989, ozone, a secondary contaminant which also exceeds the accepted limits during spring and summer, was found to exceed the permissible level between 17 and 583 times as reported by the different measurement stations. Overall, the daily ambient air quality standard for respirable particles (PM-10) was violated 100 days in 1990, 69 days in 1991, and 60 days in 1992.[23]

---

23. For a complete discussion on this topic see: The World Bank. 1994. Chile Managing Environmental Problems: Economic Analysis of Selected Issues. Report No.13061-CH. Country Operations Division, Country Department IV, LAC Regional Office.

The air pollution problem in Santiago is caused mainly by a large and antiquated fleet of more than 11,000 diesel buses and dust that is stirred up in more than 400 miles of unpaved roads around the city. This problem is aggravated by geological and atmospheric factors such as the Andean mountains that surround the city and thermal inversions that block the dissipation of polluted air in winter. Other elements that pollute the air in Chile are emissions of sulfur dioxide, arsenic and heavy metals from factories and copper-mining smelters. The particles in the air include a large proportion of particles less than 2.5 microns in diameter, which can be inhaled deeply into the lungs and thus pose a great public health risk. As discussed in Annex A, air pollution contributes to chronic respiratory diseases and is associated with lung cancer; also, heart disease can be aggravated by high levels of carbon monoxide. In addition, air pollution causes discomfort in the daily life of the population as a result of irritation of the eyes, nose, and throat, as well as diminished tolerance of physical activity. In the United States, it has been estimated that pollutants are associated with 2 percent of all cancer deaths and that elevations of respirable pollutants, such as sulfur dioxide and carbon monoxide, are associated with transient increases in daily mortality rates of 4-16 percent.[24]

## Occupational hazards

Several studies[25] have been done in Chile on risk factors associated with occupational diseases, but there is incomplete knowledge of exposed working populations and of the incidence and prevalence of occupational diseases. The exposure to silica, which is a risk factor to COPD, is considerable, owing to the high rate of employment in mining; this exposure also occurs in the ceramic industry and in the manufacturing of glass, tiles, and abrasives. The risk of silicosis varies directly with the quantity of free silica dust in the air. Data from CODELCO-CHILE, the largest mining enterprise in the country, revealed a range of free silica at the Andina and El Teniente mines of between 25 and 30 percent. The uncontrolled exposure to arsenic in mines for smelting of copper ore is associated with lesions of the skin and respiratory tract. Lung cancer is also directly associated with exposure to arsenic. The risk of asbestosis is related to exposure to asbestos when manufacturing asbestos cement products (e.g., pipes) and gloves, apparel and boots made of fireproof fabrics, as well as in the demolition of buildings. Lead, one of the most common contaminants found in battery manufacturing and recycling factories, produce liver and brain

---

24. Ref. 3.

25. Supúlveda, J. 1989. La Salud de los Trabajadores en el Chile Actual. Cuadernos Médicos Sociales XXX(3):62-70; Trucco, M. 1989. Exposición a Substancias Químicas en el Medio Laboral. Efectos Psicológicos y Psiquiátricos. Rev. Med. Chile 117:212-218; Oyanguren, H. Epidemiología de las Enfermedades Profesionales y Evaluación del Riesgo. Cuadernos Médicos Sociales (en prensa); Ríos, E. 1989. Intoxicación Familiar por Plomo. Rev. Med. Chile 117:671-676; Oyanguren, C. 1983. Indices Biólogicos en la Exposición a Plomo. Boletín del Instituto de Salud Pública de Chile Vol. XXIV, No. 1-2; Montaña, N. 1986. Silicosis en Atacama, Frecuencia y Algunas Características Asociadas. Cuadernos Médicos Sociales XXVII, 4:159-165; Sandoval, H. 1987. Contaminación Ambiental por Arsénico en Chile. Cuadernos Médicos Sociales XXVIII, 1:30-37; Martínez, L. 1985. Epidemiológia del Cáncer Broncopulmonar en Chile. Rev. Med. Chile 113:48-54; Salazar, A. M. 1986. Epidemiología de la Sordera Profesional. Departamento de Salud Ocupacional. Instituto de Salud Pública.

damage and can increase blood pressure, one of the leading risk factors for cardiovascular disease. As many of these factories are clandestine operations, working conditions in them are deficient. Exposure to pesticides occurs mainly among seasonal agricultural laborers, who are untrained in the use of these chemicals. Exposure to solvents occurs in industrial plants, tanneries, shoe factories, and dry-cleaning plants. The usually high levels of noise in industrial and mining establishments are associated with occupational deafness.

## Interactions among risk factors

As discussed in this chapter, several health risk factors acting alone or in combination are associated with the onset of the major causes of death and disease in Chile today. Some of them are more prevalent among the uneducated poor, contributing to increase the burden of illness and disease in low income groups. Since risk factors are synergistic in their effect, the relative risk of developing non-communicable diseases and suffering injuries increases sharply when various risk factors are combined.[26] In Chile, information on the interaction of risk factors for non-communicable conditions and injuries is limited except for the results of a study[27] conducted in the late 1980's on a sample of adults in the Santiago Metropolitan Region (Figure IV-7). According to those data, close to 60 percent of individuals had two and three lifestyle-related risk factors. Among men, the two most frequent associations were between smoking and sedentarism, and between smoking, alcohol consumption and sedentarism. Among women, the associations between smoking and sedentarism and between obesity and sedentarism were the most prevalent.

26. Lilienfeld, A.M. and Lilienfeld, D.E. 1980. Foundations of Epidemiology. New York: Oxford University Press.

27. Berrios, X. and Jadue, L. 1991. Factores de riesgo de enfermedad ateroesclerótica en Chile. Boletín Esc. de Medicina, P. Universidad Católica de Chile. 20:2:76-79.

## Figure IV-7

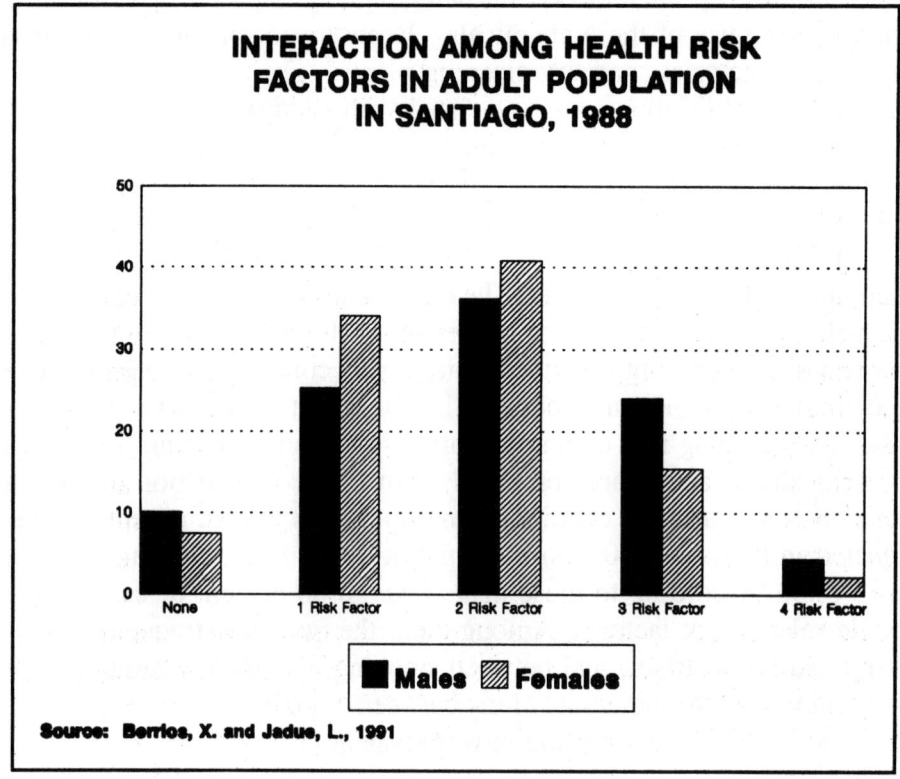

**INTERACTION AMONG HEALTH RISK FACTORS IN ADULT POPULATION IN SANTIAGO, 1988**

Source: Berrios, X. and Jadue, L., 1991

## CHAPTER V

## *FUTURE HEALTH TRENDS IN CHILE*[1]

### The Forecast Model

As discussed in detail in previous chapters, Chile is experiencing and will continue to experience morbidity and mortality patterns similar to other middle income countries. These are characterized by increasing incidence of non-communicable diseases and injuries, especially among older individuals. At the same time, the country's health care system must continue to provide health services for communicable diseases that are common in lesser developed countries. As a result of these two divergent demands on the health care system, policy makers and health planners must carefully assess future health care needs and set priorities accordingly.

In assessing future demands on the Chilean health system, there are three critical factors that must be considered. These are: (a) the changing demographic profile as determined by changing birth patterns in the recent past, increasing life expectancy at birth, and decreased risk of death at younger ages; (b) changes in lifestyles, diet, and exposure to environmental and occupational risk factors; and (c) the emergence of non-communicable conditions after long latency periods, with their incumbent increased demands for diagnosis, treatment, and follow up care.

Based on data from Chile and other countries, a forecast model was constructed for this study to provide estimates of likely future trends for the main non-communicable illnesses. Although forecast models only provide an "order of magnitude" approximation of future health care needs, such models can quantify the inevitable demographic shifts that are already in process, the fairly certain effects of continued and increasing exposure to health risk factors, and the long incubation periods of many non-communicable diseases.

The forecast model developed for this study projected morbidity and mortality trends in Chile using currently available data on cause-specific mortality rates and current distributions of major risk factors. Data on recent mortality trends, expected birth patterns, and changes in risk factors were also included. The model uses a Markov chain model whose cells represent risk factor states associated with non-communicable illness morbidity and mortality to simulate the effects of changes in the probability of transition from one state to another (e.g., from healthy state to presence of risk factor to death). By examining successful strategies of prevention elsewhere, the model was able to estimate the impact which effective disease prevention strategies could have on future health care requirements. The impact of health interventions is seen through modification of transition probabilities. The key assumptions and mechanisms of the model are described in Box V-1.

---

1. This chapter was prepared on the basis of information from the health modelling exercise by H. Dennis Tolley.

**Box V-1**

### Assumptions and Mechanisms of the Simulation Model

**Assumptions:**

- Each individual can be placed into a health or risk factor state described by the presence of any number of the following risk factors: high blood cholesterol; hypertension; current smoker; former smoker; heavy drinker.

- The probability of death is a function of age, gender and the specific risk factors present, as identified in the medical literature.

- During each year simulated, an individual may change his/her risk factor profile or may die of a specific cause of death.

- Probabilities of causes of death and risk factor incidence are estimated using Chilean data.

**Mechanism of Simulation:**

- The initial profile of risk factors in the population is estimated using current data on risk factor prevalence and recent patterns of smoking.

- Beginning with 1990, mortality/risk factor experience for each year is simulated through the following steps:

  1. Determine the number of individuals in each risk factor state who die of each cause of death. These are removed from the live population.
  2. Determine the number of the remaining individuals in each risk factor state who change risk factor states by either increasing their risk factors or by reducing them.
  3. Age the individuals by moving all alive to one year older.
  4. Determine the number of individuals who enter the adult population at age 15. World Bank projections were used to determine size of the incoming cohort of 15 year-olds.
  5. Advance the calendar year by one, return to step 1 and repeat.

- For each year the number of deaths by age, gender and cause are tabulated along with the number of individuals in each risk factor group. These are the basis for analysis.

Two scenarios were considered in the model. The **baseline scenario** reflects current trends as they might continue into the future if no preventive interventions are adopted. This means that the forecast obtained under the baseline scenario is what Chile might expect to see if health risk factors and health care practices continue as they are currently. The **optimistic scenario** represents an improvement in the health profile as reflected in the reduction of risk factor prevalence and a decline in age-specific mortality from different causes.

Within this context, it is important to note that as countries develop, the mortality rate falls even though the prevalence of some risk factors increases (e.g., consumption of alcohol, animal fats, and tobacco). The correlation of increasing national wealth and per capita income with a decrease in overall mortality has been clearly observed in data world wide. However, as yet no definitive explanation of the phenomenon has been put forth. The increase in longevity seems to occur even without health care and nutrition improvements, indicating the presence of one or more latent positive risk factors associated with general development. Chile has been the beneficiary of such an overall reduction in mortality for the past several decades and will undoubtedly continue to be so. This was assumed in mortality projections for Chile prepared by the World Bank independently of this study.[2] These projections show roughly a 7-9 percent reduction every 5 years in the overall 5-year adult mortality rate.

The trend in overall mortality rate reduction as Chile continues to develop and increase in wealth was included in the stochastic model as follows. Since projected decreases in overall mortality do not mean cause specific mortality rates will decrease, it was necessary to examine the recent trends (last 20 years) for causes specifically identified in the model. The causes not specifically identified were assumed to have an across-the-board 10 percent decrease in the five-year mortality rate for adults of all ages and for both sexes. Changes in the identified causes were altered according to recent trends and changes in the risk factor distribution. The primary causes of death affected by this across-the-board reduction are "Infectious Diseases" and "Other Causes." The result was that the forecast mortality rate under baseline conditions was similar to but slightly higher than the World Bank projections. The probable cause for the slightly higher rate was the explicit inclusion of anticipated increases in risk factors and certain causes of death dealt with only implicitly in the previous World Bank projections.

**Basis for the optimistic scenario**

The basic parameters for the likely effects of proposed interventions were obtained through discussions with officials of the MOH and other Chilean researchers concerning the various levels of intervention they believed possible (e.g., reductions in stroke through reduction in hypertension; reductions in injury deaths accomplished by improved safety measures; reductions in respiratory disease through improved environmental control and improved work conditions in factories). The proposed targets for Chile were also set taking into account actual reductions in risk factor prevalence and mortality achieved in several prospective intervention studies in developed countries, including the Multiple Risk Factor

---

2.  See: Vu, M.T., Bos, E., and Levin, A. 1993. Latin America and Caribbean Region Population Projections (1992-93 Edition). Washington, D.C.: The World Bank.

Intervention Trial in the United States.[3] The optimistic scenario is thus considered attainable in the Chilean context with concerted effort.

The intervention strategy contemplated by the optimistic scenario results in reductions in the probability of death by certain causes and in reductions in the prevalence of risk factors. These reductions are in addition to any reductions (or increases) in risk factor levels that were assumed to occur naturally under the baseline case. A summary of the reductions in risk factor prevalence are given in Table V-1. For example, within 10 years (i.e., the year 2000), the prevalence of hypertensive males in the Chilean population will be reduced 3.6 percent by the optimistic scenario over what the prevalence is forecast to be under baseline conditions.

## Table V-1
### Reductions in Risk Factor Prevalence Under
### Optimistic Scenario

|  | 10 Years | 20 Years | 40 Years |
|---|---|---|---|
| **MALES** | | | |
| Hypertension | 3.6% | 8.4% | 10.0% |
| Cholesterol | 3.6% | 9.1% | 17.4% |
| Smoking | 9.4% | 21.4% | 34.7% |
| Alcohol | 9.1% | 10.0% | 10.3% |
| **FEMALES** | | | |
| Hypertension | 3.7% | 8.0% | 12.2% |
| Cholesterol | 3.4% | 9.7% | 17.4% |
| Smoking | 9.8% | 22.4% | 26.0% |
| Alcohol | 9.3% | 9.8% | 11.2% |

---

3. Multiple Risk Factor Intervention Trial Research Group. 1982. Multiple risk factor intervention trial. JAMA 248:1465-77.

Hypertension Detection and Follow-Up Program Cooperative Group. 1988. Persistence of reduction in blood pressure and mortality of participants in the hypertension detection and follow-up program. JAMA 259:2113-22.

Muldoon, M. F., Manuck, S. B., and Mathews, K. A. 1990. Lowering cholesterol concentrations and mortality; a quantitative review of primary prevention trials. British Journal of Medicine 301:309-14.

Holme, I. 1990. An analysis of randomized trials evaluating the effects of cholesterol reduction on total mortality and coronary heart disease incidence. Circulation 82:1916-24.

U. S. Department of Health and Human Services. 1991. Strategies to Control Tobacco use in the U. S. NIH Monograph #92-3316.

Table V-2 gives the reductions in the likelihood of death by specific causes under the optimistic scenario. These reductions are in addition to those projected under baseline conditions. They are intended to reflect the improved prognosis of individuals resulting from improved medical care. For example, therapy, either drug or otherwise, which reduces hypertension and blood cholesterol among those with these risk factors would be expected to reduce the likelihood of death due to stroke and coronary heart attack. Thus the interventions proposed under the optimistic scenario not only include reduction of the incidence of risk factors, but also an increase in health care for those who possess the risk factor.

The results of the forecast exercise may help sharpen the focus on priority areas and on intervention strategies that will help reduce the burden of death and disease in Chile in the long term. It should be noted that the model allows for modification of any of the assumed risk and mortality reductions, so as to permit revision of the projections based on different expectations of the likely effects of non-communicable disease interventions.

## Caveats concerning the forecast model

Since the model focuses on adult health, particularly those conditions and mortality patterns influenced by the above health risk factors, only the adult population was considered. This means that all tables are for the population aged 15 years and older. New births in the population are new entrants aged 15. Thus possible improvements in infant and child health are reflected in the model only through the increase in the number of individuals who enter the 15 and older population.

A second point regarding the model is the list of risk factors and causes of death considered. There are many non-communicable illnesses of interest that might have been included. The restricted list used in the model was determined by several factors. First was the availability of relevant data. Those for which good data were not available were grouped in the "all other causes" category. Second was the strength of relationship to some known health risk factor of interest. Smoking, for example, is a risk factor for many non-communicable diseases. However, only major conditions such as lung cancer, heart disease, and increased likelihood of stroke were included. Third, the list of conditions was constructed with an eye toward health intervention. If there was no risk factor or health intervention that would affect the future pattern of a condition, the condition was included in the "all other" category without affecting the model's results.

Table V-2
Reductions in Probability of Death Under
Optimistic Scenario

|  | 5 Years | 10 Years | 20 Years |
|---|---|---|---|
| **MALES** | | | |
| Stroke | 10% | 20% | 35% |
| Coronary Heart Disease | 15% | 25% | 40% |
| Traffic Accident | 10% | 20% | 20% |
| Respiratory Disease | 10% | 20% | 40% |
| **FEMALES** | | | |
| Stroke | 10% | 20% | 20% |
| Coronary Heart Disease | 15% | 25% | 40% |
| Traffic Accident | 10% | 20% | 20% |
| Respiratory Disease | 5% | 10% | 10% |

## Demographic considerations

As noted above, the population profile used in the forecast model was based on predicted numbers of individuals entering the adult population (aged 15 and older) and the mortality rates for those in this age group under the baseline scenario. The forecast profile for males is given in Figure V-1.

As seen in this figure, the rate of new entrants into the Chilean adult population will follow a smooth positive growth pattern until about 2015 at which time the rate of new entrants will level off to almost a constant value. The overall growth rate for the entire adult population, however, will be much faster as indicated by the "wave" in the figure moving into middle age, from age 30 in 1990 to about age 65 by 2030, increasing the risk pool for non-communicable illness.

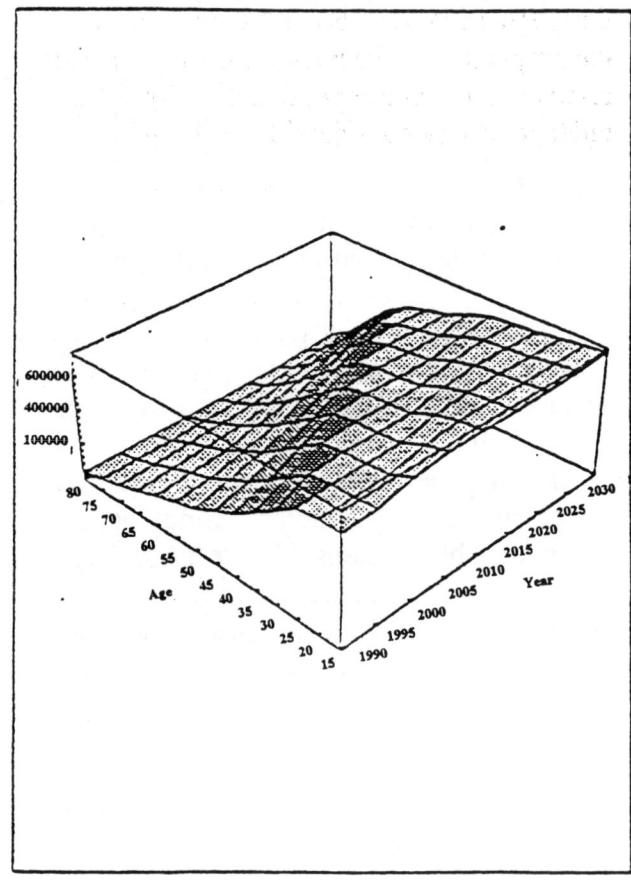

Figure V-1: Population age profile, males.

The wave seen in Figure V-1 is a result of a "baby boom" effect occurring about 1960-65 coupled with decreased infant/young adult mortality rates over the last two decades. As a result of this wave of population growth, the prevalence of certain age-dependent non-communicable conditions and the types of health services demanded will change. It should be expected, therefore, that those health care needs and demands that are correlated with aging will show relative increases in Chile as this wave ripples through the age groups.

Figure V-2 gives the population profile for females. The profile here resembles that for males. Although not evident from the two figures, the number of females is larger than the number of males. This is illustrated in Table V-3, where the male-female ratio remains essentially constant over time. The ratio is also the same among the population aged 60 and over. However, the proportion of the population over 60 years relative to the entire population 15 years and older increases considerably with time.

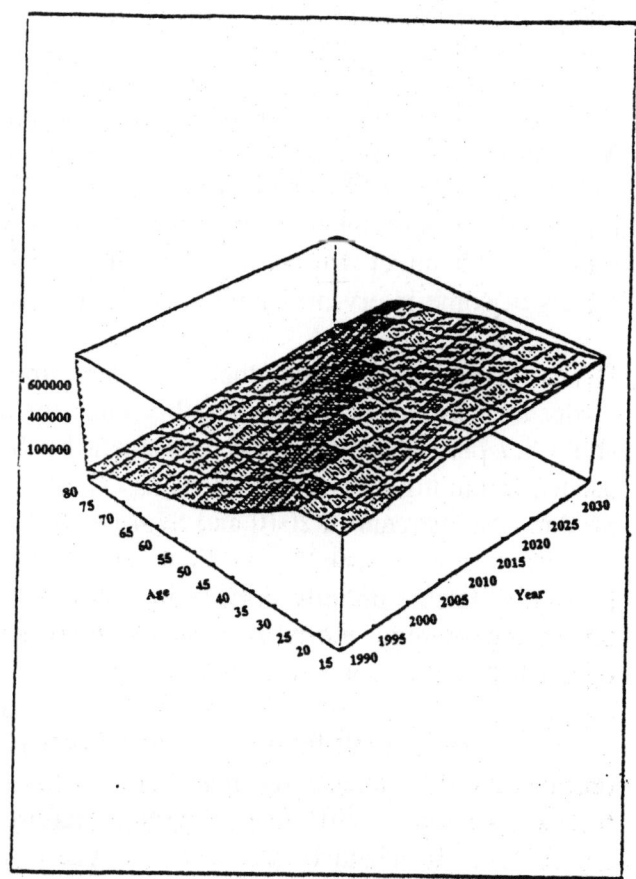

Figure V-2: Population age profile, females.

**Table V-3**
**Chile:  Population Projections--Adult Age Group  (in '000)**

| Year | Age 15-59 | Age 60+ | Percent 60+ | % Males 15-59 | % Females 15-59 | % Males 60+ | % Females 60+ |
|------|-----------|---------|-------------|---------------|-----------------|-------------|---------------|
| 1990 | 7,853     | 1,126   | 12.5        | 49.7          | 50.3            | 42.0        | 58.0          |
| 2010 | 10,671    | 2,030   | 16.0        | 49.9          | 50.1            | 43.4        | 56.6          |
| 2030 | 11,873    | 3,872   | 24.6        | 49.9          | 50.1            | 44.7        | 55.3          |

Source:  World Bank estimates from projection model.

In general, the adoption of effective disease prevention strategies in Chile will have very little effect on the shape and size of the population waves observed in Figures V-1 and V-2 since the future adult population is already born.  These strategies, however, will help to reduce the societal burden of non-communicable diseases and injuries, particularly among middle-age groups, improving their well-being and productivity.  Under the optimistic scenario, this effect will be visible for many causes of death in as little as 10 years.  The effects of some interventions will take longer to emerge among the elderly.

Table V-4 illustrates the major demographic effects of the intervention strategy.  Under the baseline scenario mortality rates for the entire adult population will increase by about 8.7 percent by 2010 and 35 percent by 2030, with much of the increased deaths occurring among middle-aged persons.  The probability of survival to 60 will increase from 84.2 to 85.7 percent in 2010 and 87.4 percent in 2030.

Under the optimistic scenario, as a result of the adoption of an effective disease prevention strategy, mortality will increase much more slowly among the adult population.  By 2010 there will be almost a 3 percent decrease, and by 2030, a 20 percent increase, compared to 1990 (Table V-4).  Most of the deaths will occur among the elderly.  The probability of survival to age 60 will be higher in 2010 and in 2030 than under baseline conditions.  Both male and female life expectancy at 15 years will also be higher.  Chile may be able to avoid by 2010 about 9,900 premature adult deaths per year and by 2030 about 14,100 annual premature adult deaths.  As a consequence, under the optimistic scenario Chile's adult population will increase by about 81,000 by 2010 and by 321,500 by 2030 over the baseline scenario.  As discussed in Chapter II, as a larger number of adults survives to older ages, they will claim a proportionally larger share of health and other social resources, posing a major challenge to the organization, financing, and delivery of social services.

**Table V-4**
**Main Demographic Effects of Preventive Strategy**

| | Year | Baseline | Optimistic |
|---|---|---|---|
| Annual Adult/Elderly Deaths (15-79) | 1990 | 64.5 | -- |
| (Thousands) | 2000 | 79.6 | 74.7 |
| | 2010 | 98.9 | 89.0 |
| | 2030 | 149.9 | 135.8 |
| Mortality Rate (15-79) | 1990 | 724.7 | -- |
| (Per 100,000) | 2000 | 740.9 | 695.0 |
| | 2010 | 787.8 | 705.1 |
| | 2030 | 974.9 | 867.6 |
| Excess Adult/Elderly Deaths (15-79) | 2010 | 9.9 | |
| (Thousands) | 2030 | 14.1 | |
| Net Population | 2000 | | 7.0 |
| (Thousands) | 2010 | | 81.0 |
| | 2030 | | 321.5 |
| Survival | 1990 | 84.2 | -- |
| Probability (%) | 2010 | 85.7 | 87.7 |
| (Age 15 to 60) | 2030 | 87.4 | 89.5 |
| Male Life Expectancy | 1990 | 70.6 | -- |
| (Given Survival to Age 15) | 2010 | 71.4 | 73.4 |
| | 2030 | 72.6 | 74.8 |
| Female Life Expectancy | 1990 | 75.9 | -- |
| (Given Survival to Age 15) | 2010 | 77.6 | 78.3 |
| | 2030 | 78.7 | 79.7 |

Source: World Bank estimates from projection model.

## Epidemiological Impact

The forecast model measures the interactive impact of demographic (i.e., the aging of the population) and epidemiological (i.e., changing health risks) variables on the future health profile of the Chilean adult population. In this section, projected mortality patterns for both the baseline and optimistic scenarios are presented for six of the leading groups of non-communicable conditions. These are: coronary heart disease, stroke, lung cancer, traffic injuries, chronic respiratory diseases, and cirrhosis of the liver. A summary of the findings for the six selected causes of death is given in Table V-5. Other non-communicable conditions (e.g., various cancers) that will contribute to shaping the future mortality and morbidity profile in Chile are not considered in this section. Also discussed is the projected reduction in the number of deaths for these causes resulting from effective disease prevention interventions under an optimistic scenario.

Under baseline conditions, by 2010 these six causes will account for about 46 percent of total adult deaths and about 53 percent by 2030. With a disease prevention strategy under an optimistic scenario, their share of total deaths will increase to 43 percent in 2010 and 52 percent in 2030. The pattern of future mortality under baseline and optimistic conditions also indicates that improvement as measured by number of lives saved is very uneven. Lung cancer deaths, for example, will increase under the optimistic scenario. The cause of this uneven effect is explained below. Table V-6, which gives the expected deaths per 100,000 population, gives essentially the same picture as Table V-5. Here, however, after adjusting for population, the changes in mortality by cause are easier to see. Only in the case of lung cancer are the age/gender-specific mortality rates for individuals under the optimistic scenario higher than the baseline scenario. The aggregate effects of a changing population profile and competing causes of death seem to explain observed changes that are small or even negative relative to the forecast baseline situation.

In general, mortality from these six leading causes will increase in the future as a result of the demographic transition taking place in Chile, growing exposure to major health risk factors, and the eventual emergence of non-communicable diseases which have been developing over a long incubation period.

**Coronary heart disease**

As shown in Table V-5, by the year 2030 the number of deaths from various coronary heart diseases will be three times the current number. This will result in a significant increase in demand for related health care services. It is important to note that the baseline conditions assumed a decrease in the coronary heart disease death rate over time but an increase in the risk factors for this condition (e.g., smoking, hypertension and high blood cholesterol prevalence). Hence, the effects of the decrease in coronary heart death rate per 100,000 that were assumed to occur for each age group over time under the baseline model are offset by the increase in risk factors in the population. In other words, increases in blood cholesterol, hypertension, and smoking that are forecast for the future make up for the decrease in coronary death rate assumed to take place in the future (e.g., due to improved treatment procedures). Naturally, the two forces do not exactly cancel each other out. As a result, the death rate per 100,000 for individuals over 65 actually dips about 7 percent in the year 2000 before the effects of the increased risk factors increase deaths per 100,000 to the approximately current values. This pattern of approximately constant coronary heart death rates per 100,000 holds for both males and females.

**Table V-5**
**Projected Adult and Elderly Mortality and Effects**
**of a Preventive Strategy for Six Leading Non-Communicable Conditions**
**(Ages 15-79)**

| Cause | Year | # deaths Baseline | % of total deaths | # deaths Optimistic | % of total deaths | Lives saved (per year) |
|-------|------|-------------------|-------------------|---------------------|-------------------|------------------------|
| Lung Cancer | 1990 | 1411 | (2.19) | | | |
| | 2000 | 3770 | (4.74) | 3779 | (5.06) | 9 |
| | 2010 | 6184 | (6.25) | 6326 | (7.11) | -142 |
| | 2030 | 13146 | (8.77) | 13065 | (9.62) | 81 |
| Chronic Respiratory Diseases | 1990 | 1736 | (2.69) | | | |
| | 2000 | 2698 | (3.39) | 2199 | (2.94) | 299 |
| | 2010 | 4055 | (4.10) | 2884 | (3.24) | 1171 |
| | 2030 | 8786 | (5.86) | 6106 | (4.50) | 2680 |
| Coronary Heart Disease | 1990 | 9419 | (14.60) | | | |
| | 2000 | 11889 | (14.93) | 10246 | (13.71) | 1643 |
| | 2010 | 16982 | (17.17) | 12473 | (14.01) | 4509 |
| | 2030 | 33368 | (22.25) | 24422 | (17.98) | 8946 |
| Stroke | 1990 | 6618 | (10.26) | | | |
| | 2000 | 6921 | (8.69) | 7094 | (9.50) | -173 |
| | 2010 | 10111 | (10.22) | 8642 | (9.71) | 1469 |
| | 2030 | 18240 | (12.16) | 15830 | (11.65) | 2410 |
| Injuries from Traffic Accidents | 1990 | 906 | (1.40) | | | |
| | 2000 | 1116 | (1.40) | 894 | (1.20) | 222 |
| | 2010 | 1326 | (1.34) | 1075 | (1.21) | 251 |
| | 2030 | 1683 | (1.12) | 1388 | (1.02) | 295 |
| Cirrhosis of the Liver | 1990 | 3765 | (5.83) | | | |
| | 2000 | 5172 | (6.50) | 4910 | (6.57) | 262 |
| | 2010 | 6879 | (6.96) | 6551 | (7.36) | 328 |
| | 2030 | 10336 | (6.89) | 10014 | (7.37) | 322 |
| Total Adult/Elderly Deaths | 1990 | 64531 | | | | |
| | 2000 | 79611 | | 74723 | | 4888 |
| | 2010 | 98887 | | 89006 | | 9881 |
| | 2030 | 149945 | | 135833 | | 14112 |

Lung cancer deaths increase under the optimistic scenario because of reductions in the number of older individuals dying of other risks; smokers who were "saved" by reductions in cholesterol and hypertension and decreasing death rates from coronary heart disease are at greater risk of dying of lung cancer.

Source: World Bank estimates from projection model.

In the optimistic scenario the prevalence of both hypertension and high blood cholesterol is reduced.  The scenario also assumes a reduction in the initiation rate for smoking.  The results of the preventive strategy (e.g., smoking cessation, hypertension control, increasing exercise, better management of diabetes) indicate that preventive interventions have a positive effect from the very beginning in terms of reducing the number of deaths for each age group.  This effect is small initially but becomes more noticeable around the year 2005 with reductions in the number of deaths of about 10 to 20 percent for those over 60 years of age.  The effect of the intervention appears to hold relatively constant after about 2010.  As presented in Table V-5, the annual number of lives saved from premature death due to coronary heart disease increases significantly by 2010.  However, it should be noted that the reduction in mortality from coronary heart diseases is obtained from improved medical treatment (e.g., regular screening to identify people with hypertension and treatment of hypertension with drugs) rather than a risk factor reduction.  As experience in developed countries indicates, some of these preventive treatments are costly, contributing to increased health care expenditures (e.g., in the United States, propranolol, the most cost-effective drug for the treatment of hypertension, costs an average of US$16,000 per year of life gained[4]).

## Lung cancer

As indicated in Table V-5, even with an effective preventive strategy, Chile can expect to bear a burden of approximately 13,000 annual lung cancer deaths among adults by 2030.  While lung cancer deaths for men are expected to increase over time, no significant change occurs in lung cancer deaths for women.  Over time, the number of deaths by age group for lung cancer for males and females under baseline conditions are similar to those for coronary heart disease.  However, the projections show that rates increase in the future. The maximum absolute burden is expected to occur among those persons between the ages of 55 and 70 years.  When the rates per 100,000 are examined instead of the absolute number of deaths, an important pattern arises.  Specifically, after adjusting for the differential population profile over time, the incidence rate of lung cancer is not constant but rather increasing.  This is partially the result of an increased smoking prevalence forecast for the future.  The deleterious effect of this increase is evident in the forecast.  The conclusion is that the health care needs associated with lung cancer will increase much more rapidly than the population at any particular age group in Chile.

Table V-6 gives the reduction in number of deaths due to lung cancer as a result of a health intervention (e.g., smoking cessation, legislation/regulation on advertising and promotion, increasing taxes on cigarettes).  This picture can be somewhat discouraging for policy makers because the reduction (presented in number of deaths reduced per 100,000 adult population) is not large.  The forecast reduction in deaths reaches only about 10 per 100,000 for those aged 55 to 65 beginning about 2010.  Forecast reduction in deaths for younger ages is less, being almost zero for ages under 50 even to the year 2030.  For

---

4.  Russell, L.B.  1993.  The Role of Prevention in Health Reform.  N. Engl. J. Med. Vol. 329:352-354.

individuals over 70, the reduction is negative, meaning that there are more deaths from lung cancer under the optimistic scenario. This is the result of two interrelated factors in the epidemiological dynamic. First, the intervention reduces initiation of tobacco consumption and increases cessation. However, for individuals over 50, the cessation rates are not very high. Thus an increase in cessation rates has only a small effect. At the same time, very few persons begin smoking after age 35. Thus, it will take a long time for the reduction in initiation rates to affect mortality patterns for the elderly. In fact, a significant reduction in lung cancer deaths only begins to emerge by 2030. The second component of the dynamic is that the number of individuals dying of other competing risks has been reduced. These smoking individuals who have been "saved" by reduction in cholesterol and hypertension as well as decreased death rates from coronary heart disease are now at risk of dying of lung cancer. The increased number is sufficient at the older ages to give the health intervention an apparent negative effect on lung cancer deaths. The aggregate effect, across all ages, is in fact negative for many years.

**Stroke**

Table V-6 presents mortality rates for stroke per 100,000 adult population under the baseline and optimistic scenarios. The reduction in the number of deaths resulting from a health intervention for stroke (e.g., smoking cessation, control of hypertension) is very similar to that seen for other diseases for males. For females, the stroke rate goes up, resulting in a negative number of lives saved. As indicated in Table V-5, about 2410 deaths per year due to stroke may be averted as a result of a preventive strategy. In general, stroke will continue to be an important cause of death in Chile because mortality will rise as the population ages.

### Table V-6
### Projected Mortality Rates per 100,000 Adult Population
### for Leading Non-Communicable Conditions

| Cause | Year | Rate Baseline | Rate Optimistic |
|---|---|---|---|
| Lung cancer | 1990 | 15.9 | |
| | 2000 | 35.2 | 34.7 |
| | 2010 | 49.1 | 50.0 |
| | 2030 | 85.3 | 83.3 |
| Chronic Respiratory Diseases | 1990 | 19.4 | |
| | 2000 | 25.4 | 20.4 |
| | 2010 | 32.4 | 23.0 |
| | 2030 | 56.8 | 39.0 |
| Coronary Heart Disease | 1990 | 105.3 | |
| | 2000 | 110.8 | 95.3 |
| | 2010 | 135.3 | 98.8 |
| | 2030 | 216.6 | 155.7 |
| Stroke | 1990 | 74.0 | |
| | 2000 | 64.2 | 57.8 |
| | 2010 | 80.3 | 66.6 |
| | 2030 | 118.6 | 101.1 |
| Injuries From Traffic Accidents | 1990 | 10.4 | |
| | 2000 | 10.4 | 7.9 |
| | 2010 | 10.4 | 8.4 |
| | 2030 | 10.8 | 8.9 |
| Cirrhosis of the Liver | 1990 | 42.6 | |
| | 2000 | 48.0 | 45.6 |
| | 2010 | 55.0 | 51.5 |
| | 2030 | 67.3 | 63.9 |
| Total | 1990 | 723.7 | |
| | 2000 | 740.9 | 695.0 |
| | 2010 | 787.8 | 705.1 |
| | 2030 | 973.9 | 867.6 |

Source: World Bank estimates from projection model.

## Chronic respiratory diseases

Table V-6 presents the mortality rates per 100,000 adult population for chronic respiratory diseases. The reduction in the number of deaths resulting from a preventive intervention (e.g., smoking cessation, reductions in pollution and occupational exposure) is very similar to the pattern for deaths due to coronary heart disease. A notable variation is that deaths from chronic respiratory diseases are forecast to have a slight increase in rates per 100,000 over time. Part of this may be attributable to increased smoking. As indicated in Table V-5, the number of deaths from chronic respiratory diseases that can be averted as a result of preventive interventions is about 2680 per year.

## Injuries from traffic accidents

Table V-6 gives the projected death rates due to injuries from traffic accidents. The picture here is very different than that for previous causes of death. The major concern is the obvious difference in age distribution of those who die. It is well recognized that the nemesis of younger adults in developed countries is death due to injuries from traffic accidents. The economic and social loss of younger adults is usually considered higher than that for older adults. Thus the potential burden on Chilean society for deaths by injuries would be expected to be large, both in terms of costly medical care and economic losses foregone. This pattern is borne out in the forecast deaths due to injuries from traffic accidents where rates reach a peak among individuals between the ages of 20 and 35 years and taper off with increasing age. The result of this pattern is that the health care demands related to injuries due to traffic accidents would be made by a considerably younger cohort than those made from individuals suffering from the non-communicable diseases discussed above.

About 15 and 25 percent of deaths could be averted if a preventive strategy (e.g., education/information, improved occupational safety, improved emergency services) is adopted. Most of this reduction is realized by 2005. Note that this strategy assumes a flat percentage reduction across ages. Because of the removal of competing causes of death and changes in the demographic profile, the intervention effect attenuates somewhat over time.

## Cirrhosis of the liver

Table V-6 gives the death rates for cirrhosis of the liver under baseline and optimistic conditions. The age group pattern here is between that for non-communicable diseases and deaths from injuries. Although the social loss of younger individuals is often high, the problem of deaths from cirrhosis of the liver is exacerbated by the fact that these deaths are preceded by a diseased, nonproductive period of life which usually adversely affects others. The baseline scenario forecasts a very serious problem in that the number of deaths by cirrhosis would remain approximately constant per 100,000 for each age group and that the peak number of deaths would continue to be for those aged 50 to 60 years old. During the recent past, the consumption of wine and other alcoholic beverages has not shown a dramatic increase per capita. If the current consumption pattern continues, deaths per 100,000 for cirrhosis would be reduced by about 10 percent among males and 2 percent among females. Any reduction in alcohol consumption will have a positive benefit.

The simulation exercise indicates a very nominal positive benefit in the reduction in the number of deaths from cirrhosis resulting from a preventive intervention (e.g., education/information, controls on alcohol availability, alcoholic rehabilitation). As shown in Table V-5, with a continuation of past trends, by 2010 about 6,879 persons will die prematurely each year of cirrhosis of the liver, and this may rise to perhaps 10,336 by 2030. Only 332 deaths per year by 2030 will be averted with an effective preventive intervention. In this case, the intervention entails a 10 percent reduction in the number of people who are heavy drinkers. It is important to note that the effect of an alcohol intervention is felt much faster than the effects of interventions to reduce hypertension and blood cholesterol. It also yields more immediate benefits than do interventions to reduce tobacco consumption. Although there will be little overall effect, the reduction in males is still positive. Part of the reason for the poor showing of the alcohol intervention is the same competing risk/demographic profile problem discussed for lung cancer and smoking.

### What is the Likely Impact of a Future Preventive Strategy on DALYs Lost?

In the preceding sections, future changes in Chile's health profile have been illustrated using mortality patterns. As was discussed in Chapter III, the use of DALYs permits the assessment of the likely impact of health changes on both life lost and disability. The predicted global burden of disease under the optimistic scenario was calculated using the method described in Chapter III. In Table V-7, the forecast DALYs under both the baseline and optimistic scenarios are given for specific years for males and females. From this table, it can be seen that under the baseline scenario, DALYs lost will grow to 1,379,000 for males and 867,000 for females by 2010. Approximately 48 percent of DALYs lost for males and 42 percent of DALYs lost for females will be due to premature mortality. This is approximately the same as current patterns.

The preventive strategy under the optimistic scenario will decrease DALY losses considerably. Specifically, DALYs for males and females are forecast to decrease 9 percent and 6.5 percent, respectively. Because of the longer life afforded by the optimistic scenario, it is likely that the share of DALYs lost attributed to mortality will increase. The forecast bears this out for males, with mortality loss increasing from 48 percent to 52 percent of total loss. For females, the mortality loss increases from 42 percent to 48 percent.

It is also evident in Table V-7 that the positive effect of the preventive strategy on DALYs saved can be obtained relatively quickly--i.e., after only the first 10 years of implementation. Part of the reason for this is that the optimistic scenario assumed that most of the reductions in risk factor prevalence and in cause-specific death rates would be realized by 2000-2005. The health intervention after that time is to simply maintain the levels of risk factor prevalence and death rates achieved.

**Table V-7**
**Total DALYs for All Causes for Chilean Adults and Elderly**
**By Type of Loss and Forecast Year**
**(Thousands)**

| | YEAR | | | | |
|---|---|---|---|---|---|
| | 1990 | 2000 | 2010 | 2020 | 2030 |
| **MALES** | | | | | |
| Baseline | | | | | |
| Mortality | 429 | 563 | 658 | 756 | 830 |
| Disability | 622 | 672 | 721 | 758 | 766 |
| Total | 1051 | 1235 | 1379 | 1514 | 1596 |
| Optimistic | | | | | |
| Mortality | -- | 489 | 539 | 625 | 698 |
| Disability | -- | 651 | 686 | 730 | 752 |
| Total | -- | 1140 | 1225 | 1355 | 1450 |
| **FEMALES** | | | | | |
| Baseline | | | | | |
| Mortality | 271 | 307 | 364 | 420 | 467 |
| Disability | 452 | 475 | 503 | 512 | 506 |
| Total | 723 | 782 | 867 | 932 | 973 |
| Optimistic | | | | | |
| Mortality | -- | 296 | 339 | 385 | 421 |
| Disability | -- | 470 | 493 | 498 | 487 |
| Total | | 766 | 832 | 883 | 908 |

Source:  World Bank estimates from projection model.

## Policy Issues Concerning Future Health Trends

It is quite evident from the discussion above that the establishment or strengthening of disease prevention programs will help to reduce the burden of mortality and disability from various non-communicable diseases and injuries, benefitting in particular middle-aged persons.  The impact of these mortality reductions on the well-being of the Chilean population is conditioned, however, by the dynamic of demographic and epidemiological factors which mediate the effects of relative mortality declines for specific causes and age groups.  First, the mortality-reduction effects of non-communicable disease interventions will only be visible in the long term, since mortality in the coming years has largely been determined by risk factor patterns of the past 20-30 years.  Second, non-communicable disease control will benefit primarily middle-aged persons, enabling them to enjoy an average of 20 or more years of life, but have limited effects on increasing overall life expectancy.  Non-communicable disease interventions in general only reduce or postpone, but not eliminate, the burden of illness and may be expected to add only a few years of life to older age groups, since these individuals will die, on average, within a few years from other causes.

The forecast changes in total DALYs due to a preventive strategy suggest a more positive result in that reductions in overall DALYs lost are realized fairly quickly (i.e., after the first 10 years of implementation), a timeframe which is more persuasive to policymakers than 30 to 40 years. The DALYs "saved" resulted not only from reductions in disability, but also in mortality, due to the higher weighted value of deaths prevented in middle age (i.e., deaths postponed to later ages).

The net effect of non-communicable disease prevention and control will be a somewhat older but healthier population. However, as shown in a study on declining mortality in the United States,[5] it should be clear that reductions in mortality among older adults and the elderly will not be associated with generalized reductions in morbidity at each age, but rather with increases in the variance of health status at each age. The latter implies that as medical progress advances, the best-off members of a given cohort will improve their health status, while the health of marginal survivors will remain poor, putting additional pressure on the health system since they are most likely to be in need of sustained care.

Despite constraints on the benefits of non-communicable disease control, the projection model shows that in the future, as the population ages, an even larger number of premature deaths and illnesses and disability cases may occur if effective measures are not introduced to deal with the main risk factors associated with the onset of non-communicable conditions. This means that while the benefits of preventing non-communicable diseases may not be as palpable as those yielded from control of communicable diseases, the costs of not initiating preventive programs early in the health transition are very high.

An urgent task for Chilean policymakers, therefore, is to continue to reform the health care system to adequately manage the large predicted increases in the demand for medical services. Since the reforms underway are almost exclusively reforms of curative health services, it is now timely to consider parallel reforms and upgrading of preventive health services. It is also important to focus on preventive care because it does not always save resources, but rather has been shown to contribute to rises in health spending, despite the widely-held view that savings accrue to the health system because prevention lowers disease incidence, with its associated costs. An example of preventive services that are not cost-effective are certain cancer screening tests, the cost of which exceeds the savings that could be accrued from foregone treatment of the illnesses prevented.[6] But other preventive services do save money or are good "buys" from the public perspective because they produce more health for the resources invested than do alternative services. This latter standard should be considered as a criterion for determining those preventive and curative services in which to invest. A guiding principle for these reforms, then, should be that the services provided be effective from a medical perspective and that priority should be given to those that are the most cost-effective.

---

5.  Poterba, J.M. and Summers, L.H. 1987. Public Policy Implications of Declining Old-Age Mortality. Cambridge: National Bureau of Economic Research, INC.

6.  Russell, L.B. 1986. Is prevention better than cure? Washington, D.C.: Brookings Institution.

# CHAPTER VI

## IMPLICATIONS FOR HEALTH CARE COSTS[1]

The expected evolution of risk factors and non-communicable diseases and injuries among adults in Chile has major consequences for health care demand. This chapter examines available information on health care spending and costs in Chile, focussing on hospital costs. Based on projected scenarios for the prevalence of risk factors and non-communicable illnesses discussed in Chapter V, the health care cost implications of Chile's changing epidemiological profile are analyzed in terms of changes in hospital costs.

### Current Health Spending in Chile

Total health spending in Chile, including direct household expenditures for medical care and pharmaceuticals, has expanded as a percentage of GDP from an estimated 3.3 percent in the 1960's to an estimated 5-6 percent in the early 1990's. As seen in Figure VI-1, Chile's share of GDP spent on health care is comparable to that in several middle-income Latin American countries but lower than the median of 8 percent in OECD countries.

### Figure VI-1

**DISTRIBUTION OF HEALTH SPENDING, 1990**
**CHILE AND OTHER COUNTRIES**
**(Share of Total Health Expenditures in Total Domestic Expenditure)**

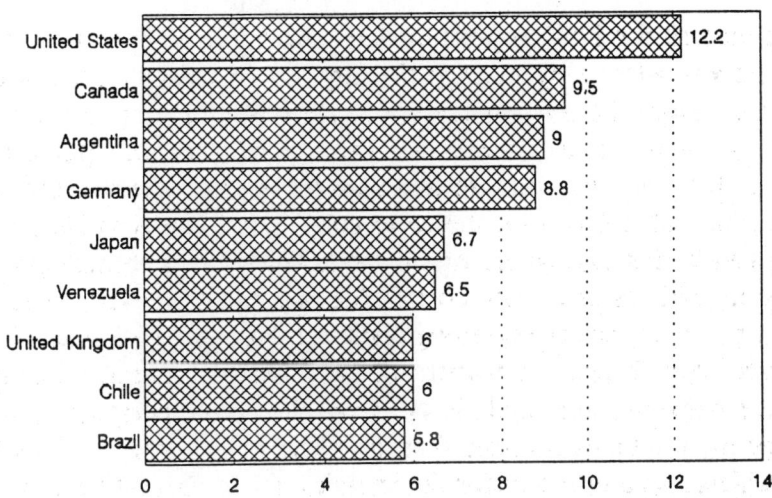

Source: OECD 1993, PAHO 1994.

---

1. This chapter was prepared on the basis of information from background papers by César Oyarzo and Rony Lenz (current hospital costs), and H. Dennis Tolley (forecast of hospital costs), respectively.

Public and private health expenditures, including expenditures by the NHSS and the ISAPREs and excluding copayments in the ISAPREs, expenditures by the armed forces medical program, direct expenditures by high income groups not affiliated with the ISAPREs and by other patients, as well as expenditures by the mutual funds, were estimated at approximately US$1.7 billion in 1992. As shown in Box VI-1, per capita expenditure in health is about US$116, far lower than in OECD countries (e.g., less than 8 percent of Canada's and 6 percent of U.S. per capita expenditures for health care), but comparable to several middle-income countries in Latin America. Public expenditures in health (including maternal leave payments for FONASA affiliates) are about 2.6 percent of GDP or 59 percent of total health expenditures, while ISAPREs expenditures account for about 1.8 percent of GDP or 41 percent of total expenditures. Annual expenditures per beneficiary in the public sector (including subsidies and medical care for FONASA affiliates and indigents) amount to approximately US$100, and in the ISAPREs, US$232.

**Box VI-1**

### HEALTH AND WEALTH, 1991, CHILE AND OTHER COUNTRIES

| Country | GNP per Capita (US$) | Health spending per person (US$) |
|---|---|---|
| Chile | 2,160 | 116 |
| Uruguay | 2,840 | 141 |
| Brazil | 2,940 | 132 |
| Argentina | 2,767 | 234 |
| Britain | 16,550 | 1,039 |
| Japan | 26,930 | 1,538 |
| France | 20,380 | 1,869 |
| Canada | 20,440 | 1,945 |
| United States | 22,240 | 2,763 |

Source: World Bank, 1993.

## Recent trends in public health spending

As shown in Table VI-1, in 1992 public expenditures in health (excluding the subsidies provided to ISAPRE affiliates) amounted to about US$952 million or 12.23 percent of total public expenditures, up from about US$717 million or 10.66 percent in 1989. It is estimated that public health expenditures in 1993 would amount to about US$1.08 billion or 11.81 percent of total public expenditures. Because of the variety of programs and transfers covered by the public health expenditures, only about 60 percent of total public health expenditures actually finances the direct delivery of medical services in public facilities. Of public sector expenditures for direct services, the largest share (about 85 percent) is estimated to be channeled into hospital-based services. For this reason, and because the largest share of hospital services are consumed by adults with non-communicable conditions, this chapter focuses on the costs of hospital services and their implications for the Chilean health system.

### Table VI-1
### Public Expenditures on Health
### (In Millions of US$ of October 1993)

|  | 1989 | 1990 | 1991 | 1992 | 1993 (7) |
|---|---|---|---|---|---|
| Service Delivery in HSA Facilities (1) | 360 | 362 | 419 | 477 | 567 |
| Curative Services Under PPS | 98 | 90 | 96 | 109 | 120 |
| Workman's Compensation(2) | 48 | 44 | 42 | 42 | 45 |
| Primary Care at Municipal Level(3) | 57 | 62 | 75 | 86 | 89 |
| PNAC Distribution | 59 | 54 | 61 | 63 | 63 |
| Administrative Costs(4) | 16 | 16 | 22 | 27 | 33 |
| Other(5) | 23 | 40 | 42 | 42 | 51 |
| Subtotal Operating Expenditures | 664 | 670 | 760 | 835 | 970 |
| Investments | 21 | 15 | 19 | 84 | 88 |
| Total MOH Expenditures | 685 | 685 | 780 | 933 | 1,060 |
| FNDR Investments | 31 | 18 | 23 | 19 | 24 |
| Total Public Expenditures on Health(6) | 717 | 704 | 804 | 952 | 1,084 |
| Public Expenditure on Health/Total | 10.66 | 11.06% | 11.51% | 12.23% | 11.81% |

(1) Expenditures for goods and services and HSA personnel, excluding FAPEM.
(2) Includes all types of subsidies for FONASA affiliates, i.e., curative, preventive, and maternal subsidies paid by the HSAs and the CCAF.
(3) Primary health care services financed by FAPEM and municipal contributions.
(4) Expenditures for personnel; goods and services in MOH executive agencies (i.e., FONASA, INSP, SISP, and Central Supply Facility.
(5) Expenditures for production of goods and services, prior year's operations, financial, investment, and other obligations.
(6) Excludes expenditures in foreign currency, cash balances, and debt service.
(7) Projected figures.
Source: Ministerio de Hacienda, 1994.

## Recent trends in ISAPRE spending

Although financial data are not available for the ISAPREs prior to 1986, analysis of information from 1986 to 1992 as indicated in Table VI-2 shows that income of the ISAPREs has more than tripled (284 percent increase), their operating surplus has more than doubled (114 percent increase), and health service delivery costs have more than tripled (325 percent increase). The higher growth of health service delivery costs over income has raised the ratio of costs/income from its low of 72 percent in 1986 to 79 percent in 1992 (down from a high of 82 percent in 1988). The ISAPREs have managed to contain the growth of administration and marketing costs, which have actually declined relative to income, from 24 percent in 1986 to 18 percent in 1992.

Table VI-2
Financial Status of ISAPRE System
1986-1992
(In Millions of US$ of July 1993)

|  | 1986 | % | 1988 | % | 1990 | % | 1992 | % |
|---|---|---|---|---|---|---|---|---|
| Income | 147 | 100 | 246 | 100 | 404 | 100 | 565 | 100 |
| Health Service Delivery | 105 | 72 | 202 | 82 | 307 | 76 | 446 | 79 |
| Gross Margin | 41 | 28 | 44 | 18 | 97 | 24 | 119 | 21 |
| Administrative/Mktg Cost | 35 | 24 | 53 | 22 | 81 | 20 | 104 | 18 |
| Operating Surplus | 7 | 5 | 10 | 4 | 16 | 4 | 15 | 3 |

Source: ISAPREs, FONASA, 1992.

Despite success in improving administrative efficiency, the ISAPREs have not been any more successful than the public sector in controlling the growth of operating costs. The average cost per ISAPRE beneficiary has grown in real terms from US$114 in 1986 to US$149 in 1992, a 30 percent increase. The increase in costs is apparently not the result of increases in the total number of services provided to each beneficiary. During the 1986-1992 period, several indicators of service utilization in the ISAPREs exhibited declines. The number of consultations per beneficiary decreased from 4.25 in 1986 to 3.26 in 1992, and similar trends occurred for laboratory services (from 2.99 to 1.98), X rays (from 0.68 to 0.45), surgical procedures (from 0.14 to 0.06) and hospital bed days (from 0.44 to 0.21). These trends suggest that while the ISAPREs may have attempted to lower costs by limiting the use of services, these efforts were not sufficient to compensate for increases in the prices charged by service providers.

## Costs of Hospital Services in the NHSS

Although health expenditure data are ready available in Chile, there is little corresponding information about the actual level and evolution of health care costs. One source of information is SIGMO (Sistema de Información Gerencial y Monitoreo), a hospital management data base which relates resources used to services produced. Established in 1985, SIGMO presently collects data from approximately 70 public hospitals of varying levels of complexity, as defined by number of beds and clinical specialties and level of monthly expenditures. However, not all of these hospitals have been reliable in reporting information. In addition, the data in SIGMO are aggregated at the clinical service level; there is no information on unit costs for individual services. Private hospitals do not report to SIGMO, and no information is available about costs in private facilities.

Despite these limitations, information from a sample of 23 hospitals[2] that regularly report to SIGMO was analyzed for this study in order to estimate the cost of hospital services in Chile. Four different clinical services used for the diagnosis and treatment of adult health complications were included in the analysis: Internal Medicine (e.g., chronic respiratory diseases, diabetes, cardiovascular diseases), Surgery (e.g., gallstone removal, appendicitis, injuries), Trauma (e.g., fractures), and Obstetrics-Gynecology (e.g., obstetrics-related diagnoses, benign uterine tumors). Oncology services for the treatment of cancer patients were not included because information was not available. The four clinical services were chosen because they account for a majority of all hospital discharges in Chile (see Table VI-3). Of these services, Obstetrics-Gynecology accounted for the majority of hospital discharges in the country (13.5 percent) and 56.4 percent of the discharges analyzed for this study. Internal Medicine accounted for 24.4 percent of all discharges included in the sample, followed by Surgery which accounted for 16.4 percent. Trauma was the least representative service, accounting for 1.7 percent of the national discharges and 2.8 of all the discharges included in the study.

The costs analyzed in this study are expressed in terms of cost per hospital discharge and cost per occupied bed day, calculated for each clinical service and for each level of hospital complexity. All costs were converted to constant dollars, using the exchange rate prevailing in December 1991. Cost per hospital discharge was calculated by dividing the total cost (including personnel, supplies, and indirect costs) for each of the four clinical services by the total number of discharges from the respective service in the sample hospitals. Given that the composition of the sample was not based on representative statistical criteria, this potential bias was corrected by weighting costs for each level of hospital complexity by the corresponding proportion of total discharges at the national level for each level of hospital complexity. The weights used were based on the distribution of discharges in public hospitals for 1990.[3]

---

2. Hospitals in the sample by level of technological complexity: **maximum**: Hospital Van Buren, Hospital de Valparaíso, Hospital San Juan de Dios, Hospital Barros Luco; **high**: Hospital de Antofagasta, Hospital de Talca, Hospital de Temuco; **medium**: Hospital de San Felipe, Hospital de Curicó, Hospital de Linares, Hospital de Chillán, Hospital de Osorno; **low**: Hospital de Vallenar, Hospital de Buin, Hospital de Parral, Hospital de Cauquenes; **minimum**: Hospital de Teno, Hospital de Molina, Hospital de Hualañe, Hospital de Curepto, Hospital de Constitución, Hospital de San Javier, Hospital de Chanco.

3. The weights used for **medicine** were: 11.6 percent, maximum; 14.7 percent, high; 20.4 percent, medium; 25.1 percent, low; and 28.2 percent, minimum. For **surgery** were: 20.4 percent, maximum; 25.5 percent, high; 27.6 percent, medium; 24.6 percent, low; and 1.9 percent, minimum. For **traumatology** were: 25.7 percent, maximum; 34.8 percent, high; 39 percent, medium; 0.0 percent, low; and 0.5 percent, minimum. For **obstetrics-gynecology** were: 22.1 percent, maximum; 28.6 percent, high; 19.8 percent, medium; 18.6 percent, low; and 10.8 percent, minimum.

Cost per occupied bed day was calculated using the total cost for each clinical service and dividing it by the number of occupied bed days for that service. As it was not possible to obtain information on occupied bed days by level of hospital complexity, the study used as a proxy variable the number of beds in each facility weighted by the average rate of occupation for the HSA in which the hospital was located.

## Cost per discharge by clinical service

The average cost per hospital discharge for each clinical service for the hospitals in the sample is shown in Table VI-4. The cumulative increase in costs from December 1987 to March 1991 was 25.1 percent. The highest increase in costs during this period were in Surgery and in Internal Medicine, which had a cumulative increase of 50.4 percent and 21.4 percent, respectively. The increase in costs for Obstetrics-Gynecology was below the average by 36.4 percent. While the costs for Trauma services increased the least of all the services with a cumulative variation of 10.1 percent, the actual cost for these services was higher than all other services. By 1991 the cost per discharge for Trauma was US$ 307.0 or 59.3 percent higher than the average for all other clinical services.

**TABLE VI-3**
**PUBLIC HOSPITAL DISCHARGES BY TYPE OF DIAGNOSIS**
**1989**

| DIAGNOSIS | NUMBER OF DISCHARGES | % OF ALL DISCHARGES | CUMULATIVE |
|---|---|---|---|
| Total | 1,389,937 | | |
| Obstetrical complications | 187,757 | 13.5 | 13.5 |
| Normal Delivery | 170,955 | 12.3 | 25.8 |
| Pneumonia | 58,721 | 4.2 | 30.0 |
| Causes Related to the Perinatal Period | 54,713 | 3.9 | 34.0 |
| Cholelithiasis and Cholecystitis | 50,502 | 3.6 | 37.6 |
| Abortion | 46,294 | 3.3 | 40.9 |
| Undefined Intestinal Infections | 33,074 | 2.4 | 43.3 |
| Abdominal Hernia | 27,727 | 2.0 | 45.3 |
| Appendicitis | 24,668 | 1.8 | 47.1 |
| Trauma | 24,041 | 1.7 | 48.8 |
| Chronic and Non-infectious Bronchitis | 19,269 | 1.4 | 50.2 |
| Blood Vessel Injuries | 16,568 | 1.2 | 51.4 |
| Infections of the Skin or Cellular Tissue | 12,324 | 0.9 | 52.3 |
| Chronic Tonsillitis and Adenoidal Growths | 12,127 | 0.9 | 53.1 |
| Diabetes | 10,786 | 0.8 | 53.9 |
| Benign Uterine Tumors | 9,985 | 0.7 | 54.6 |
| Acute Bronchitis and Bronchiolitis | 9,724 | 0.7 | 55.3 |
| Fractured Shoulder, Cubitus, and Radius  (arm) | 9,460 | 0.7 | 56.0 |
| Fractured Tibia, Fibula and Ankle        (leg) | 9,286 | 0.7 | 56.7 |
| Burns | 9,112 | 0.7 | 57.3 |
| Hypertensive Disease | 7,477 | 0.5 | 57.9 |

Source: Oyarzo and Lenz, 1992.

**Table VI-4**
**Cost Per Hospital Discharge By Clinical Service**
**Based On Sigmo Data**
**(US$ of December 1991)**

| CLINICAL SERVICE | DECEMBER 1987 | DECEMBER 1988 | | DECEMBER 1989 | | MARCH 1991 | | CUMULATIVE VARIATION |
|---|---|---|---|---|---|---|---|---|
| | Cost | Cost | % Change | Cost | % Change | Cost | % Change | |
| Internal Medicine | 157.0 | 165.9 | 5.6 | 162.4 | -2.2 | 190.0 | 17.6 | 21.4 |
| Surgery | 191.4 | 215.1 | 12.4 | 203.5 | -5.4 | 287.7 | 41.4 | 50.4 |
| Traumatology | 279.1 | 298.4 | 7.0 | 280.0 | -3.5 | 307.0 | 6.7 | 10.1 |
| Obstetrics-Gynecology | 105.1 | 103.5 | -1.5 | 108.9 | 5.2 | 122.6 | 12.7 | 16.8 |
| Average for all Clinical Services* | 154.1 | 164.8 | 6.9 | 167.2 | 1.5 | 192.5 | 15.0 | 25.1 |

* Includes clinical services listed above and all other services.
Source: Oyarzo and Lenz, 1992.

Several reasons can be postulated to explain the overall increase in cost per discharge in the period studied: a fall in productivity due to shortages of inputs and to the deterioration of medical equipment and infrastructure as measured by a longer average length of stay; higher rates of hospital-related infections; or possibly changes in the mix of patients treated. During the period studied, there was a rise in the cost of inputs such as drugs and wages; the increase in wages was particularly significant for 1990, when Law 19,005 mandated increases in salaries by 5.0 percent in real terms. In addition, another 5 percent increase in real terms of the total cost of salaries is estimated to have resulted from the reclassification of HSAs personnel to higher wage categories. However, there is not sufficient information to assign responsibility for the rise in costs solely to any of these factors.

## Cost per discharge by level of hospital complexity

As seen in Table VI-5, the highest costs per discharge occurred in hospitals of maximum and high complexity. The cost per discharge at hospitals of maximum complexity was 48 percent higher that the average in March 1991, while in hospitals of high complexity, cost per discharge was 28 percent higher than the average.

**Table VI-5**
**Cost Per Hospital Discharge By Level Of Complexity**
**Based On Sigmo Data**
**(US$ of December 1991)**

| LEVEL OF COMPLEXITY | DECEMBER 1987 | DECEMBER 1988 | | DECEMBER 1989 | | MARCH 1991 | |
|---|---|---|---|---|---|---|---|
| | Cost | Cost | % Change | Cost | % Change | Cost | % Change |
| Maximum | 223.4 | 249.0 | 11.47 | 241.7 | -2.97 | 284.7 | 17.8 |
| High | 207.8 | 217.5 | 4.75 | 216.4 | -0.5 | 246.0 | 13.7 |
| Medium | 117.2 | 126.4 | 7.8 | 150.0 | 18.7 | 153.3 | 2.2 |
| Low | 101.6 | 107.0 | 5.3 | 102.7 | -4.0 | 135.2 | 31.7 |
| Minimum | 87.1 | 85.7 | -1.5 | 88.5 | 0.3 | 100.3 | 13.4 |
| Average | 154.1 | 164.8 | 6.9 | 167.2 | 1.5 | 192.5 | 15.0 |

Source: Oyarzo and Lenz, 1992.

## Cost per occupied bed day by clinical service

As seen in Table VI-6, the increase for all services in cost per occupied bed day during the period analyzed was 15.7 percent. The cost per occupied bed for Internal Medicine was US$24 in March 1991, 15 percent less than the average for all services. This represented a cumulative 12.1 percent increase for Internal Medicine as compared to the 15.7 percent cumulative increase for all services. The greatest total increase occurred with surgical beds, which increased in cost per day for the 1987-1991 period by 24.2 percent. However, the highest actual cost per bed day was for Obstetrics-Gynecology beds, which had a cumulative cost per occupied bed day 14.4 percent higher than the average. When compared to the average for all of the services, obstetrical services had the highest costs but the lowest real annual growth. The only decrease in costs was for Trauma. The cost per occupied bed day for Trauma was 6.9 percent lower in 1991 than it had been in 1987. This is especially low compared to the 15.7 percent growth seen in the average for all services during this same period.

## Cost per occupied bed day by level of hospital complexity

Once again the hospitals of maximum complexity had the highest cost. Table VI-7 shows that the cost per occupied bed day in a hospital of maximum complexity in March 1991 was 30 percent higher than the average. All other levels of complexity showed an average cost per occupied bed day in March 1991 less than the sample average, indicating the relative weight of maximum complexity hospitals in the production of total occupied bed days (accounting for 34.5 percent of all bed days).

**Table VI-6**
**Cost Per Occupied Bed Day By Clinical Service**
**Based On Sigmo Data**
**(US$ of December 1991)**

| CLINICAL SERVICE | DECEMBER 1987 | DECEMBER 1988 | | DECEMBER 1989 | | MARCH 1991 | | 1991 ACCUMULATED CHANGE |
|---|---|---|---|---|---|---|---|---|
| | Cost | Cost | % Change | Cost | % Change | Cost | % Change | |
| Medicine | 21.2 | 24.5 | 14.6 | 22.0 | -9.8 | 23.9 | 8.56 | 12.1 |
| Surgery | 23.9 | 25.8 | 7.3 | 24.2 | -6.4 | 29.8 | 23.7 | 24.2 |
| Traumatology | 18.3 | 21.2 | 16.0 | 20.7 | -2.5 | 17.2 | -17.7 | -6.9 |
| Obstetrics-Gynecology | 28.8 | 28.5 | -0.4 | 30.7 | 7.5 | 32.0 | 3.6 | 11.0 |
| Average for all Clinical Services* | 24.2 | 26.3 | 8.6 | 24.7 | -5.9 | 28.0 | 13.2 | 15.7 |

* Includes clinical services listed above and all other clinical services.
Source: Oyarzo and Lenz, 1992.

**Table VI-7**
**Cost Per Occupied Bed Day By Level Of Complexity**
**Based On Sigmo Data**
**(US$ of December 1991)**

| LEVEL OF COMPLEXITY | DECEMBER 1987 | DECEMBER 1988 | | DECEMBER 1989 | | MARCH 1991 | | CHANGE 1987-91 |
|---|---|---|---|---|---|---|---|---|
| | Cost | Cost | % | Cost | % | Cost | % | % |
| Maximum | 29.6 | 33.1 | 12.1 | 32.8 | -0.4 | 36.3 | 10.5 | 22.6 |
| High | 22.9 | 25.5 | 12.2 | 17.5 | -31.6 | 23.7 | 35.1 | 3.5 |
| Medium | 19.4 | 21.2 | 9.1 | 23.9 | 13.1 | 24.2 | 1.1 | 24.7 |
| Low | 21.8 | 19.4 | -11.3 | 19.6 | 1.4 | 23.4 | 19.6 | 7.3 |
| Minimum | 14.5 | 14.8 | 2.4 | 15.9 | 7.1 | 17.5 | 10.9 | 20.7 |
| Average | 24.2 | 26.3 | 10.2 | 24.7 | -6.2 | 28.0 | 13.2 | 15.7 |

Source: Oyarzo and Lenz, 1992.

## Projected Hospital Costs

### Some caveats on the forecasting exercise

At the outset, it is important to signal a strong cautionary note against the tendency to "believe" health care cost forecasts, especially for budgeting purposes. It has been well documented that health care needs and demand have little to do with actual health care costs. Growth of health care expenditures is driven more often by changes in the relative equity of the distribution of wealth and access to health care in a country, increases in feelings of entitlement, technological developments, or rises in labor costs of medical professionals.[4] Thus, changes in actual demand may have little to do with real changes in expenditures. Consequently, forecast increases in health care costs based solely on changes in the demographic profile or health needs will likely bear little relation to actual future expenditures. Additionally, the gross domestic product of a country may increase as fast or faster than health care expenditures, resulting in a relative decrease in total health spending as a percentage of GDP.

The use of the terms "cost" and "health care costs" in this exercise are predicated on the assumption that the distribution of wealth, entitlement programs, health care systems, and other factors that strongly influence medical care spending are fixed. Only in this context are cost forecasts made measured in 1990 dollars. As such, these cost projections are not intended to be used for budgetary purposes, but rather serve only to determine the relative increases in hospital and outpatient care that can be attributed to demographic trends and changes in risk factor profiles.

### Forecast assumptions

One of the critical issues facing public policy makers in Chile is how to plan for the future costs of health care. As noted above, there are many factors that drive increases in health care costs. Unfortunately, many of these are not related to changes in need. Therefore, predicting changes in need resulting from shifts in the demographic and the risk factor profiles of a country will not explicitly result in an accurate prediction of future health care costs. Similarly, an escalation of health care expenditures does not imply a change in need. However, in view of the growing importance of non-communicable diseases and injuries affecting the adult and elderly populations, it is informative to relate changes in these populations to resultant changes in health care need. In this section, this need will be translated into costs as measured by hospital bed days and proportionate outpatient services.

To examine such a future health care cost burden, this study projected the age profile of individuals, causes of death, bed days associated with such a death, and the costs of these

---

4. Schwartz, W.B. 1987. The Inevitable Failure of Current Cost-Containment Strategies. Why They Can Provide Only Temporary Relief. JAMA 257(2):220-224.

bed days for Chile for the next 40 years. In addition, health maintenance, as measured as a proportion of the population in the various health states, was forecast over the same period. Forecasts were made using disease and injury cost data on patients receiving care from public sector facilities. Rates of hospitalization resulting from the projected prevalence of risk factors and disease-specific morbidity and mortality were based on actual rates for public sector users in Chile. Projected numbers of individuals dying of specific causes or with specific risk factors were based on projections discussed in Chapter V.

Hospitalization costs were derived by multiplying projected numbers of bed days by the average cost per occupied bed day. As discussed in the previous section, the average cost per hospital bed day in Chile was estimated at US$28. For 1990, MOH discharge data (**Anuario de Egresos Hospitalarios**) reported approximately 10,490,000 bed days of care provided in public hospitals in Chile. At a cost of $28 per day, this translates to US$293.7 million or about 69 percent of the total medical care expense for hospitalization. The remaining 31 percent of total medical expenditures was for all other direct health care activities, including hospital outpatient and primary health care services.

Of the total public hospital bed days of care provided, approximately 7,981,000 days or 76 percent was provided to individuals 15 and older. Under the assumption that the total medical care costs for individuals 15 and older is in the same relationship as the total bed days, an estimate of the total medical costs in public facilities for individuals 15 and older is US$322 million[5] of which approximately US$223 million is for hospitalization and US$99 million is for all other health care activities.

In assessing future trends, it should be kept in mind that the estimates in this Chapter refer only to public sector health care expenditures; however, based on ISAPRE experience and experiences in other countries, medical care costs in the private sector can be expected to rise as fast or faster than rates in the public sector.

The following assumptions were made in performing the calculations:

a) health care costs for hospitals will stay in approximately the same proportion to total costs as at present. Nevertheless, as the number of hospitals increases or the capacity of existing hospitals improves beyond that required to service the growing population, this assumption will be violated and the proportion of health care costs spent for hospital care will increase;

b) hospital costs can be divided into two components: i) the health maintenance component (treatment costs for non-fatal illnesses and injuries), and ii) the mortality component (treatment costs for fatal illnesses and injuries);

---

5.  Based on 76 percent of the total medical care expense in 1990 of US$ 424 million, as shown Table VI-1.

c) there will be no general price increases in the Chilean economy as a whole or medical inflation due to increased levels of technology or services. This assumption forecasts costs under current conditions without distortions introduced by inflationary forces. Certainly, this assumption is unlikely to hold. Actual future health care expenditures could be much higher than presented here when general price increases, medical inflation, and other factors that contribute to cost escalation are considered.

## What can be expected in view of the changing demographic and epidemiological profiles?

Under these assumptions, the pattern of the total health costs for individuals 15 and older for Chile who receive care in public facilities is given in Table VI-8. As can be seen from the entries in this table, costs are expected to increase by 13 percent by the year 2000 and by 38 percent by the year 2030. The two major components of the projected cost increases are: a) an increase in the size of the Chilean adult population, and b) changes in the composition of the adult population.

When adjusted for population change, per capita[6] costs, given in Table VI-9, steadily decrease over time. The reasons for this projected decrease are the following. First, the overall decrease in mortality rates is assumed in the forecast to coincide with a decrease in morbidity. The forecast also assumes that the amount of health care unit consumed for each illness and for each death in the future will remain the same as the current amount. As a consequence, the overall decrease in general mortality will more than offset the increases in specific causes of mortality associated with risk factors known to be on the rise. In addition, the model assumed that even with increases in certain risk factors, the age-specific mortality rates for specific causes associated with some of these risk factors will decrease in the future.

Experience in other countries, however, indicates that per capita health care costs usually do not decrease. In reality, decreases are unlikely to be realized in Chile either. It is likely that in order to attain decreases in disease-specific mortality rates, the amount of health care provided per individual will have to increase. It is also probable that there will be a growth in the provision of health care stemming from the additional revenue in the system.

---

6. Per capita costs represent costs per adult user of public health facilities. In 1990, it was estimated that 71 percent of Chile's 13 million population used public sector health facilities (approximately 9,230,000 people). Since currently 70 percent of the Chilean population is aged 15 and older, the total population of adult users of public health facilities is estimated at 6,461,000.

**Table VI-8**
**Forecast Hospital Costs and Other Medical Costs**
**For Individuals 15 and Older**
**(in thousands of US$)**

| COST | YEAR | | | | |
|---|---|---|---|---|---|
| | 1990 | 2000 | 2010 | 2020 | 2030 |
| Hospital | 223,000 | 252,623 | 271,149 | 288,144 | 307,377 |
| Other | 99,000 | 112,176 | 120,402 | 127,949 | 136,489 |
| Total | 322,000 | 364,799 | 391,551 | 416,093 | 443,866 |

Source: World Bank estimates from projection model.

**Table VI-9**
**Forecast Per Capita Hospital Costs and Other Medical Costs**
**For Individuals 15 and Older**
**(in US$)**

| COST | YEAR | | | | |
|---|---|---|---|---|---|
| | 1990 | 2000 | 2010 | 2020 | 2030 |
| Hospital | 34.51 | 23.51 | 21.61 | 20.43 | 19.95 |
| Other | 15.32 | 10.44 | 9.59 | 9.07 | 8.86 |
| Total | 49.83 | 33.95 | 31.20 | 29.50 | 28.81 |

Source: World Bank estimates from projection model.

It is important to bear in mind that Tables VI-8 and VI-9 forecast costs under baseline conditions only. That is, these are the estimated total costs and per capita costs if Chile continues under current conditions, without taking into account increased use of health services or higher levels of technology. As noted above, changes in the distribution of wealth, entitlement programs, and availability of services have a large impact on the quantity of health services delivered. Since baseline conditions forecast per capita decreases if the current "system" continues as it is with respect to the amount of care provided to each individual, it seems clear that there will be considerable pressure to increase the system's capability to deliver care. Put in other words, if individuals remain willing to pay the same per capita costs as currently paid, there will be an approximate 40 percent increase in the amount of revenue available to provide the same services as currently provided. This revenue in turn could be used to expand care. What technology and services should be purchased with this additional revenue ought to be a major concern for health policy planners in Chile. Simply allowing the growth to evolve according to uncontrolled market forces may not be optimal.

**What can be expected if a successful disease prevention strategy is implemented?**

It is instructive to note the changes in health care costs that can be expected under the different health scenarios. In Table VI-10, the costs shown in Table VI-8 for the baseline scenario (i.e., deterioration in the health status of the population due to increases in the prevalence of health risk factors and in the major causes of disease and death reflecting an increasingly industrialized society) are compared with projected costs under a successful disease prevention scenario (i.e., improved health status due to the reduction of health risk factors and in the age-specific causes of death for particular diseases). When a successful disease prevention strategy is simulated, the effect of the intervention is a reduction of total costs by about 10 percent, saving approximately US$40 million over the 40-year period-- about US$1 million per year. Interestingly, over US$27 million or more than half (68 percent) of the total 40-year savings accrue in the first ten years--a strong incentive to policymakers to invest in preventive activities now.

**Table VI-10**
**Forecast Hospital Costs and Other Medical Costs**
**For Individuals 15 and Older**
**Baseline and Optimistic Scenarios**
**(in thousands of US$)**

| | YEAR | | | |
|---|---|---|---|---|
| **BASELINE** | 2000 | 2010 | 2020 | 2030 |
| Hospital | 252,623 | 271,149 | 288,145 | 307,377 |
| Other | 112,176 | 120,402 | 127,949 | 136,489 |
| Total | 364,799 | 391,551 | 416,093 | 443,866 |
| | | | | |
| **OPTIMISTIC** | | | | |
| Hospital | 241,631 | 252,457 | 265,892 | 280,042 |
| Other | 107,295 | 112,102 | 118,068 | 124,351 |
| Total | 348,926 | 364,559 | 383,959 | 404,394 |

Source: World Bank estimates from projection model.

## Policy Issues Concerning Future Health Care Costs

The increases in adult health care costs forecast here demonstrate the cumulative effects of Chile's current adult and elderly population age and health risk factor distribution. Much of the potential increase resulting from the demographic and risk factor shifts discussed in Chapters V and VI is offset by general reductions in morbidity and mortality. However, this rough forecast is based upon assumptions that are not likely to hold. For example, if the number of hospitals increases faster than the per capita need, based on current utilization, health care costs will increase beyond the predictions contained here. In addition, medical inflation resulting from improved technology, increased care, or expanded scope of care will all increase costs much faster than predicted. With increased specialty care and long-term care facilities, it is likely that the per capita health care cost for the elderly, especially those over 80 years old, will increase. This will be particularly costly as the Chilean population ages. Currently, the elderly receive considerably less care than younger individuals when considered on the basis of bed days per death.

It may be concluded from this analysis, therefore, that even under the best of circumstances, the costs in real terms of adult health care provided by public facilities may be expected to increase significantly beyond the simulation provided here. Moreover, this analysis has not addressed regional or private sector variability in health care costs which undoubtedly exist. This variability can be due in part to differences in population and risk factor profiles. However, the major differences will be in the capabilities of health facilities in the various regions or in the private sector. The forecast increases in health care costs will probably not be uniform over the country. Therefore, without careful planning, regional increases in facilities and health professionals may not be optimal with regard to need. In such cases, health care costs will increase even further in order to maintain the same level of health care throughout the country. If the current cost increases in the ISAPRE system continue, they will only exacerbate the future escalation of total health care costs. Moreover, it should be expected that as income levels rise in the future, there will be an ever-expanding appetite for more health services, as patients expect to raise their quality of life through medical care, further increasing the total health care bill.

All of the above suggests, as shown elsewhere,[7] that even with vigorous preventive efforts, health care costs may increase in the future relative to possible savings that might be attainable through improvements in the delivery of health services or that might obtained by making consumers bear a larger fraction of health care costs. It is imperative, therefore, that Chile begin implementing strategies now that will contain health care costs and mitigate the financial burden of future increases in demand for health services. As will be discussed in detail in Chapter IX, another emerging policy issue for Chile will be to assess alternative

---

7. See Ref.8 in Chapter V.

United States General Accounting Office. 1994. Long-Term Care: Demography, Dollars, and Dissatisfaction Drive Reform. Washington, D.C.: GAO/T-HEHS-94-140.

approaches for mobilizing additional resources needed to finance the health care needs of adults and the elderly, including a wide array of long-term care services for the chronically ill, the elderly, and the disabled.  Otherwise, Chile may likely face an overwhelming task of containing health care costs while expanding benefits to a population increasing in numbers and longevity.

# CHAPTER VII

# CONTROLLING NON-COMMUNICABLE CONDITIONS[1]

## Overview of the Challenge

Many non-communicable illnesses and injuries are preventable, and their associated risk factors can be modified or reduced through carefully designed interventions. This chapter presents recommendations for strengthening and expanding the primary, secondary, and tertiary prevention programs and actions of the Chilean health system, based on a review of current efforts and in light of the morbidity, mortality, and risk factor patterns discussed in previous chapters.

## Current Programs and Activities

A list of the main adult health programs and activities undertaken by public and private agencies is shown in Table VII-1.

### Preventive programs and activities

The bulk of the NHSS's health promotion and non-communicable disease prevention efforts are clustered under the MOH's Adult Health Program (AHP), one of the MOH's three basic service programs. Currently, the AHP includes the following subprograms: Tuberculosis, Sexually Transmitted Diseases, AIDS, Cholera, Hypertension, Diabetes and Epilepsy. In addition to these, two independent non-communicable illness programs exist in the MOH: Cancer and Mental Health.

The AHP, which was created in the early 1980's, was revised in 1991 to propose, for the first time, integrated control measures, i.e., control of risk factors common to many non-communicable diseases, such as cardiovascular disease, hypertension, diabetes and cancer. The AHP has supported activities such as anti-smoking public information and education campaigns. Also, a series of health promotion activities supported by non-governmental organizations (NGOs) have been carried out (e.g., pilot projects against smoking in the primary and secondary schools and against alcohol abuse among adolescents). With respect to specific MOH's subprograms, improvements have been made since the early 1990's to standardize diagnostic and therapeutic guidelines and to increase coverage and diagnostic reliability of cervical cancer screening, although overall coverage is still very low (i.e., less than 20 percent of women aged 25 to 64 years). The National Chemotherapy Program has improved and help to standardize cancer treatment. The mental health program is well integrated with other health services and works in coordination with other social services agencies.

---

1. This chapter draws on background papers commissioned for this study prepared by Cecilia Albala, María C. Escobar, Luis Martinez, Ernesto Medina, Eduardo Medina, Alfredo Pemjean, María I. Pino, Jaime Rozovski, Cecilia Sepúlveda, and Erica Taucher.

The public health system's infrastructure for secondary and tertiary prevention is limited. Public hospitals, particularly outside of Santiago, lack basic diagnostic and treatment equipment and suffer from shortages of specialized personnel, resulting in common delays in treatment, especially for radiation therapy, chemotherapy and supporting laboratory services. The growing aged population will only exacerbate this problem by increasing the demand for diagnostic and treatment services.

**Other measures**

For the prevention of injuries due to traffic accidents, Chile has establish a fairly broad legal framework, including traffic regulations, obligatory use of seat belts, and driver tests prior to the issuance of licenses. Media campaigns have also been launched to educate the public about the use of seat belts by car drivers and passengers. These efforts are complemented by police ticketing of offenders. In spite of the latter efforts, the use of seat belts is still not widespread; seat belt users are concentrated among better educated groups.

Occupational health and safety has been the focus of numerous Chilean laws since 1916 which have mandated employer coverage of occupational diseases and injuries occurring to their employees and set standards for health and safety in the work place. As noted in Chapter I, Law No. 16.744 of 1968 mandates obligatory social insurance against work-related injuries and diseases. The NHSS, through the MOH's ISP, has oversight responsibility for the enforcement of this law. Very little information is available, however, on the prevalence of occupational exposure to hazardous and carcinogenic substances, and awareness of occupational risks on the part of both workers and managers is limited. The MOH initiated in 1992 a pilot program to undertake activities in high-risk industries identified by HSAs, including field consultation and monitoring by engineers and health professionals, as well as occupational health education and training.

The country also has legislation governing the protection of the environment, but basic environmental data are either lacking or collected independently by sectoral agencies and are not compiled in an integrated manner to facilitate planning and monitoring. The National Environment Commission (CONAMA), an inter-agency body, was established 1990. An ongoing project is under implementation to strengthen CONAMA's institutional capacity to play a catalytic role in defining and administering environmental policies. In 1988, an automatic monitoring network was installed, constituting a major advance in air pollution control. Also, a strategic plan to reduce pollution in the Santiago Metropolitan Region, including the reduction in the number of diesel cars and the control of industrial emissions, began to be implemented in 1990.

**The issue**

The picture which emerges from the review of current efforts in Chile is that a great number of programs and activities aimed at preventing or ameliorating non-communicable illnesses and injuries exist, but that their effectiveness is constrained by several important limitations. Chief among the latter are limited resources for preventive health activities. It is estimated that in 1993 the MOH spent approximately US$7.8 million or less than 1 percent of its total budget on preventive health programs, including activities related to AIDS, cholera, cervical cancer, diabetes, tuberculosis, mental health, occupational health, and other adult-health related initiatives. As a result, preventive health activities have not been continuous or systematic and have not been implemented consistently throughout the country. Despite some improvements since 1991, the current structure of activities related to adult health in Chile is fragmented, impeding the dissemination of guidelines and standards and the organization of comprehensive control efforts. Coverage of some programs, such as those for the detection and control of hypertension, remains low, and there are no programs to address certain problems of unquestionable importance, such as breast, stomach, and gallbladder cancer. Weak coordination with other sectors and NGO's, and lack of data on the prevalence of many risk factors and conditions, have also hindered the above efforts.

The following sections outline steps which could serve to strengthen and extend current activities in light of projected demographic and epidemiological trends and a broad understanding of the cost and effectiveness of interventions.

**Table VII-1**
**Current Preventive Programs and Activities Related to Adult Health**

| Program/Activity | Objectives | Activities | Annual Budget[a] |
|---|---|---|---|
| Cancer[b] | Reduce cancer deaths | Three priority interventions: cervical cancer, tobacco control, chemotherapy | N.A. |
| Tobacco control | Increase public awareness | Public: Promote legislation, education, information dissemination, smoking cessation<br>Private: Public education, smoking cessation training for health personnel | N.A. |
| Cervical cancer | Increase coverage of Pap smear screening among women 25-64 | New guidelines developed, upgraded screening and diagnostic capabilities, improved follow-up/treatment of positive cases | 255 |
| National Chemotherapy | Increase availability of chemotherapy | Standardized therapies, centralized financing of chemotherapy for NHSS beneficiaries | N.A. |
| AIDS[c] | Prevent HIV infection | Public education campaigns | 2,451 |
| Hypertension[c] | Increase diagnosis and treatment | Updated diagnostic and treatment guidelines; pilot project to control risk factors | N.A. |
| Diabetes[c] | Early detection and case management | Public: Patient education/counseling, development of training/educational materials<br>Private: Patient education, rehabilitation | 70 |
| Mental health[b] | Prevention and rehabilitation | Expanded availability of community-based services, patient counseling | 445 |
| Alcohol/drug abuse | Prevention, rehabilitation | Public: Pilot school-based education programs<br>Private: Alcoholic rehabilitation programs | N.A. |
| Occupational health and safety | Risk monitoring, education | Health education, training, detection of occupational risks, monitoring of exposed workers | 320 |
| Environmental health | Pollution control in Santiago | Special commission created to lead intersectoral coordination and implement policies | N.A. |
| Injury control | Increase awareness and prevention | Public education campaigns, establishment of traffic regulations, school crossing guards, monitoring | N.A. |
| Cardiovascular disease | Increase public awareness | Public: Very limited<br>Private: Education campaigns for the control of risk factors, cholesterol screening | N.A. |
| Chronic obstr. pulmonary disease | Public education and patient assistance | Public: Very limited<br>Private: Mass education, research on home therapies, procurement of drugs at low cost, oxygen therapy program | N.A. |

[a] 1993 central level MOH budget, in thousands of U.S. dollars of July 1993 (430.89 Chilean pesos: US$ 1.00).
[b] Considered an independent program of the MOH apart from the Adult Health Program.
[c] Designated as a sub-program of the MOH Adult Health Program.

## What Should Be Done: Principles and Recommended Actions

### A framework for intervention

Successful international experiments in the control of risk factors[2] suggest certain principles which should guide prevention strategies. First, it is critical to begin such actions promptly. As discussed in Chapter IV, the prevalence of many key risk factors is very high in both sexes. Nevertheless, Chile's mortality rates from these conditions are below the figures in industrialized countries. This suggests that the natural history of these diseases in Chile has still not reached the stage at which they produce all fatal effects, which justifies the immediate implementation, or in some cases, strengthening of preventive measures, particularly those aimed at modifying risk factors among adolescents and young adults.

The complex etiology of non-communicable illnesses and injuries--which have behavioral, social, economic and legal dimensions—warrants a coordinated, multisectoral approach to prevention. While the Chilean MOH may assume a leadership role in developing interventions, their implementation will often require the participation and cooperation of diverse government agencies, as well as the private sector. This is particularly important in educational and informational activities, where it is critical that the various actors involved transmit consistent messages.

Prevention strategies should target the control of multiple risk factors. Traditionally, control of non-communicable illnesses has focused on control of a single pathology. Yet because most non-communicable diseases have certain shared risk factors (e.g., smoking, alcohol and drug abuse, sedentary lifestyles, obesity) and because risk factor combinations tend to have synergistic effects, multi-faceted interventions have been shown in many cases to be more effective and efficient than single-focus efforts.

### Intervention strategies

Interventions to reduce non-communicable illnesses and injuries can be grouped into three categories, according to their focus (individual vs. population) and location (community, work place, health facility):[3]

---

2. One example is the North Karelia Project in eastern Finland established in 1972 to control cigarette smoking, obesity, and fat consumption, and to increase detection and treatment of hypertension, as means to reduce noncommunicable disease mortality. Another is the demonstration project initiated at Stanford University in the late 1970's, where health education was used as a tool against multiple risk factors associated with chronic diseases. This information was reported in: Litvak, J., Ruiz, L., Restrepo, H., and McAlister, A. 1987. The Growing Noncommunicable Disease Burden. A Challenge for the Countries in the Americas. PAHO Bulletin 21:1561-171.

3. U.S. Department of Health and Human Service. 1991. Healthy People 2000: national health promotion and disease prevention objectives. Washington, D.C.: Government Printing Office (DHHS publication no. (PHS) 91-50213).

**Health Promotion**: Refers to primary prevention strategies related to individual lifestyles. These address physical activity and fitness, nutrition, tobacco, alcohol and drugs, and mental health, and can have a powerful influence on personal health. Educational and community-based programs can address individual lifestyle in a cross-cutting fashion.

**Health Protection**: Encompasses actions related to the environment or which provide protection to large segments of the population, involving a community-wide rather than an individual focus. These would include the prevention of injuries through traffic safety measures, occupational health and safety, reduction of environment pollution, fluoridation of water to prevent cavities, and control of foods and drugs.

**Disease Prevention**: Includes screening, counseling, and prophylactic interventions for individuals in clinical settings. Priority areas include heart disease and stroke, cancer, diabetes, HIV infection, and sexually transmitted diseases.

The social environment may be the most important factor in behavioral change to improve health. Health promotion and protection strategies, therefore, must typically exceed the traditional boundaries of the health sector to effectively reach the target population, with most activities taking place beyond the confines of health facilities. Educational and community programs have a multiplier effect and can help prevent a host of risk factors. Secondary and tertiary disease prevention activities tend to rely on clinical settings, although many innovative strategies for non-communicable disease screening and management have adopted community-based approaches. A comprehensive approach to non-communicable disease and injury control, as well as risk factor prevention and management thus integrates appropriate actions at all levels.

As will be discussed later in this chapter, disease prevention and management strategies should direct resources to those interventions proven to be cost-effective. The selection of interventions to be included in a basic package of preventive services, therefore, requires thorough demographic and epidemiological analysis and economic evaluation of the various options.

## Health Promotion

Based on an integrated program, health promotion objectives must consider common risk factors throughout the population. Efforts should focus on smoking, diet and nutritional habits, physical exercise, alcohol and drug use, and mental health.

**Smoking**. In order to prevent new smokers and encourage smoking cessation, it is necessary to develop strategies that target the social environment. These include, among others, a decrease in the social acceptability of smoking, motivation for people to seek specialized help (e.g., smoking cessation assistance programs at the primary care level), an increase in the cost of cigarettes (e.g., the experience of developed countries indicate that the application of this measure can deter smoking[4]), and restrictions on smoking in public and work areas. It is also important to construct strategies that directly support the individual's decision not to smoke. The main strategies are education and information, taxes and regulatory measures to deter tobacco consumption, including higher prices for cigarettes and restrictions on tobacco advertising and promotion, as well as treatment of smokers, which together have a synergistic effect.

These strategies should be targeted to specific population groups on whom they can have the greatest impact. In particular, given data on smoking initiation and experience from pilot studies conducted in the primary schools, elementary school children should be targeted. It is also important to reduce tobacco consumption among health and education workers because of their status as role models and the high prevalence of smoking among them. At the level of secondary prevention, health care providers need up-to-date scientific information on smoking cessation techniques that have proven effective in developed countries.

**Diet and nutritional habits**. Dietary factors are associated with many of the leading causes of death in Chile. While the available data on diet in Chile show a pattern in line with international recommendations, obesity is prevalent, especially among lower-income women, and osteoporosis is a growing problem among the elderly. A nutritional evaluation of the adult Chilean population is needed, including a nutrition survey to assess the food intake and nutrition status across socioeconomic and age groups and geographic regions. Most of the surveys done previously were confined mainly to the Santiago Metropolitan Region.

Prevention of obesity may be the only effective means of control, since the treatment of obesity has a high failure rate even in programs for young people and has an 80 percent or more recidivism at the end of five years among successful cases. Prevention of osteoporosis should also begin during childhood, adolescence and youth, with a view to reaching adulthood with adequate bone mass. To this end, the consumption of calcium-rich foods and physical activity should be encouraged. Nutritional objectives should also focus on the prevention of a possible deterioration in diet, as has occurred in developed countries.

To attain these objectives, programs must be implemented at all levels of the educational system, capitalizing on the nutrition components in primary and secondary school curricula to emphasize health education. Dietary standards should be formulated for the prevention of non-communicable diseases in adults, and consistent nutritional messages

---

4. U. S. Department of Health and Human Services. 1992. Smoking and Health in the Americas. A 1992 Report of the Surgeon General, in collaboration with the Pan American Health Organization. Atlanta: U.S. Department of Health and Human Services, Public Health Service, Centers for Disease Control, National Center for Chronic Disease Prevention and Health Promotion, Office on Smoking and Health, DHHS Publication No. (CDC) 92-8419.

developed. The use of the mass media to attain the proposed objectives should have a great impact in Chile because: (a) literacy is very high; (b) most urban dwellers, among whom non-communicable illnesses are most predominant, have a radio, a television set or both; and (c) distribution of newspapers and magazines is widespread.

**Physical activity and fitness**. Regular physical activity improves the quality of life at any stage, increases life expectancy, and helps the elderly to maintain functional independence. Exercise benefits a wide range of non-communicable diseases and is an essential component of obesity control programs. Physical activity improves muscle mass, which protects against bone and joint diseases, injuries, and disability. Its effect on blood lipoproteins has also been established, as physical activity helps to reduce cholesterol.

Program efforts should seek to combat sedentary lifestyles among the general population and to increase physical activity and the time engaged in sports by adolescents and young adults. Obviously, these general objectives should be closely linked to nutritional messages.

Experience shows that changing a sedentary lifestyle is one of the most difficult behaviors to modify in adults. It is therefore necessary to strengthen programs offered through primary education and to conduct intensive community efforts using existing social organizations to promote physical activity. In this regard, strategies must target physical education teachers who, together with the health team, should be the key promoters of physical activity.

**Alcohol abuse**. On the supply side, prevention of alcoholism can be approached by dealing with the availability of alcoholic beverages through the regulation of production, distribution, prices, access (particularly for minors), and advertising. Efforts to modify demand should include education and information to promote moderate consumption of alcohol and increase awareness of the adverse consequences associated with its abuse, aimed at the general population, adolescents, pregnant women, drivers of automotive vehicles, family members of alcoholics, and supervisory personnel in the work place.

The most useful public policy tools appear to be regulation of the supply of alcohol and restriction of advertising to messages compatible with healthy lifestyles. Prevention in schools also seems very promising. Health professionals, through training and advisory assistance to teachers and community volunteers, can provide key support in achieving these educational goals. In addition, stronger laws related to driving under the influence of alcohol and drugs and their strict enforcement are effective means to reduce alcohol and drug abuse.

**Drug abuse**. Preventive measures should distinguish between forms of use, which can be experimental, occasional, or habitual. Prevention aimed at experimental and occasional use should be fundamentally educational, for both the general public and vulnerable groups such as adolescents and young adults. Educational activities should be intersectoral, enlisting the cooperation of the justice system and the municipalities. Health education about the consequences of drug abuse should also be integrated into school curricula.

Special attention should be given to bringing drug abuse prevention programs to the community level through the family mental health community centers and the work of NGOs. In the latter case, the role of health personnel should be to provide training and technical assistance to those in charge of these activities. There may be some advantage to associating these efforts with other activities aimed at the prevention of alcoholism.

**Mental health**. In order to reduce the impact of mental health problems, health authorities should vigorously implement existing plans to develop mental health activities in conjunction with other primary care activities, emphasizing their integration at the community level. These plans address the control of problems related to the use of alcohol and drugs as well as the prevention of violent and abusive behavior. Additionally, the health-related efforts should be linked with other social support mechanisms to help patients and their families cope with problems and reinsert discharged patients into the community.

## Health Protection

Health protection actions should emphasize the prevention of injuries and occupational health and safety.

**Injuries**. There are certain known risk factors that can be used in planning strategies for the control of injuries. Such strategies must take into account the variety of causes (e.g., exposure to electrical shocks, mechanical or thermal energy, oxygen insufficiency) and whether the injury is involuntary or intentional (i.e., homicides, assaults, suicides). Also, many injuries are caused by a multitude of factors, necessitating multi-faceted solutions.

To reduce deaths from involuntary causes, measures being carried out to prevent injuries must be maintained and/or stepped up (e.g., laws for expanding the use of seat belts in cars and protective helmets when riding motorcycles, improvements in roadway design and markers, injury prevention education campaigns). The MOH must play a leadership role in injury prevention initiatives and ensure coordination with alcohol and drug programs. The MOH should also formulate specific secondary and tertiary prevention programs in this area, ensuring, among other measures, that well-designed emergency services are available to reduce fatalities and disability.

**Occupational health**. Work-related accidents particularly impact upon those persons 25 to 40 years old. Prevention of occupational injuries requires specific measures involving the basic principles of machine safety, job design, protective equipment, and monitoring of the work place to prevent accidents.

To decrease risk factors, both labor and management must be sensitized as to threats to worker safety. Education in this area is particularly important owing to the high return on efforts to promote self-regulation of hazards and proper use of protective equipment. The Government must more fully play its role in surveillance of occupational health and ensure early detection of work-related pathologies. This requires having sufficient trained personnel, which is not now the case, as well as specialized equipment.

The strategies for achieving these objectives include a first phase of early detection and diagnosis of occupational diseases through epidemiological monitoring programs and the training of health personnel in occupational health. Surveillance efforts should include development of databases to track exposure and the number of cases over time, which would provide a clearer picture of the magnitude of the problem and the risk factors involved. In addition, the Government must rigorously monitor and enforce compliance with regulations, as well as provide assistance to small firms in setting up and implementing work health and safety programs.

To improve prevention and control activities, as well as expand coverage of workers against occupational risks, Law Number 16.744 should be revised; increased human, physical, and financial resources should be given to each occupational health unit; the occupational health department of the ISP should be strengthened; an efficient computerized information system should be established to serve as a basis for program planning and the evaluation of results; and continuous training should be given to workers, managers, and health personnel.

**Environmental Health**. Air pollution is a particular problem in Santiago, which is home to 40 percent of the country's population. In recent years, the Government has made protection of the environment an important part of its economic and social agenda. The Government should support the establishment of systems to track and evaluate environmental exposures and diseases. To this end, mechanisms should be developed to encourage health professionals, and in particular the research community, to work closely with the agencies involved in pollution control to identify linkages between health outcomes and contaminants, levels of exposure to contaminants, as well as types of interventions to reduce environmental risks.

### Secondary and Tertiary Prevention

Prevention of non-communicable diseases through the health services delivery system involves early secondary prevention and diagnosis to prevent progression of the disease, complications, disability, and death. The priority areas should be cardiovascular disease, cancer and diabetes.

**Cardiovascular disease**. As discussed in Chapter IV, the major risk factors for cardiovascular disease are hypertension, high cholesterol, and smoking. A reduction in these risk factors has been shown to have a significant impact on cardiovascular mortality.

With regard to hypertension, those with uncontrolled hypertension have a three to four times greater risk of developing coronary disease and a seven-fold risk of having a coronary event than those with normal blood pressure. Partial studies done in Chile show prevalence of 12-18 percent, of which only one third are aware of their condition, and of those, only a third are receiving treatment. Accordingly, early detection and timely treatment of this pathology would result in a major reduction in cardiovascular mortality. Unfortunately, since the disease in its early stages is asymptomatic, early detection is difficult, and adherence to treatment is often low.

High cholesterol, as discussed in Chapter IV, is not a highly prevalent problem in Chile, although it exists among higher income groups and is related to diet. Smoking is widespread among men and women in Chile, and has a significant impact on cardiovascular mortality.

Strategies for reducing mortality from cardiovascular diseases include: (a) screening at the local level, work place, and among high-risk groups; (b) expanded accessibility, coverage, quality, and timeliness of care, including follow up programs; and (c) inclusion of health education and community participation in program activities to improve the control of risk factors and compliance with treatment.

**Cancer**. Cancer is the second leading cause of death in Chile. A number of epidemiological studies have shown that the risk of cancer can be significantly reduced by preventive measures. Also, early detection has a major impact on cancer mortality.

**Cervical cancer**. Despite the availability of PAP smear tests at all primary care centers, there has not been a decline in cervical cancer deaths in the last 20 years. Studies done by the MOH have identified deficiencies and made it possible to adjust the cervical cancer program accordingly.

Strategies for increasing coverage of women 30 and older with periodic PAP smears and improving the quality and reliability of screening and diagnosis include: (a) having trained nurse-midwives at the primary care establishments to take PAP smears; (b) improving diagnostic capabilities and quality control in cytopathology laboratories; and (c) educational activities in health centers, in the work place, and through community organizations in order to increase coverage of women who are not covered by maternal and child health programs.

**Breast cancer**. As there are certain breast cancer risk factors that have been identified and effective screening methods exist, such as physical examination and mammography, strategies can target prevention through early detection. However, mammography requires costly equipment and trained staff, which means that a program cannot be implemented in the short run.

Strategies to increase coverage of screening mammography and physical breast examination and reduce deaths from breast cancer include: (a) carrying out educational campaigns on manual breast self-examination through the print and broadcast media, NGOs, and primary care facilities; (b) having trained nurse-midwives perform physical breast examinations whenever PAP smears are taken; and (c) conducting screening mammography in high risk patients as part of secondary care.

**Stomach and gallbladder cancer.** Stomach cancer, the leading cancer in men requires attention since it is not addressed by any national program. Actions to address risk factors for gallbladder cancer are limited by the lack of international experience, since its high prevalence is peculiar to Chile. The undertaking of a major epidemiological study to determine possible etiological factors in Chile should be given priority. However, as noted in Annex A, gallbladder cancer is associated with the high prevalence of stones in the biliary tract, a risk factor that has been sufficiently identified and which in Chile is very common. Although for operational reasons, control of gallbladder cancer is not realistic over the short run, this must be a goal in the medium and long term. To reduce mortality, increased screening of patients with suspected gall stones is needed, as well as a reduction in waiting time between diagnosis and surgery. Public health personnel need to be trained in detection of gallbladder cancer and be offered the opportunity to upgrade their skills for treatment with new procedures such as laparoscopic surgery, which seems to be more cost-effective than traditional surgery.

**Diabetes.** Primary prevention of diabetes is feasible in part through health promotion efforts such as physical activity, appropriate diet, and control of obesity. As this is a pathology whose importance is largely due to its complications (e.g., blindness, renal insufficiency, cardiovascular and neurological complications) and because its control is critical in the prevention of complications, a secondary prevention program is necessary at the primary care level.

Primary care strategies must include early detection in high risk groups such as the obese and pregnant women, and effective follow-up and monitoring of all cases diagnosed. Orientation on proper management of diabetes for nursing assistants, teachers, and community volunteers can have a multiplier effect on basic actions carried out among patients and their family members.

### What are the Priority Health Interventions?

The call for greater actions in health protection and promotion and disease prevention cannot ignore their cost and how these services will be paid for. It is clear that the NHSS's resource constraints would require reallocation of existing funds in order to finance expanded prevention programs. Naturally, such reallocation will depend on a clear policy decision by the MOH to assign greater priority to these types of efforts.

One approach that may be considered for priority setting is the comparison of the likely costs and impacts of health interventions. Since standardized cost-effectiveness data are lacking for most health interventions in Chile, Box VII-1 presents cost-effectiveness estimates for a variety of public health and clinical interventions compiled from a collection of studies on disease control priorities in developing countries.[5] Because the costs of, responses to, and effects of health interventions differ substantially between countries, this should be seen only as an attempt to provide a "sense of priority" among the various health interventions that are used for dealing with non-communicable illnesses and not as a prescription on how to rationalize the allocation of public health resources in Chile. The latter exercise is a pending activity in the Chilean health sector that will require not only the gathering of appropriate and reliable local data to adequately carry out a comparative assessment of the cost and effectiveness of health interventions under the NHSS, but a consideration of the interplay of political, social and ethical factors as well.

The health interventions included in Box VII-1 can be compared because their effectiveness is measured in the same unit of DALYs.[6] Based on the unit cost of a DALY, which measures the cost-effectiveness of an intervention, a health intervention priority ranking has been established. The lower the cost of an intervention to achieve one additional year of healthy life the higher its ranking. From the information in Box VII-1 it is clear that many non-communicable illnesses can be controlled with highly (less than US$250 per DALY saved) and moderately cost-effective interventions (US$250 to US$999 per DALY saved). For example, given that the control of smoking may provide multiple benefits (e.g., reduce the incidence of lung cancer, heart disease, and chronic obstructive pulmonary disease), it should likely receive top priority. Although not included in Box VII-1 because of lack of data, the probably high cost-effectiveness of alcohol control makes it another "good buy," along with certain other behavioral changes that are favorable for health outcomes (e.g., change in sedentary lifestyles). Naturally, as discussed in this chapter, the efforts to modify behaviors in individuals need in some instances to be complemented with governmental policies to further influence them (e.g., taxation policies for tobacco and alcohol). It is also apparent from Box VII-1 that there are various clinical interventions of moderate cost-effectiveness that can be considered as "good buys" assuming that the health infrastructure needed to treat these conditions exists. In view of the above, as argued in Chapter V, it is clear that assessments of the cost and effectiveness of health interventions can potentially serve as a valuable public policy tool to define the composition of preventive and curative health programs and redirect health resources toward those interventions with high and moderate cost-effectiveness and away from those with low cost-effectiveness.

---

5.  Jamison, D.T, et al., eds. 1993. Disease Control Priorities in Developing Countries. New York: Oxford University Press.

6.  For a complete discussion on the cost and effectiveness of health interventions see ref. 5 and World Bank. 1993. World Development Report 1993. Investing in Health. New York: Oxford University Press.

## Box VII-I

# Cost-Effectiveness of Public Health and Clinical Interventions

| Potential Intervention | Strategy | Objective | Target Group |
|---|---|---|---|
| **US$25 per DALY[A/]** | | | |
| Smoking prevention or cessation programs | Public Health: Behavior change | Primary prevention plus secondary prevention | Adults |
| Use of condoms to prevent sexually transmitted diseases | Public Health: Behavior change | Primary prevention | Adults |
| Blood Screening for HIV | Clinical: Local hospital, referral hospital | Primary prevention | Adults |
| **US$50 per DALY** | | | |
| Annual breast examination to screen for breast cancer (women after the age of 50) | Clinical: Primary care | Primary prevention plus secondary prevention | Adults |
| **US$75 - $250 per DALY** | | | |
| Public preventive package for most cardiovascular risk factors | Public health: Behavior change | Secondary prevention | Adults |
| Insulin therapy for non-insulin dependent diabetic individuals | Clinical: Primary care | Rehabilitation plus secondary prevention | Adults/Elderly |
| Management of stable angina with medication | Clinical: Primary care | Rehabilitation plus secondary prevention | Adults/Elderly |
| Management of post-myocardial or post-stroke patients | Clinical: Primary care, Public health, Behavior change | Secondary prevention | Adults/Elderly |
| Low cost medical management of unstable or myocardial infarction | Clinical: Local hospital | Rehabilitation plus secondary prevention | Adults/Elderly |
| PAP Smear at five-year intervals to screen for cervical cancer | Clinical: Primary care | Secondary prevention | Adults |
| Cancer pain management | Clinical: Primary care | Palliation | All ages |
| Schizophrenia or manic-depressive illness treatment with medication | Clinical: Primary care | Rehabilitation | Adults |
| **US$250 - $US1,000 per DALY** | | | |
| Referral of pharyngitis cases for antibiotic prophylaxis to prevent rheumatic fever and rheumatic heart disease | Public health: screening and referral | Primary prevention | Childhood |
| **US$1,000 per DALY** | | | |
| Medical and surgical management of chronic obstructive pulmonary disease | Clinical: Referral hospital | Rehabilitation plus palliation | Adults/Elderly |
| Surgery for rheumatic heart disease | Clinical: Referral hospital | Rehabilitation plus secondary prevention | Adults |
| Management of moderate hypertension with medication | Clinical: Primary care | Secondary prevention | Adults/Elderly |
| High-cost management of myocardial infarction or unstable angina | Clinical: Local Hospital | Secondary prevention | Adults/Elderly |
| Management of coronary artery disease with surgery | Clinical: Referral hospital | Rehabilitation plus secondary prevention | Adults/Elderly |
| Medical and surgical management of cancer | Clinical: Referral hospital | Care plus palliation | All ages |

A/ DALY = Disability-Adjusted Life Years

Source:   Adapted from tables 1A-3 and 1A-6 in Jamison, D.T. et. al., eds. 1993. Disease Control Priorities in Developing Countries. New York: Oxford University Press.

## Policy Issues Concerning the Control
## of Non-Communicable Illnesses and Injuries

There are three main reasons why reforms affecting preventive services should be contemplated to go hand-in-hand with reforms of curative services currently underway in Chile:

(a)   Reallocation of resources from curative to preventive services would, in general, enhance equity, since the major risk factors for disease are more prevalent among the poor, who therefore benefit disproportionately from investments in prevention.

(b)  Reallocation of resources from curative to preventive services would, in general, enhance efficiency because preventive interventions tend to be more cost-effective (in terms of $ per DALY gained) than curative interventions.

(c) The reform of curative services provides specific opportunities to incorporate incentives for prevention, both for medical professionals and for the general population.  For example, the reform of the National Health Service in the United Kingdom allowed the contracts of general practitioners to be modified to incorporate financial incentives for health promotion and screening.

To this end, a national constituency-building initiative on disease prevention and health promotion and protection priorities should be launched to raise public awareness of individual, community, and societal responsibilities in health.  The following steps should be considered:  (a) the development of national health goals, including specific targets for selected preventable conditions and their risk factors; (b) the creation of popular and political consensus on these goals; and (c) the development of a plan to achieve these goals, incorporating regulation, public education, and appropriate incentives to individuals, businesses, and providers.  The development of health goals and intervention strategies should be based on consideration of the magnitude of the problem (both prevalence and severity), its susceptibility to modification, and the cost and effectiveness of the interventions proposed.

More comprehensive data are needed on the prevalence of risk factors and non-communicable illnesses and on the characteristics of groups at highest risk in order to feed into the setting of priorities and targets and the design and evaluation of interventions.  Given limited resources, accurate information is also needed on the costs and expected effectiveness of interventions to guide the selection of priority health promotion and prevention strategies, as well as investment in technologies for secondary and tertiary prevention.  These issues should be addressed in the current initiatives underway to strengthen the management information and epidemiological monitoring systems of the MOH.

The current fragmentation of activities to combat non-communicable illnesses and their risk factors among different MOH programs argues for development of a more comprehensive organizational structure so as to facilitate greater integration of prevention strategies to address multiple risk factors. Also, for many of the adult health problems discussed in this study, a broader intervention approach is needed to more fully utilize the range of policy mechanisms available to promote and protect health and prevent non-communicable illness, particularly those measures that go beyond the traditional boundaries of the health sector. The MOH will need to continue to exercise a leadership role while finding ways to strengthen coordination with other ministries and government institutions, particularly the Ministry of Education. By the same measure, the MOH must find ways to enlist greater cooperation and participation of the private sector (i.e., ISAPREs, NGOs, private practitioners) in health education concerning non-communicable disease risk factors. Given the decentralized nature of the Chilean health system, the role of the MOH should be to foster the development and implementation of appropriate and timely disease prevention efforts by local governments, HSAs, municipal health authorities, NGOs, and practitioners.

The establishment of funding mechanisms for health promotion and disease prevention should also be accorded priority. A promising approach to stimulate innovative activities might be the creation of a demand-driven fund managed by an intersectoral group headed by the MOH and financed by public and private sources that could channel resources to public and private organizations, including community groups. Activities that could be financed by such a fund would include pilot interventions or their replication at the community level, media campaigns, and applied research on risk factor prevalence and effectiveness of interventions.

# CHAPTER VIII

## MANAGING HEALTH TECHNOLOGY IN CHILE[1]

Health technology is often thought of only in terms of equipment or devices, yet it encompasses drugs, procedures and programs used in health care as well. The past 30 years have seen an explosion in the variety and complexity of technology employed in health care worldwide, especially for the diagnosis and treatment of adult health problems. The unbridled acquisition of advanced medical technology is an important source of medical care cost escalation. The challenge of effectively addressing the health needs of the aging Chilean population with limited financial resources lends special importance to how new technology is incorporated into the health system. To understand the effects this pressure for increased technology will have on the health sector, it is important to first examine the current availability of major types of medical equipment in Chile. Given that the public sector provides a majority of all health services, the review of available technology will focus primarily on public health facilities.

### Recent Health Investment Trends

As shown in Table VIII-1, during the 1980's public sector capital investment in health practically came to a halt. Budget figures for the last decade show declining allocations for hospital investments, maintenance, operating budgets, and even staffing. The average investment in equipment and facilities in the HSAs during 1986-90 barely exceeded US$10 million per year. In 1991 only two percent of all public expenditures in health were allocated to investments such as construction and equipment for hospitals. This situation, however, began to change in 1992 as a result of governmental efforts intended to address the deterioration of public hospitals and the vacuum created in the health system by the lack of specialized ambulatory care facilities. It is estimated that in that year investment spending as a percent of total public health care expenditures increased from 2.4 percent to 7.9 percent. In contrast, a strong infusion of investment funds from FNDR helped expand and update the primary health care network nationwide. FNDR health investments averaged about US$19.5 million per year in the last 5 years.

---

1. This chapter was prepared on the basis of background papers commissioned to César Oyarzo and Rony Lenz, and Renaldo Battista and Matthew Hodge, respectively. Additional information is from: World Bank. 1992. Staff Appraisal Report. Chile Health Sector Reform Project. Report No. 10987-CH.

**Table VIII-1**
**Composition of Public Sector Health Expenditures**
**1980-1992**

| | Percent of Total Health Expenditures | | | |
|------|-------|-----------------|------------|-------|
| Year | Wages | Goods & Services | Investment | Other |
| 1980 | 36.6 | 20.8 | 3.8 | 38.9 |
| 1981 | 36.9 | 18.8 | 2.7 | 41.6 |
| 1982 | 36.9 | 19.2 | 2.3 | 41.9 |
| 1983 | 36.8 | 21.5 | 0.8 | 40.9 |
| 1984 | 37.6 | 21.8 | 1.7 | 39.0 |
| 1985 | 37.3 | 21.8 | 2.3 | 38.5 |
| 1986 | 38.0 | 21.7 | 1.6 | 38.7 |
| 1987 | 39.1 | 23.6 | 1.5 | 35.8 |
| 1988 | 40.3 | 23.5 | 2.4 | 33.8 |
| 1989 | 39.2 | 22.0 | 3.0 | 35.7 |
| 1990 | 33.5 | 27.8 | 2.2 | 36.5 |
| 1991 | 32.6 | 27.3 | 2.4 | 37.7 |
| 1992 | 26.7 | 27.5 | 7.9 | 37.9 |

Source: Chilean MOH, 1992.

Amid limited resources, both new construction and equipping of hospitals, as well as modernization and maintenance of existing hospitals, was virtually abandoned in favor of expansion and upgrading of primary care facilities. As a result, physical plant and equipment within the public hospital network deteriorated. Negligible investments led to a failure to adopt new technologies, even in such critical areas as care for high-risk newborn infants and trauma, as well as in outpatient departments. In spite of recent governmental efforts, many hospitals still suffer from antiquated or inoperative equipment, even in such basic areas as X-ray machines. This obsolescence is not limited to medical equipment, but has also affected supportive services such as kitchens, communications, and information systems. In addition, some hospitals suffer from serious defects in their physical plants, plumbing, heating/cooling systems, and sanitary systems.

### Availability of advanced medical equipment in public hospitals

The above situation was documented in a MOH study[2] undertaken in 1991 focusing on health service needs in the HSAs of Metropolitan Santiago, Llanchipal, and Antofagasta, which cover approximately 50 percent of the total population in the country. The study evaluated all medical and industrial equipment in hospitals with a replacement value of over US$ 3,000, and an inventory of the estimated residual life use of this equipment was made. For each piece of equipment information was gathered on: total possible years of use;

---

2. Ministerio de Salud, Oficina del Proyecto MINSAL-Banco Mundial. 1992. Proyecto HSRP - Catastros de Equipamiento (Anexo XII). Santiago, Chile

residual life use; general condition; and operational state. The overall findings for each HSA are presented in Table VIII-2. In almost all of the HSAs surveyed, the majority of equipment had less than 10 years of residual life use implying that within the next decade most of it may have to be replaced.

**Table VIII-2**
**Residual Life Use of Hospital Equipment by HSA, 1992**

| Health Service Area | Percent of Equipment With Residual Life Use of: | | |
|---|---|---|---|
| | 0-2 years | 3-9 Years | 10+ Years |
| Metropolitan Santiago - North | 9 | 56 | 35 |
| Metropolitan Santiago - Central | 9 | 62 | 29 |
| Metropolitan Santiago - West | 15 | 44 | 41 |
| Metropolitan Santiago - East | 15 | 51 | 34 |
| Metropolitan Santiago - South | 5 | 60 | 35 |
| Metropolitan Santiago - Southeast | 6 | 54 | 40 |
| Llanchipal | 36 | 41 | 23 |
| Antofagasta | 44 | 42 | 14 |

Source: Chilean MOH, 1992.

MOH estimates indicate that the cumulative effect of the deterioration of the public hospital network contributed to reducing bed utilization by 20 percent. In some facilities, beds often remain empty because of incidental reasons such as the disrepair of buildings or a breakdown of heating or plumbing systems. In addition, other hospital activities have been affected, such as: (a) round-the-clock emergency care for injuries and other medical emergencies, due to the lack of technology necessary to respond to a changing patient mix (e.g., trauma cases); (b) outpatient care, because of insufficient equipment and staffing, especially weak diagnostic capabilities, as evidenced by waiting lists and slow processing of patients; and (c) hospital admissions, due to the inadequate capacity of hospitals to provide timely inpatient care, particularly for specialized services such as orthopedics, cancer treatment, and surgery.

The 1991 MOH study also gathered information on the availability of advanced medical equipment, providing a glimpse of the degree of incorporation of new technology into the Chilean public health system to meet the clinical needs of adults and the elderly. Table VIII-3 presents findings by type of medical equipment surveyed.

## Table VIII-3
### Residual Life of a Sample of Hospital Equipment by Type, 1992

| Type of equipment | No. of machines in hospitals surveyed | Percent equipment with residual life use of: | | |
|---|---|---|---|---|
| | | 0-2 years | 3-9 years | 10+ years |
| Surgical Microscopes | 35 | 46 | 49 | 6 |
| Anesthesia Machines | 191 | 21 | 63 | 16 |
| Endoscopes | 25 | 36 | 48 | 16 |
| Colonoscopes | 10 | 40 | 40 | 20 |
| Bronchoscopes | 12 | 25 | 67 | 8 |
| Mammography Units | 3 | 0 | 33 | 67 |
| Computerized Tomography Scanners | 5 | 0 | 20 | 80 |
| Ectomagraphs | 17 | 12 | 41 | 47 |
| Respirometers | 20 | 50 | 20 | 30 |

Source: Chilean MOH, 1992.

## Comparison with the private sector

The availability of medical technology in private facilities is far greater than in the public sector in Chile. While it not possible to undertake a full comparison of technology in the two sectors, to illustrate the situation, a small survey was done for this study evaluating the availability of CT scanners in Metropolitan Santiago. As indicated in Table VIII-4, the survey found that there were 15 CT scanners available in the private sector compared to the 5 in the public sector. In addition, while the private sector first introduced CT scanners in 1978, the public sector did not acquire its first scanner until 1982.

### Table VIII-4
### Availability of CT Scanners in the Public
### and the Private Health Sectors,
### Metropolitan Santiago, 1990

| BRAND | Generation[a] | Hospital | Installation Date |
|---|---|---|---|
| **PRIVATE SECTOR** | | | |
| PICKER | Fourth | Hospital Militar | 1983 |
| OHIO NUCLEAR | Fourth | Fleming | 1978 |
| OHIO NUCLEAR | Second | Indisa | 1981 |
| PHILIPS | Fourth | Dipreca | 1985 |
| C.G.R. | Fourth | Hospital Fach | 1985 |
| PFIZER 200 | Second | Dr. Humeres | 1990 |
| SIEMENS | Third | Universidad Católica | 1985 |
| SIEMENS | Third | Fleming | 1987 |
| SIEMENS | Third | Santa Maria | 1987 |
| EMI | Second | C. Scanner | 1978 |
| GENERAL ELECTRIC | Third | Clínica Alemana | 1988 |
| GENERAL ELECTRIC | Third | Mutual de Seguridad | 1990 |
| GENERAL ELECTRIC | Third | Dr. Casals | 1990 |
| EMI | Second | Hospital Parroquial | 1990 |
| EMI | Second | S. San Bernardo | 1990 |
| **PUBLIC SECTOR** | | | |
| PFIZER | Second | Universidad de Chile | 1986 |
| PFIZER | Second | Hospital Barros Luco | 1987 |
| PFIZER | Fourth | San Juan de Dios | 1990 |
| TOSHIBA | Second | Neurocirugía | 1982 |
| EMI | Second | Hospital del Salvador | 1986 |
| **Total Number of CT Scanners in Santiago** | | | 22 |

[a] Indicates how modern the equipment is. First generation CT scanners are those that were first available on the market, and fourth generation are the machines most recently introduced and thus the most advanced.

Source: Oyarzo and Lenz, 1992.

**Ongoing investments**

As a result of declining investments in the public health sector throughout the 1980's the present state of Chile's health technology is deficient. Hospitals are in need of repair, the majority of equipment has a residual life use of less than ten years, and new equipment is required. The deteriorated technological capability of public health facilities hinders the delivery of services to adequately meet the health care needs of an aging population. Also, routine maintenance and repair of both infrastructure and equipment is limited in public health facilities.

As discussed in Chapter I, the Government of Chile recognizes this situation and has begun to implement a series of reforms to upgrade medical technology at all levels of care. Since the present public health system provides primary care through a network of low-technology dispensaries of varying size, and outpatient specialized care is only available at the overcrowded ambulatory departments of tertiary hospitals, a new network of ambulatory care facilities --rural outposts, rural dispensaries, urban clinics, reference centers, and diagnosis and treatment centers-- is being established with the support of international donors to provide care of progressive complexity at different levels of the system. The rehabilitation and upgrading of hospitals and the provision of resources for their appropriate operation and maintenance is starting to receive high priority.

The central element of the ongoing reform program is the creation of two new specialized outpatient facilities: the Health Referral Center (**Centro de Referencia de Salud**, CRS), and the Diagnostic and Treatment Center (**Centro de Diagnóstico y Tratamiento**, CDT). The CRS is an outpatient center of medium technological complexity to be located in small cities (10,000-15,000 inhabitants), as a free-standing facility or attached to a Type 3 hospital, or in medium (50,000-100,000 inhabitants) or large cities (more than 100,000 inhabitants) as part of the network of urban health centers, where it can be attached to a Type 2 or 3 hospital. This facility is proposed to serve as a specialized referral center for 4-6 urban health centers, covering on average a target population of 150,000 to 250,000 inhabitants. The CRSs would be staffed with physicians trained in the four basic medical specialties (internal medicine, pediatrics, obstetrics/gynecology, and general surgery), psychiatric personnel, dentists, and nursing and auxiliary personnel, and would be equipped with basic diagnostic equipment (e.g., X-ray) and laboratories for basic tests, including electrocardiograms. The CRSs would also have beds for the provision of short-term inpatient care on an emergency basis, and ambulances for transferring patients to higher level facilities.

The CDT is a specialized ambulatory care facility located in the principal city of an HSA, endowed with higher level technology (e.g., laboratories for specialized tests, sonograms, CT scanners, and ambulatory surgery equipment) for the provision of complex diagnostic and therapeutic services, such as oncology, neurology, and traumatology. These facilities would be attached to a Type 2 or 1 hospital, with catchment areas of more than

100,000 and 500,000 inhabitants, respectively. The CDT staff would include physicians trained in all clinical specialties, dentistry, and nursing and auxiliary personnel.

It is expected that the reformed public health system would serve a great number of patients in health facilities closer to their residence in those places currently lacking them, with less time and travel costs incurred by the patients. By making specialized services available on an ambulatory basis, it is expected that the users of public health services would be encouraged to seek care at local, lower cost facilities rather than overcrowding outpatient departments at the tertiary care hospitals. The shifting of patients from hospitals to less complex facilities should result in a less costly service provision, although the improved access may result in an increase in total costs through increased utilization.

### Role of Health Technology Assessment

In view of the need for new investment in conjunction with the construction of new facilities and the rehabilitation of existing ones, but given limited resources and concerns about escalation of health costs, it is vital that a rational process for making decisions regarding health care technology be established in Chile. As the pressure for advanced technologies intensifies, it will be necessary to more carefully evaluate the cost-effectiveness of different health interventions prior to investment. Experience in OECD countries[3] indicates that although new disease diagnosis and treatment devices and techniques have contributed to unparalled improvements in medical care in the past 40 years, their unrestrained acquisition and the recurrent costs thereby engendered have accelerated the growth of health care expenditures at an unprecedented rate. In the United States, for example, the cost escalation effect of the adoption or diffusion of new health technologies is clearly illustrated by liver transplant technology, which provides effective treatment but at a cost of about US$200,000 or more, with an additional US$20,000 for follow-up care and drugs. Similar examples of this phenomenon include open heart surgery to replace clogged arteries, at an average cost of US$46,000, and ultrasound technology such as the PET (positron emission tomography) scanner that aids in the detection of heart disease at a cost of US$1,800 per test.[4] Below, lessons for Chile from approaches to health technology assessment in selected OECD countries are reviewed.

---

3.  OECD countries are those that are members of the Organization for Economic Cooperation and Development (OECD). These include: Australia, Austria, Belgium, Canada, Denmark, Finland, France, Germany, Greece, Iceland, Ireland, Italy, Japan, Luxembourg, the Netherlands, New Zealand, Norway, Portugal, Spain, Sweden, Switzerland, Turkey, the United Kingdom, and the United States.

4.  Weisbrod, B. A. 1991. The Health Care Quadrilemma: An Essay on Technological Change, Insurance, Quality of Care, and Cost Containment. Journal of Economic Literature XXIX:523-552.

## What is health technology assessment (TA)?

Formal appraisals of the costs and benefits of health technology have become increasingly used in OECD countries to influence medical practice, provide a framework for decision-making about the acquisition of sophisticated technology, and for controlling escalating medical care costs. Technology assessment (TA) has been defined as a comprehensive form of policy research examining short- and long-term consequences (i.e., benefits, costs, and risks) of the application of technology.[5] Its defining feature is its interdisciplinary character, drawing on information including the technical properties, feasibility, efficacy, effectiveness, and safety of health interventions, efficiency evaluations with respect to value for money, assessment of both intended and unintended social consequences of technology use, ethical implications of technology, and the acceptability, availability, accessibility and indications for use of technologies.

Technology assessment bodies have taken on a variety of forms in OECD countries, ranging from government entities, a university-centered model, a non-governmental body, or consulting committees. Because of the broad scope of most technology assessment processes, conducting TA requires the participation of scientists, practitioners, managers, and consumers.

## What are the main applications of TA?

TA is of particular use in two related spheres: procurement of goods and services and medical practice. TA's main application has been to procurement and funding decisions. TA of this form has been carried out through a variety of organizations, both governmental and non-governmental. In Canada, two provincial health care technology assessment bodies in Quebec and British Columbia act at arms-length from the political process, producing evaluations to support policy deliberations of the provincial governments and other health care decision-makers. Physicians are less often a primary audience for such evaluations, in contrast to practice-focused TA. In France, L'Assistance Publique de Paris, which is in charge of administering all public hospitals in the city of Paris, created a TA committee in 1982 to help hospital managers make better decisions with respect to the adoption of new technology. In the United States, a variety of federal bodies have had roles in health care TA. For example, the Office of Technology Assessment (OTA) advises Congress on the social impact, safety, efficacy, and cost-effectiveness of all types of technology, including health care technology. In addition, the United States has been the site of an innovative proposal for technology assessment involving public consultation to prioritize health services for government financing in the State of Oregon.[6]

---

5. Coates, J. 1971. Technology assessment: the benefits..the costs..the consequences. Futurist 5:225.

6. Hadorn, R. N. 1991. Setting health priorities in Oregon. J. Am. Med. Assoc. 265:2218.

TA's other main thrust has been directed towards medical practice has generally taken the form of guidelines produced by consensus panels or expert task forces.[7] The other general approach involves a semi-permanent group of experts who engage in an iterative process of evaluating scientific evidence on the effectiveness of medical treatments and producing practice guidelines (i.e., when various treatments work and for whom).[8] Guidelines for medical practices, such as those produced by the Panel of the National Consensus Conference on Aspects of Cesarean Birth in Canada,[9] are now frequent in North America and in Europe. In pursuing these efforts, the goal is to improve the quality of patient care and to reduce operating costs. For example, recent studies in the United States have estimated that the rates of "inappropriate" use of a variety of procedures (e.g., coronary angiography and coronary-artery bypass graft surgery) in different settings range from about 15 to 30 percent, reaching as high as 40 percent for particular procedures at individual institutions[10] If inappropriate care, which results in unnecessary hospital days, procedures, and medications, were avoided, then it is estimated that the United States' annual health care bill could be cut by US$100 billion without a negative impact to patients.[11] [12]

Effective guideline development processes in OECD countries have managed to position themselves primarily as tools for increasing quality of care rather than as mechanisms set up to control physician behavior. Guidelines that are directive while not coercive and that reduce uncertainty are less likely to meet resistance from medical practitioners. There is also a move to promote greater involvement of practicing physicians in the development of guidelines so as to increase their credibility. As indicated by a survey of hospitals and obstetricians in Canada, guidelines for medical practice may predispose

7.   Perry, S. The NIH Consensus Development Program. A decade later. N. Engl. J. Med. 317:485.

8.   Woolf, S. H., Battista, R. N., Anderson, G. M., Logan, A. G., Wang, E., and the Canadian Task Force on the Periodic Health Examination. 1990. Assessing the clinical effectiveness of preventive maneuvers: Analytic principles and systematic methods in reviewing evidence and developing clinical practice recommendations. J. Clin. Epidemiol. 43(9):891-905.

9.   Panel of the National Consensus Conference on Aspects of Cesarean Birth. 1986. Indications for cesarean section: final statement on the Panel of the National Consensus Conference on Aspects of Cesarean Birth. Can. Med. Assoc. J. 134:1384-52.

10.  Phelps, C. E. 1993. The Methodologic Foundations of Studies of the Appropriates of Medical Care. N. Engl. J. Med. 329(17):1241-45.

11.  Siu, A. L., Sonnenberg, F. A., Manning, W. G., et al. 1986. Inappropriate use of hospitals in a randomized trial of health insurance plans. N. Engl. J. Med. 315:1259-66.

12.  Brook, R. H. 1989. Practice guidelines and practicing medicine: are they compatible? JAMA 262:3027-30.

physicians to consider changing their behavior.[13]  However, rapid change in actual practice would not occur if barriers to their implementation (e.g., economic incentives to perform elective cesarean section as opposed to vaginal delivery, perceived threats of malpractice litigation) are not removed.

TA's ultimate objective is to improve decision-making by using scientific knowledge in the policy debate.  For example, as is illustrated in Box VIII-1, a ministry of health might ask a TA body to produce a summary document on the costs and benefits of a potential breast cancer screening program.  A ministry of health might also request advice not only on scientific matters but on their implications for policy decisions.  An example would be a request to examine the effectiveness of transplantation and, if effectiveness is established, to determine the optimal distribution of transplant centers in a given region.

In general, OECD country experiences suggest that technology use can be managed effectively and efficiently when demand is evaluated at the macro level and incorporated into micro-level planning and procurement.  In those cases where technology acquisition decisions are made at the level of institutions, micro-level aggregate capacity is likely to exceed local demand, and the resulting search for economies of scale and, in some systems, operating profit, creates powerful incentives to expand use to marginal indications or even to situations producing no marginal gain from technology use.[14]  These incentives may be further strengthened by government subsidization of capital outlays required for a given institution to acquire a particular technology and by systems of third-party insurance which exclude payers from providers' decision-making about technology use.  Such a system of supply engendering demand is reinforced when physicians are paid on a fee-for-service basis, such as in Canada and the United States, rather than by capitation, as in the Netherlands and the United Kingdom.  Fee-for-service reimbursement schemes produce incentives for expansion and an increasingly intensive approach to each patient and disincentives to rationalization or increased efficiency for a given level of expenditures.[15]  In contrast, if demand were evaluated at a macro level (e.g., all hospitals in one or more regions) and then incorporated in planned micro-level procurement and siting, such aggressive utilization would be less likely, for owners of a given technology would be closer to the break-even point on the average cost curve from the time of first use.

If TA is to have any effect, it must be linked with legislative or financial power to ensure that policies lead to action.  Beyond simply paying for health care, financial power

---

13.  Lomas, J., Anderson, G. M., Dominick-Pierre, K., Vayda, E., Enkin, M. W., and Hannah, W. J.  Do Practice Guidelines Guide Practice?  The Effects of a Consensus Statement on the Practice of Physicians.  N. Engl. J. Med. 321:1306-1311.

14.  Evans, R. G.  1990.  Tension, compression, and shear:  directions, stresses, and outcomes of health care cost control.  J. Hlth. Politics, Policy and Law 15:101.

15.  Deber, R.  1982.  Trends in health care costs - the contribution of technology.  Dimens. Health Serv. 59:16.

implies also some ability to influence market behavior. Thus, when a Canadian provincial government decides not to reimburse practitioners for a given service, its use rapidly declines since there are no other financing sources to which practitioners can turn for reimbursement. It is conceivable that a non-governmental payer would be of sufficient size that its decisions about payment for use or procurement of technologies would have de facto policy implications in the jurisdiction in which such a body provides health care. Regional health authorities in the United Kingdom and the sickness funds in the Netherlands appear to be moving in this direction.[16]

## Policy Issues Concerning Health Technology

The most pressing issue for Chile's health sector concerning health technology is the revamping of the methodology used in the public sector to define technology needs and priorities for investment in the NHSS. The process currently in use is inadequate to address concerns of efficiency, equity, and cost control. A process which takes into account population-based needs, the cost and effectiveness of technology, and which aids in balancing competing needs for scarce investment funds is urgently needed to guide the large amount of near term investment that has been proposed to upgrade Chile's ambulatory and hospital infrastructure. A related need is for the development of guidelines for medical practice based on the findings of TA, since these can contribute to improved care and appropriateness of practice while helping to reduce operating costs. This issue is of great importance because as shown in OECD countries more than any other factor the proliferation of technology contributes to the escalation of health care spending by expanding the menu of treatments and by reducing invasive procedures (e.g., exploratory surgery) that are replaced by a higher consumption of noninvasively procedures (e.g., CT scanners and magnetic resonance imaging tests).[17]

Since it is estimated that proposed investment in medical equipment in Chile over the next five to eight years is in the magnitude of US$206 million in the public sector and US$100 million in the private sector,[18] a related issue for the Government is whether to create a formal structure or to define alternative arrangements to conduct health technology assessments. At present, the only occasions in which health technology is evaluated is when analyzing commercial offers as part of bidding processes for purchasing new equipment. To this end, expert panels have been established for assessing brands, types of equipment, and post sale routine maintenance and repair support, but not the cost and effectiveness of the

---

16. Banta, H. D. Pushing the limits: technology assessment in health care. Text of an inaugural address given at the State University Limburg in Maastricht, The Netherlands, May 17, 1990.

17. Aaron, H. J. 1991. Serious and Unstable Condition. Financing America's Health Care. Washington, D.C.: The Brookings Institution.

18. Jiménez, J.' Inversiones en equipamiento médico: Proyección para década del 90. Intersal-Medcom, Julio 1993.

# Box VIII-1

### EXAMPLE OF APPLICATION OF TECHNOLOGY ASSESSMENT
Estimated Costs and Benefits of Breast Cancer Screening

**Problem:** Breast cancer is a major health problem in the Province of Quebec, accounting for about 26% of all new cancer cases diagnosed in women. For patients with breast cancer, the risk of dying depends on the stage at which the illness is diagnosed and treated. There is solid epidemiologic evidence that early detection of breast cancer through periodic screening (with or without physical examination) can prolong the lives of women with breast cancer.

**Objective:** To assist the Quebec health authorities, the Conseil d'evaluation des technologies de la santé (Quebec Province's Health Technology Council) undertook an evaluation to determine the health effects and costs of a potential breast cancer screening program.

**Estimation of effects:** Quantitative estimates of the effects of screening on breast cancer mortality were developed based on published results of four large prospective epidemiological trials of mammographic screening for breast cancer in other countries. The reductions obtained in annual mortality ranged from 24 to 54%. The individual study results were then combined statistically to estimate an overall average effect of 35% reduction in annual mortality. When the data were considered only for older women (50-69 years of age), the mortality reduction averaged 43%.

**Estimation of costs:** The direct costs of an ongoing screening program to the health care system were considered. Costs were calculated for different rates of program participation (100%, 75%, 60%); it was estimated that if all women aged 50 to 69 took part in a program of biennial screening, the cost would be C$27 million per year. With 75% and 60% participation, the costs might be C$20 million and C$16 million, respectively.

**Relation of benefits to cost:** After a start-up period, it was estimated that a program comparable to those in the reference studies might be expected to prevent about 230 deaths per year, an aggregate increase in life-expectancy of 4,700 years. If full participation was required to produce this effect, at a cost of C$27 million per year, the program would cost C$117,000 per death prevented or C$5,700 per life year. If the same benefits could be obtained with only 75% participation, the corresponding figures would be C$87,000 and C$4,300; if 60% participation yielded these benefits, the costs would decrease to C$70,000 and $3,400, respectively.

**Policy implications:** Because a considerable amount of screening mammography was already being done in Quebec (230,000 in 1989, and growing by about 20% per year) and since its cost was expected to increase in the future even if a formal program were not implemented, the relevant policy question posed to the provincial health authorities was what interventions should be enacted to optimize those screening activities which are already taking place. The alternatives proposed were: directing screening activities towards the age group which offers the greatest benefits, and improving the quality of the screening process at all levels. To do this, it was suggested the following: (i) the mammography done for screening would need to be identified and remunerated appropriately; (ii) screening outside the chosen age range would need to be discouraged through education and perhaps by the award of lower professional fees; (iii) guidelines for the purchase, maintenance and quality assurance of all equipment used, and for the training of technical and professional personnel, would have to be introduced for improving the efficacy of existing screening activities. Also, quality control measures could be introduced to assure high standards in taking and interpreting of mammograms; and (iv) a mechanism needs to be established to collect data on the extent of present screening, the ages of those screened, and the outcome of these activities in terms of the number of true and false positives, the extent of therapeutic interventions, and the increase in life expectancy for women, to assist in future policy decisions.

Source: Adapted from: Conseil D'Évaluation Des Technologies De La Santé Du Québec. 1990. Screening for Breast Cancer in Quebec: Estimates of Health Effects and of Costs. Report submitted to the Ministre de la Santé et des Services sociaux du Québec.

selected technology. These panels are not part of a permanent effort, and there is no continuity. Under the proposed decentralization plan for the public health sector, technology assessment would logically fall under the mandate of the MOH. If the MOH were given an explicit mandate for technology assessment, the boundaries and objectives of such a technology assessment process would need to be clearly set forth and disseminated. This effort, however, should not be developed in isolation from other initiatives to modify medical practice such as the ongoing health financing reforms or a future definition of cost-effective interventions as argued in Chapter VII. Based on OECD experience, it would be useful to define a role for practitioners in such a process. In-depth inspection of approaches used in OECD countries could also be of benefit to Chilean officials charged with developing a technology assessment capability.

A final related issue to the establishment of a technology assessment capacity in the MOH is how the public sector will manage competition and/or coordination with the private sector with respect to the introduction of advanced health technology. As seen in the example of CT scanners, the private sector has made a large investment in sophisticated equipment. Given the pressures of cost escalation facing the ISAPREs, it remains to be seen whether private providers can sustain their past level of investment in expensive technology. A joint public-private initiative might produce better knowledge to define criteria and set guidelines for the introduction and diffusion of technological innovations in a balanced and productive way. For example, the interrelationship between public and private sectors could very well be used in the future for the establishment of integrated high technology reference programs for certain specialized procedures, such as organ transplants, cardiovascular surgery, hip replacement, trauma interventions, or chronic dialysis. As in the case of the successful Integrated High-Technology Systems (SIAT) program in Brazil, a public or private hospital "of excellence" may define technical norms, including the type of procedures that can be done at different levels of qualified facilities, material and price standards, and evaluation and control mechanisms.[19] Again, TA may facilitate the undertaking of this initiative by ensuring equal access to information on technology effectiveness and by assisting in the definition of norms and standards.

While it is unlikely in Chile that the MOH would assume a role of regulating technology acquisition in the private sector, it is encumbent upon the Government to ensure that tax laws and health care financing mechanisms produce appropriate incentives for the private sector's rational acquisition of technology. It is also of interest to the public sector to find ways to leverage government investment in health technology to generate additional revenues through the sale of diagnostic and therapeutic services in public facilities to private providers. By the same token, in those areas where private institutions already possess sophisticated technology unavailable in public facilities, public providers should be encouraged to purchase services from private providers to avoid duplication of investment.

---

19. World Bank. 1989. Adult Health in Brazil: Adjusting to new challenges. Report No. 7807-BR., Washington, D.C.

# CHAPTER IX

## COST CONTAINMENT STRATEGIES[1]

As the population in Chile continues to age there will be a demand for more costly health services, and as discussed in Chapter VI, health care expenditures are likely to increase significantly. It is thus essential that Chile begin implementing strategies now that will contain costs in the future. In this chapter, existing cost containment measures are discussed, with recommendations made for potential strategies to mitigate the financial effects of the changing epidemiological profile.

### A Framework for the Analysis of Cost Containment Strategies in the Health Sector

A useful framework for the analysis of cost containment strategies in the health sector is shown in Box IX-1. It classifies policy options that affect supply and demand aspects of health care in terms of micro and macro management categories. This analytical framework is used below to explore the viability of various policy options for containing the likely escalation of health care costs in Chile in both the public and the private sectors.

Recently, more and more countries worldwide have been utilizing micro management strategies to contain health care costs. The focus of these are to control costs by influencing individual medical treatment. Demand side alternatives consist of requiring patients to share costs through user-fees and pre-paid premiums. On the supply side, policy options include using payment/reimbursement mechanisms, such as Diagnostic-Related Groups (DRGs) or prepaid capitation, to encourage providers to minimize the use of resources in treating patients; controls on prices of inputs (e.g., drugs, physician fees) or quantities of outputs (e.g., limits on drugs prescribed); as well as utilization reviews of medical decisions. Macro management, more often employed in nations that view health care as a social good, emphasizes regulation of the health delivery system. Demand side strategies focus on restricting the flow of funds into the health sector through such mechanisms as predetermined global budgets and expenditure caps. Supply side strategies include limiting the overall physical capacity of the health sector through limits on construction of new facilities, training of health personnel, and acquisition of technology.

---

1. This chapter was prepared on the basis of background papers by César Oyarzo and Rony Lenz (cost control mechanisms in Chile), and Enis Baris, André-Pierre Contandriopoulos and Francois Champagne (cost containment experiences in OECD countries).

**Box IX-1**

### ANALYTICAL FRAMEWORK FOR
### COST CONTAINMENT STRATEGIES

|  | MICRO MANAGEMENT | MACRO MANAGEMENT |
|---|---|---|
| **SUPPLY SIDE** | - Encourage efficiency in production through economic incentives <br><br> - Legal constraints on ownership of facilities <br><br> - Close supervision of medical decisions (e.g., utilization review) | - Regional planning to limit physical resources |
| **DEMAND SIDE** | - Conversion of patients into consumers through cost-sharing | - Predetermined global budgets and expenditure caps |

Source: Adapted from Reinhardt, U., 1990, The Health System of The United States: Lessons for Other Countries.

## What are the Lessons from OECD Countries?

A review of cost containment experiences in OECD countries was carried out as part of this study to identify relevant lessons for Chile from these countries' efforts to control the escalation of health care costs through supply and demand strategies. Despite differences in health care organization, all OECD countries have experienced common problems related to slowing the growth of overall health care expenditures and increasing the micro-efficiency of health care delivery. During the 1980's, health care expenditures grew faster than did GDP for most countries, with similar growth rates among the major components of health care spending. The health-to-total expenditure ratio in OECD countries in the early 1990's concentrated in the 7 to 9 percent range.[2] The main factors contributing to the increase in health care expenditures have been: inflation in the general economy which affects prices and wages in the health sector; changes in the size and demographic mix of the population, especially in the oldest age group (75 years and older); increases in prices and wages in the health sector above and beyond the general inflation; and growth in the volume and intensity

---

2.   OECD. 1993. OECD Health Systems. Facts and Trends 1960-1991. Volume I. Paris: OECD.

of health care services per capita. Only the last two reasons constitute major targets for cost containment in the health sector not only because they are modifiable but because they are the main factors contributing to the increase in health care expenditures. While individual examples of cost containment approaches are discussed below, the general conclusions from this review are presented in Box IX-2.

## Micro Management of Demand

Demand side micro management focuses on consumer cost-sharing for medical services. Among OECD countries, France and Japan have the most extensive set of cost-sharing rules. While in France, out-of-pocket payments account for approximately 17 percent of total payments for health, in Japan, cost-sharing ranges from 10-30 percent of costs depending on the insurance carrier and type of treatment.[3] Although this policy is principally utilized for increasing revenues, in the United States at least it has also fulfilled a cost containment role. The introduction of user fees, which should reflect the costs of production, is believed to transform the pattern of health service utilization. By making patients share in the costs of health care services as they use them, they become consumers and may opt to procure less costly services. In addition, fees may lessen overutilization of superfluous medical services. There is some evidence that cost-sharing reduces utilization, but mainly of adult ambulatory services and preventive services, without affecting service intensity. Moreover, user co-payments for outpatient care can often result in cost shifting to inpatient care, which results in ultimately higher costs for the health system. Also, user charges are not an effective cost containment tool where supplemental insurance is available to cover the patient's share as is the case in France and in the United States with Medicare patients. Most countries apply user charges very selectively--mostly for drugs and other medical goods. User charges levied against patients who are not the targeted beneficiaries of services, as in the case of high income individuals using public facilities, is an attractive revenue-generating strategy, particularly if fees paid by non-beneficiaries are higher than the costs of production and yield income to help subsidize the costs of care for beneficiary groups. Controls are needed, however, to ensure that public hospitals do not overly orient services to capture the revenue-generating market to the detriment of care for the intended beneficiaries.

---

3.   Wolfe, P. R., and Moran, D. W. 1993. Global Budgeting in the OECD Countries. Health Care Financing Review 14(3):55-76.

**Box IX-2**

### GENERAL LESSONS FROM OECD COUNTRIES FOR
### THE CONTROL OF HEALTH CARE COSTS

- To be most effective, cost containment policies should involve not only public expenditures, but be applied to total health care expenditures.

- The fewer and more centralized are the sources of health care financing, the easier it is for a country to contain health care costs.

- Supply-side macro-management strategies aimed at controlling both the price and volume-intensity of services have proven more effective in containing growth in health care expenditures than have demand-side micro-management strategies involving copayments and deductibles, and reduction in the volume and intensity of services per capita.

- The allocation of financial, human and physical resources should be done in accordance with criteria and norms set forth from a population perspective (i.e., disease prevalence or specific health needs, per capita basis) rather than from an institutional perspective (i.e., per number of doctors or hospital beds).

- The supply of personnel, especially medical specialists, should be planned in connection with demographic changes and be closely monitored.

- Fee-for-service methods of payment should be replaced by other prospective and retrospective methods (e.g., capitation, salaries, diagnostic-related groups) which remove incentives for supplier-induced demand.

- Global budgeting on a regional basis has proven effective in controlling overall expenditures while at the same time stimulating better integration of resources and services.

- The promotion of alternative service delivery modes (e.g., long-term care, ambulatory surgery) can reduce hospitalization costs.

- The introduction of new technologies and drugs should be conditional upon their proven efficacy and cost-effectiveness and the existence of needs as assessed on a regional basis.

- A mechanism for periodic, systematic review of quality, effectiveness and efficiency of services is needed to closely monitor the congruence between resources and services (productivity) and between services and outcomes (performance indicators). Such information should be used as the basis for budget decisions.

Source: Baris, E., Contandriopoulos, A. P., and Champagne, F., 1992.

**What has been the experience in Chile with micro management of demand?**

**Public sector**: As discussed in Chapter I, different copayment schemes exist in the Chilean public health system. In the NHSS, cost recovery is used to mobilize additional resources to complement regular budgetary allocations. Under the PPS, copayments are used as a cost containment tool. In this section the focus will be on the NHSS experience with copayments.

As seen in Table IX-1, during the 1981-1986 period, overall NHSS income declined appreciably; the system has only experienced real growth in income since 1987. At the same time, user charges have declined as a percentage of total income. Absolute increases in the amount of revenues generated through the sale of services since 1987 have resulted from increases in revenues from charges on hospital beds, use of surgical facilities, laboratory tests and pharmaceuticals, while income from ambulatory services has stagnated.

Table IX-1
Cost Recovery in the NHSS, 1980-1990
(in thousands of US$ of June 1991)

| Year | Total Income | % Variation From Prev. Year | Income From User Fees | % Of Total Income From User Fees |
|---|---|---|---|---|
| 1981 | 464 | | 36.7 | 7.9 |
| 1982 | 450 | -3.0 | 34.2 | 7.6 |
| 1983 | 428 | -4.9 | 29.1 | 6.8 |
| 1984 | 400 | -6.5 | 23.6 | 5.9 |
| 1985 | 402 | +0.5 | 21.3 | 5.3 |
| 1986 | 394 | -1.9 | 16.5 | 4.2 |
| 1987 | 410 | +4.0 | 20.9 | 5.1 |
| 1988 | 497 | +21.2 | 24.4 | 4.9 |
| 1989 | 524 | +5.4 | 25.7 | 4.9 |
| 1990 | 572 | +9.2 | 27.4 | 4.8 |
| AVERAGE | 454 | +2.4 | 26.3 | 5.8 |

Source: NHSS, "Balances Presupuestarios de los Servicios de Salud,"
as cited in Oyarzo, C. and Lenz, R., 1992.

The reduction in user fees since 1981 can be explained by the fact that many of the higher income public sector beneficiaries, who paid these fees in the early and mid-1980's, have since become members of ISAPREs. In addition, the economic recession of the early 1980's may have reduced the overall number of persons who could pay user fees. Lastly, there is evidence (discussed further below) that many users of public health services may be misclassified.

Currently, there are several major problems with the charging of user fees in the Chilean public sector. The first limitation is that the list of prices for medical services, from which user fees are established, is not based on the actual costs of providing the services. The relationship between the actual cost of providing a service and the price charged to consumers has been distorted, with wide variation between fees and production costs. Moreover, the level of prices has not kept pace with inflation, resulting in a serious erosion in real terms. As shown in Table IX-2, the value of a Level 1 consultation declined by about 50 percent from 1983 to 1991.

**Table IX-2**
**Evolution of Price of Level 1 Consultation**
**In FONASA PPS**
**(US$ of June of 1991)**

| Year | Price | Percent of variation |
|------|-------|---------------------|
| 1983 | 7.30  |        |
| 1984 | 6.09  | -16.6  |
| 1985 | 5.31  | -12.8  |
| 1986 | 4.44  | -16.3  |
| 1987 | 4.16  | - 6.3  |
| 1988 | 4.03  | - 3.1  |
| 1989 | 3.78  | - 6.6  |
| 1990 | 3.07  | -18.7  |
| 1991 | 3.84  | +25.1  |

Source: FONASA, as cited in Oyarzo, C. and Lenz, R., 1992.

In order to implement user fees in the public sector, a price list for services needs to be defined based on actual production costs. One possibility would be to develop two separate lists. The master list would include the full cost of providing services based on all inputs (e.g., human resources, supplies, or equipment depreciation). The second list would be the prices charged to users. This list would differ from the first list in that it would reflect the emphasis of the government in providing various services (e.g., subsidized prices for preventive health services; higher prices for non-essential elective interventions). In such a way, the MOH would be able to assist in shaping the consumption of services by beneficiaries. Along this lines, recently the MOH has begun to develop such a list of production costs for medical treatments, in conjunction with efforts to develop a prospective payment system based on diagnostic-related groups.

The second limitation on user charges relates to the classification system which determines the amount of user fees a beneficiary must pay for medical services. As stipulated in the 1985 Health Law, all NHSS users are classified into four groups according to their ability to pay for services rendered. Those classified in categories A and B as indigent or poor are not required to pay user charges in public health facilities. In 1989 a full 76 percent of all beneficiaries under the FONASA system were in these two categories and consequently exempt from paying user fees. This may not adequately reflect the ability of these persons to pay fees. It is more likely that the high percentage of persons classified in these two categories is due to the lack of financial information for classification and the lack of resources for follow-up administration, as well as to lack of willingness or experience on the part of health personnel to charge patients. To correct this situation, the Government should adjust the boundaries of the four income categories for classifying FONASA beneficiaries, so that those who cannot afford copayments effectively do not pay them and those who can afford them do. Given the current low level of cost recovery, the overall effect would be to increase financing through copayments but drawing from a wider, more equitable base. Specific proposals for modifying the FONASA cost-sharing arrangements are under review, such as copayment percentages; protection of FONASA beneficiaries from medical expenditures too high relative to their incomes; and total catastrophic protection or zero copayment beyond some expenditure ceiling.

Significant disparities exist, however, between public hospitals in their ability to capture fee-paying patients. In order to redistribute some resources from hospitals which generate high revenues from FONASA beneficiaries' copayments and fees charged to private patients to those hospitals which are not able to do so, the Government is reviewing another proposal that would require transfer of a fixed share of the discretionary revenues earned by hospitals to the NHSS for redistribution to hospitals serving primarily low-income patients. Also under review is the proposed requirement that fees for private patients be a constant mark-up over the PADs or PPPs, with each hospital free to set its own mark-up. The Government has already changed rules governing public hospitals' charging private patients for discrete services so as to induce hospital directors to tap the private market (i.e., the MOH has raised the limit to 10 percent of each hospital's total number of beds without cutting back on services for public patients).

**Private sector**: Currently, the private sector in Chile utilizes a number of micro management mechanisms to reduce demand. As noted in Chapter VI, the number of services per ISAPRE beneficiary has declined substantially from 1986 to 1992, suggesting that ISAPREs are taking some actions to control utilization. A major form of control on demand is the use of copayments. All ISAPRE beneficiaries are required to make copayments varying between 10 and 40 percent of the cost of each service, depending on the type of policy. The private sector also reduces demand by excluding older and high risk patients and costly conditions and/or by dropping affiliates once they develop non-communicable illnesses.

There has been some speculation that these practices are too pervasive within the private sector and have led to an inequitable system in which ISAPREs "dump" treatment of non-communicable or catastrophic illnesses on the public sector by refusing to cover such problems. In response to these perceived inequities, as discussed in Chapter I, the Government is currently developing legislation which would more strictly regulate the private sector's coverage practices.

## Micro Management of Supply

Micro management of supply focuses on improving efficiency in medical treatment by providing economic incentives to health care providers. The emphasis is on reducing utilization of unnecessary and inappropriate medical services. This may be done through the manipulation of the reimbursement mechanism for providers and/or improved management arrangements. The most significant micro management strategy on the supply side for control of hospital costs has been the introduction of Diagnostic-Related Groups (DRGs) in the United States in the early 1980's. The DRG method of payment relies on predetermined global payment for explicitly defined groups of diagnostic and therapeutic services. The introduction of DRGs has cut down on inpatient costs by reducing average costs per admission and average lengths of stay. As different studies[4] have documented, the implementation of the DRG-based payment system has not negatively affected the quality of care for Medicare patients, despite a reduction in the number of diagnostic and therapeutic procedures per case. On the contrary, evidence suggest that quality of care has improved during this period. However, providers have found ways to undercut the cost containment objectives of DRGs by "upcoding" diagnoses to more costly DRGs (i.e., systematic coding errors leading to higher reimbursements) and increasing overall number of hospital admissions (supplier-induced demand). Also, teaching hospitals in particular have complained that the DRG system unfairly penalizes them because their frequently higher costs of treatment are in part due to their dual function as service delivery and training institutions. Furthermore, DRGs are not applicable to ill-defined medical cases and do not cover physician fees and ambulatory services.

As differing from traditional fee-for-service systems, which encourage more consultations, diagnostic tests, overprescription of drugs, higher surgical rates, and higher costs,[5] the use of prospective payment mechanisms such as capitation also offers a vast array of incentives for providers to increase efficiency in their medical practice, since they must

---

4. Coulam, R. F. and Gaumar, G. L. 1992. Medicare's Prospective Payment System: A Critical Appraisal. Health Care Financing Review 1991 Annual Supplement:45-77.

   Wiley, M. M. 1992. Hospital Financing Reform and Case Mix Measurement: An International Review. Health Care Financing Review 13(4):119-133.

5. Shimmura, K. 1988. Effects of different remuneration methods on general practice: a comparison of capitation and fee-for-service payments. International Journal of Health Planning and Management 3:245-58.

absorb any additional cost if they exceed the fixed amount that is allocated per person for a defined package of services. Efforts need to be made, however, to adjust the capitation payment for individual risks (e.g., age, sex, place of residence) to prevent adverse selection (i.e., selection of only low-risk persons for enrollment), to prevent the referral of patients to higher level providers within a same system as a means to reduce costs, and to monitor the quantity and quality of services provided to prevent underutilization of services. For example, in the United States, some health maintenance organizations (HMOs) substract the fees for all care provided by specialized providers from the capitated fee. In the United Kingdom, a country which uses a capitated system of primary care payment, a supplemental fee for selective preventive services such as immunizations is provided to prevent underutilization of preventive services. In general, the success of this payment mechanism depends on skilled management at the different levels of the system (e.g., to negotiate contracts with providers, to monitor provider practices).

Another micro management of supply tool that has been used extensively in the United States is utilization review, whether in the form of independent boards making a retrospective review of physician use of tests and procedures, or medical practice guidelines. In Japan, aggressive peer review of doctor's spending patterns has been successfully utilized.[6] While utilization and spending reviews have been shown to reduce service intensity, they are controversial because many providers feel that such measures threaten professional autonomy. In addition, the extensive monitoring and auditing reviews needed to ensure the success of case-based reimbursement require management capacity and sophisticated information systems that are lacking in most developing countries.

**What has been the experience in Chile with micro management of supply?**

**Public sector**: At present, as discussed in Chapter I, Chilean public health care providers are paid according to the FAP fee-for-service schedule and historical fee-for-service reimbursements through FAPEM. Two main problems exist with the reimbursement of health care providers which have contributed to the escalation of costs. First, the fee-for-service nature of the reimbursement system itself acts as an incentive for providers to increase the quantity of services performed, perhaps providing services that are only marginally beneficial or even useless, in order to maintain or increase their incomes. Secondly, public sector prices paid to health providers under the PPS have suffered from wide disparities between reimbursement rates and the actual costs of services. The difference between current prices and recently estimated costs for an illustrative list of services is shown in Table IX-3.

The inconsistent relationship between reimbursement levels and costs means that some providers are paid at a rate higher than their cost for some services (e.g., stool exam), while other services are arbitrarily reimbursed at a level below cost (e.g., medical consultations for

---

6. World Bank. 1993. World Development Report 1993. Investing in Health. New York: Oxford University Press.

adults). When analyzing the above situation, it should be kept in mind that in the case of hospital reimbursements, there are two forms of payment: the FAP (fee-for-service schedule) and the historically-based budgetary allocations to cover salaries (see Chapter I). The former is intended to cover the cost of all operating expenditures except salaries, while the latter covers labor costs. The gap seen between costs and reimbursement levels in Table IX-3 may be explained by both the potential discrepancy between the cost of all operating expenditures except salaries and the FAP payments, and by the non-inclusion of labor costs. The real gap between the cost of services and reimbursement levels is unknown. The principal problem for the health system lies not in the gaps themselves, which disappear at the aggregate level, but rather in the distortion they create at the marginal level in the health facilities.

The wide disparities between reimbursement rates and costs affects both those services primarily related to infectious diseases and those related to non-communicable illnesses. The distortion between reimbursement rates and actual costs induces beneficiaries to make erroneous decisions with regard to the services consumed and creates perverse incentives for health providers. This in turn causes problems for the overall distribution of resources and may affect the financial wellbeing of hospitals which must deliver costly services without adequate reimbursement. This situation may also represent an equity issue to the extent that public facilities may be subsidizing care for ISAPRE affiliates when they use public services and pay fees that have been set on the basis of internal prices that are below production costs.

**Table IX-3**
**Cost and NHSS Reimbursement Rates For**
**Selected Health Care Services**
**(In US$ of February 1992)**

| SERVICE | Cost (US$) | Reimbursement Rate (US$) | Percent Of Cost Covered By Reimbursement |
|---|---|---|---|
| Bed Day for Intensive Care | 143.3 | 40.5 | 28 % |
| X-Ray Including Fluoroscopy | 5.7 | 8.9 | 156 % |
| Cholecystectomy and Choledochostomy | 105.8 | 170.9 | 161 % |
| Adenoma or Prostate Cancer | 91.0 | 141.1 | 155 % |
| Histopathology, Deferred Biopsy | 9.3 | 9.1 | 98 % |
| Medical Consultation for an Adult | 3.5 | 2.9 | 81 % |
| Urine Culture and Colony Count | 5.0 | 3.3 | 66 % |
| Indirect Elisa | 1.3 | 5.5 | 433 % |
| Complete Series Stool Test | 3.3 | 7.3 | 223 % |

Source: Oyarzo, C. and Lenz, R., 1992.

In order to hold down health care costs, the traditional method of paying providers needs to be replaced with a reimbursement mechanism which contains economic incentives to eliminating the provision of unnecessary care and encourages the provision of cost-effective services (e.g., some preventive care). The Chilean MOH has recently begun designing and pilot testing in various HSAs a new system which will pay providers prospectively based on a DRG-type system of payment (**pagos asociados a diagnósticos** or PADs). As a first step toward designing the new system, a revised prospective fee schedule (**pagos prospectivos por prestación** or PPP) has been prepared based on the results of a study of the actual production costs of 108 secondary and tertiary services which account for about 80 percent of costs in public hospitals. The study costed these 108 services in a nationally representative sample of 15 hospitals of all levels of complexity. Both direct (e.g., personnel, supplies, equipment usage) and indirect (e.g., administration) costs were determined.

A related study was carried out to estimate the full cost of providing patient care over the course of a hospital stay for 23 primary diagnoses which represent 60 percent of all inpatient stays in Chile. These diagnoses were selected using criteria of cost, prevalence, and degree of standardization of care for patients with such conditions. The type and quantity of services associated with each diagnosis were defined based on the judgment of 282 clinicians in different areas of medical specialty, drawn from a representative sample of 13 hospitals of different levels of complexity. The cost of treating each diagnosis was determined by applying the average cost per service to each of the required services and summing the total. The list of 23 diagnostic groups and their respective cost of treatment is shown in Table IX-4.

The new prospective payment system represents a major change from the FAP payment system, which covers all recurrent costs except personnel. Under the current system, the NHSS pays salaries of all hospital personnel directly; under the PPP schedule, each facility would be responsible for paying its own staff salaries out of income from the prospective payments eliminating separate payments for salaries. The basis for public hospital prospective funding would be fixed PAD payments which would be expected to cover all of the discrete services associated with the treatment of each diagnosis.

Additionally, the resource transfer system based on a schedule of charges for individual services (FAPEM) provided by primary care facilities at the municipal level would be replaced by a fixed capitated rate system for paying the complete primary care of enrolled patients. On the basis of actual FAPEM outlays from a sample of municipalities, the basic capitation rate would be set prospectively to cover the full cost of care according to norms for each of four categories of primary care (child care, maternal care, adult care, and oral hygiene). The estimated number of users of each primary care service would be multiplied by the annual recommended norm of visit frequency and services per user. The rate would include the labor costs of providing the recommended level of services, administrative costs, and a percentage allowance for non-labor input costs such as pharmaceuticals. The estimated total costs of a primary health facility would be converted to per capita costs by dividing total costs by the area population. This payment mechanism would allow private providers to participate in the delivery of primary care services at the municipal level, particularly in large urban areas, fostering competition among public and private providers and offering a wider choice to the users.

Under this new prospective payment schemes, the public health system in Chile would pay for complete treatments rather than for specific services, thereby creating a strong incentive for providers to improve efficiency and productivity as well as to increase quality of care at the lowest possible cost. This strategy will likely induce efficiency into the system but will not be sufficient to contain costs without concomitantly modernizing management in the health sector. At present, planning capability in Chile is weak, particularly in regard to multi-year strategic planning that responds to national policies and norms while recognizing the specificity of local conditions. Also, there is limited capability for balancing short-term investment and operational needs with longer-term investment requirements. Training of management personnel and development of appropriate information systems are needed to facilitate cost containment, as is the refurbishment of the public sector's physical infrastructure.

**Table IX-4**
**Estimation Of Costs For 23**
**Principal Diagnostic-Related Groups (DRGs/PADs)**
**(In US$ of February 1992)**

| DIAGNOSTIC-RELATED GROUP | COST (US$) |
|---|---|
| Chronic Cholecystitis | 337 |
| Cholangitis | 140 |
| Appendicitis | 205 |
| Peritonitis | 294 |
| Umbilical Hernia | 175 |
| Inguinal Hernia | 175 |
| Inguinal Hernia with Gangrene | 541 |
| Stomach Cancer | 1415 |
| Non-operable Stomach Cancer | 181 |
| Gastric Ulcer | 587 |
| Non-operable Gastric Ulcer | 89 |
| Duodenal Ulcer | 407 |
| Non-operable Duodenal Ulcer | 74 |
| Normal Birth | 141 |
| Elective Caesarean Birth | 241 |
| Ectopic Pregnancy | 371 |
| Spontaneous Abortion | 196 |
| Induced Abortion | 210 |
| Septic Abortion | 366 |
| Complicated Pregnancy | 344 |
| Chronic Tonsillitis | 109 |
| Adenoid Growths | 121 |
| Enlarged Prostate | 549 |

Source: Oyarzo, C. and Lenz, R., 1992.

As discussed in Chapter I, in a strategy intended to make health services management more responsive to local needs and conditions, the Chilean Government has decided to decentralize the health care delivery system, removing all operational responsibilities from the MOH's central administration and completely delegating service provision to the 26 HSAs. Under the proposed decentralized scheme, the MOH's central administration would have solely a normative, supervisory, and quality control role. MOH plans to delegate service delivery responsibilities to the HSAs by establishing annual service provision agreements with each HSA, estimating the type and number of health services to be provided and the level of resource allocation and transfer payments, as well as determining performance indicators to monitor achievement of the mutually agreed upon annual targets. Under this proposed arrangement, the PPP/PAD would help link the planning process to resource allocation in the production and delivery of services at the hospital level. The PPPs and the PADs would be paid prospectively according to the annual service provision agreements between the MOH and the HSAs, which are to become the planning instrument for the operation of the HSAs. The differences between services planned and those actually provided would be reviewed at the end of each planning or payment period.

The process of delegating authority from the MOH's central administration to the HSAs and the NHSS's autonomous agencies will be gradual and take several years to complete. The speed of implementation will depend on the introduction of legal changes, the development of the necessary support systems, especially the training of senior and middle level managers, and the upgrading of the information system.

**Private sector**: At their inception, in order to attract new clients, the ISAPREs made available a wide range of medical services. Over time this has created a situation whereby ISAPRE providers are dispensing increasing amounts of health care, particularly costly treatments. The ISAPREs need to develop supply side mechanisms to contain their costs in order to ensure their long-term financial well-being and should look to the public sector which has already begun developing mechanisms to do so. One method that is increasingly being adopted by the ISAPREs is the vertical integration of health care providers, which implies the direct provision of services by providers hired as staff of the respective ISAPRE. As a result, an important part of the private health care infrastructure is now controlled by the ISAPREs.

## Macro Management of Demand

The most common tool used in macro management of demand is prospective global budgeting for health services. This may be done through a centralized authority or through negotiations with agents that intervene in the process of health provision, such as provider associations. OECD countries with centralized control of hospital budgets (such as Denmark, Great Britain, Canada, and Spain) have been rather successful in controlling inpatient care costs through prospective budgets, which have resulted in lower admission rates, shorter lengths of stay, and lower costs per patient. As a result, global budgeting is being adopted by more and more countries for hospital care.

A more contentious approach to demand side macro management is placing limits on the compensation of physicians, particularly for ambulatory services. Attempts at placing caps on physician earnings or fee levels have generally not succeeded because of the resistance of medical associations. Governments have been more successful in linking physician fees to expenditure targets, with excess utilization resulting in reduction in fee payments or in annual fee increases. In Canada expenditure targets are set based upon utilization patterns of the previous year and estimations of influential factors such as population growth. In both Germany and France expenditure targets are set through negotiations between physician associations and the insurance funds. However, one of the limitations of expenditure targets in France is that they do not cover ambulatory services. In the Netherlands the success of expenditure targets has also been limited due to the lack of sanctions when targets are exceeded.

Pharmaceuticals, which often consume a sizeable portion of health care expenditures, have been shown to be quite susceptible to demand-side cost containment strategies applied both to consumers and providers. Currently, there are three main types of pharmaceutical cost control in OECD countries: price controls, negative listing, and prescription control. In France, high pharmaceutical expenditures have prompted the government to institute regulations to control drug prices, to limit the number of pharmacies, to periodically increase cost-sharing, and to develop negative lists of drugs with high prices and dubious efficacy. In Germany, the measures for curbing pharmaceutical expenditures have been of similar nature: negative drug lists, fixed payments for almost 55 percent of prescription drugs on the market, disincentives for prescription of more expensive drugs instead of their less expensive equivalents, authorization of pharmacists to dispense generic equivalents of branded pharmaceuticals, monitoring of physicians' prescribing patterns, periodic adjustments of cost-sharing in prescription drugs and publication of prices for comparable drugs. In the Netherlands, although the government does not control drug prices, the dispensing fees of pharmacists are set by negotiations between the insurers who fully reimburse prescription drugs, the Central Agency for Health Care Tariffs and the association of pharmacists. A fixed reimbursement price is planned to be introduced for similar drugs. Any price difference between the prescribed drug and the reference price is borne by the patient. In Great Britain, the introduction of prospective drug budgets for general practitioners is on the reform agenda. In some OECD countries the application of these measures has been highly successful. For example, in Germany the controls on prescriptions and pharmaceutical prices contributed to a 20 percent drop in spending on medicine and prescriptions, which will bring total savings of US$925 million to the health insurance system in 1993.

**What has been the experience in Chile with macro management of demand?**

**Public sector**: In Chile, the health budget for the public sector is determined annually by the Ministry of Finance. Thereafter, spending is strictly controlled so as to avoid significant financial deficit. The restrictions imposed by federal spending policies reverberate through the entire sector as the MOH controls the HSAs and the HSAs in turn control the health facilities. One limitation to global budgeting in Chile is that the process of developing budgets in the HSAs and the health facilities is very crude and does not facilitate financial management. For global budgeting to be truly effective, greater interaction is needed between the central authorities and the HSAs in budget negotiations, both to standardize the basis for HSA budgets and to achieve commitment on the part of providers to their negotiated budgets. The newly established Service Provision Agreements should provide a structure for budget negotiations and assist in reaching a compromise between providers and the government.

A second limitation to global budgeting has been the erosion of the public sector's monopolistic power as the principal financier of health care services. Without doubt, the development of the ISAPREs in the 1980's weakened the ability of the government to impose cost containment policies on providers. One solution would be for the public sector to work with major ISAPREs to agree on prices, thereby strengthening their mutual ability to negotiate curbs on costs with provider associations.

**Private sector**: For the private sector, global budgets will be extremely difficult to implement. Not only is the market power of the ISAPREs alone not sufficient to allow them to fix prices for providers, but also private providers must guard against relinquishing their share of the consumer market. In contrast to the public sector, private providers will lose beneficiaries if waiting lists develop or quality of care is perceived to have been reduced, both of which are possibilities given the constraints of global budgeting.

## Macro Management of Supply

Macro management of supply focuses on restricting the physical capacity of the health sector such as limiting the supply of providers and facilities. Perhaps the most important aspect of supply macro management is controlling the introduction of new technology. As discussed in Chapter VIII, one of the principal sources of inflationary pressure in the health sector has been the introduction of technologies which are clearly medical advances but which are also quite costly. Medical technology impacts on the costs of a health care system in a number of ways: (a) the initial investment, capital costs, are often quite high; (b) in some countries, once purchased, equipment frequently remains unused (due to lack of trained personnel, incompatibility with existing equipment, and mechanical problems combined with a lack of access to parts), however, it still adds to the operational costs of a facility; (c) in order to cover the purchasing and operating costs of new technology the price of other, unrelated, services may rise; and (d) there could be demand inducement by providers with new technologies, especially if the availability of certain equipment exceeds the needs of the population.[7]

As discussed in Chapter VIII, economic criteria can be used as a tool for making decisions about the acquisition of new technology, since the most technically advanced equipment is not always the most cost-effective. National technology policies and structures are essential to deflect pressure from medical groups pushing to accelerate technological advancement. Even in some OECD countries, where much of the health care infrastructure is privately owned, the regulatory powers of the federal or state government are used to restrict construction of new facilities and restrict acquisition of new medical equipment through national planning and technology assessment and regulation (France) or through negotiations between the government and physician associations (Germany). In the Netherlands, while acquisition of new medical technology can be financed by private sector loans, new investments still must conform to national plans set by the government. An innovative approach has been adopted in Sweden whereby all capital expenditures must be approved by community councils.

With the exception of the United States, most OECD countries have also set regulations to limit the influx of new physicians through restrictions on admission to medical schools, on licensing for registration and practice rights for new graduates, and on the number of posts for specialty training. In addition, almost all countries have sharply reduced immigration of foreign graduate physicians.

**What has been the experience in Chile with macro management of supply?**

**Public sector**: As alluded in Chapter VIII, at present there are no clear policies in Chile with regard to the physical capacity of the health sector. This lack of clarity is reflected in a number of ways including: the lack of an explicit investment policy; the lack of a standard methodology to evaluate health investment projects; problems in defining the optimal size of hospital facilities; problems of reinforcing the hospital network; the lack of a policy for the introduction or diffusion of new technologies in the sector. However, as the MOH takes on a more supervisory role, many of these issues may be resolved. With regard to new medical technology, the Chilean public sector has not kept current with many technological developments in common use in developed countries, particularly those related to the diagnosis and treatment of adult health complications, and in fact probably suffers losses in productivity due to outdated and in many cases, inoperable equipment. Upgrading of medical technology in public sector hospitals is currently being addressed by the Technical Assistance and Hospital Rehabilitation Project (TAHRP) and Health Sector Reform Project (HSRP), as well as by other investment projects, being implemented by the Government of Chile.

---

7. Yang, B. 1993. Medical technology and inequity in health care: the case of Korea. Health Policy and Planning 8(4):385-393.

Within the public sector, the agency in charge of evaluating investment for equipment is the Ministry of Planning (MIDEPLAN). In evaluating investments, MIDEPLAN uses a methodology[8] which analyzes level of deterioration of existing equipment, susceptibility to repair, and the life use of equipment and facilities. This approach focuses on present needs and defines what will be needed in the short and medium term. However, this methodology does not adequately relate current demand for services with equipment needs, nor does it assess the cost and effectiveness of the required technology. This is particularly critical in planning for the acquisition of high cost technology used in the treatment of adult health problems. Another limitation of the current methodology is inadequate planning for handling the recurrent costs of equipment investment (e.g., inputs, maintenance, personnel required to operate).

As discussed in Chapter VIII, given the large amount of procurement of medical technology contemplated by the public sector, it is urgent that the Government improve its approach to evaluating investments in medical technology, particularly taking into account needs posed by the growing importance of non-communicable illnesses and injuries.

**Private sector**: The private sector in Chile has used macro management of supply quite successfully to contain costs. By contracting with the public sector for facilities and equipment, a number of ISAPREs have reduced investment and maintenance costs. However, the rising competition for new patients will increasingly lead to cost escalation as ISAPREs try to maintain their edge by offering state-of-the-art medical equipment.

### Policy Issues Concerning the Control of Health Care Costs

Chapter VI of this study examined the costs of treating adult health problems in Chile, with particular emphasis on trends in hospitalization costs, which account for some 65 percent of all medical care expenditures. During the period December 1987 through March 1991, the average cost per hospital discharge grew by 22.3 percent in real terms (an annual growth rate of over 6.9 percent). The cost per bed day during the same period rose by 15.7 percent in real terms (5.0 percent annual growth). The largest cost increases were seen in surgical services, which grew by 50 percent. The projected increases in prevalence of non-communicable illnesses, and the inflationary pressures of new technologies used in the prevention and treatment of many of these illnesses, can be expected to increasingly drive the growth in hospital care costs. As presented in Chapter V, the results of the forecast model of risk factors, morbidity and mortality for non-communicable illnesses and injuries affecting adults, indicated that Chile will also experience a substantial increase in health care costs as a result of its changing demographic and risk factor profile. These expected increases will compound those increases due to inflation and more intensive use of high cost technology.

---

8. "Guidelines for Formulation and Presentation of Public Investment for Medical Equipment, Industrial Equipment and Vehicles in Health Facilities", developed by MIDEPLAN in collaboration with the Ministry of Health.

Faced with this panorama of rising costs and increasing numbers of patients afflicted with non-communicable illnesses, effective control over health care costs assumes ever-greater urgency. The easiest way to control costs is obviously to limit the extent of the service benefits or the population covered. Though attempts have been made towards this end in the United States (e.g., the Oregon experiment with Medicaid services which are now covered only if they are included on a list of services ranked in a hierarchical order according to their score of cost-effectiveness) it is not an accepted concept in many countries. The challenge, therefore, is to control costs without jeopardizing equity, freedom of choice, or quality. Indeed, cost containment is but one of the means towards the attainment of optimal equilibrium between three competing objectives of most health care systems: equity, freedom of choice, and efficiency. It is important only to the extent that increasing total health expenditures may be less productive in improving health than investing in other sectors of the economy capable of creating wealth. In fact, the analysis of life expectancy in selected OECD countries clearly shows that beyond a certain level of wealth the differences in the level of health expenditures make little difference in the health status of the population. It does make a difference, however, in the satisfaction of the population with the accessibility and overall quality of care. Within this context, the discussion of currently planned or implemented cost containment measures in Chile, and the lessons drawn from OECD countries, raise a number of issues for consideration by Chilean policymakers.

Since near universal access to health care has been achieved in Chile, concern should now focus on the efficiency and the effectiveness of the entire system (i.e., the delivery of quality health services, to meet the needs of an aging population, at minimum cost). Based on OECD experience, Chile's currently proposed reforms of resource allocation are promising (e.g., switching from fee-for-service reimbursement to other prospective or retrospective systems like capitation and DRGs; eventual integration of costs of personnel and other inputs into payment mechanism, instead of separate payment of salaries; HSA service provision agreements as mechanism for regionally-based prospective global budgeting). The implementation of the proposed reforms would provide incentives for improving efficiency and productivity in the NHSS, and would facilitate a more equitable resource allocation across HSAs. Critical to the success of these measures will be the development of practical procedures for negotiation and monitoring of global budgets, along with transfer of financial management to give local managers greater financial responsibilities. With respect to the PPP system, it may be useful to examine the experience of the United States with DRGs to identify ways of overcoming pitfalls in implementing this type of system (e.g., the case categories should be well designed to control the incentive to select certain types of patients, but not so detailed so as to make them administratively unworkable; the number of case categories should be manageable; and there should be small variation in resource use for different cases within the same category[9]). The experience of the United Kingdom and the Netherlands with capitated systems may offer valuable lessons for establishing the capitation scheme at the primary health care level,

---

9. Barnum, H., Kutzin, J., and Saxenian, H. 1995. Incentives and Provider Payment Methods. HROWP51. Washington, D. C.: PHN Department, The World Bank.

particularly in relation to alternative capitation models that have been devised to mitigate the problems of adverse selection and windfall profits or losses for insurers (e.g., capitation payments based on, among other, diagnostic information from previous hospitalization).[10]

Concerning the acquisition of sophisticated medical technology, it has been noted in Chapter VIII that a more systematic approach to determining need and evaluating the cost-effectiveness of specific technologies must be developed in Chile. Because of the importance of technology as a source of medical inflation in both the public and private sectors, rational planning of technology procurement should not be limited to the public health system. The approaches used in several OECD countries to assess technology and regulate its incorporation into health care may provide useful models for Chile.

Similarly, because of the rising number of adults and the elderly, who are consumers of high cost pharmaceuticals for the prevention and treatment of many non-communicable illnesses, the Government should examine approaches used in OECD countries to curb pharmaceutical expenditures while assuring availability of efficacious drugs. In the early 1990's the public and private sectors in Chile spent an estimated US$390 million, or US$30 per capita, on pharmaceuticals.[11] This per capita amount is similar to those in other middle-income Latin American countries such as Mexico (US$28), Uruguay (US$29), and Argentina (US$44), despite a lower per capita income in Chile. The challenge for the Government, therefore, is to define and implement policies to improve the selection, acquisition, and use of pharmaceuticals, including promoting the use of generic drugs.

Another issue that merits in-depth assessment in Chile is the skewed health personnel mix. As pointed out in Chapter I, a striking aspect of Chile's physician market is the low number of general practitioners and the growing number of specialists. The three conditions needed to alter this situation are not met in Chile today. These are: (a) emphasis on general practice in the medical curriculum; (b) requirement for post-graduate specialization in general practice (making general practice a "speciality"); and (c) reimbursement schemes which give successful general practitioners a level of remuneration similar to hospital-based specialists. The medical schools at both major universities in Santiago have post-graduate training programs in general practice, but demand for such training will be weak unless such specialist training becomes mandatory for those pursuing a career in general practice. To this end, medical education should be reformed to: (a) rationalize the content and the objectives of the medical curriculum to produce a medical graduate who knows the health problems of the country and the medical professional's role in addressing them; (b) reorient early training toward problem solving at the ambulatory level, with special emphasis on prevention and health education; (c) expand opportunities for specialization to all graduates,

---

10. Van Vliet, R.C.J.A., and Van De Ven, W.P.M.M. 1993. Capitation Payments Based On Prior Hospitalizations. Health Economics 2: 177-188.

11. World Bank. 1993. World Development Report 1993. Investing in Health. New York: Oxford University Press.

including residency training in general medicine for adults and children; (d) increase the number of residency training slots for general medical internists and pediatricians, using secondary level facilities as the principal teaching sites; (e) increase the capability of physicians to deal with complex issues surrounding health care by reinforcing in the medical school curriculum ethical, legal, management, and economic topics, including the application of cost-effectiveness criteria to the selection of diagnostic, treatment, and preventive procedures in clinical practice; and (f) train undergraduates and residents to work effectively in teams with other health personnel.[12] Also, the training of nurses and auxiliary personnel should be supported by strengthening nursing education programs to focus on training new personnel, expanding post-graduate training opportunities for existing nurses, and upgrading the knowledge of auxiliaries to become registered nurses.

A related issue is the geographical maldistribution of physicians and the low number of available nurses vis-a-vis the evolving needs of the primary care system. Again, OECD country experiences might provide relevant lessons for Chile. In these countries, supply side macromanagement strategies have been concerned with "rationing" not only physical but human resources as well, through rational planning and allocation methods that do not necessarily jeopardize equal access to care (i.e., regardless of socioeconomic status and location). The allocation of human resources in Chile should be done in accordance with criteria and norms set from a population perspective (i.e., needs and demands) and not from an institutional one (i.e., number of doctors).

The reorientation of health personnel training and utilization would facilitate the development of a labor market for all specialities in the health sector that results in optimal prices and quantities of each speciality and that favors competition and not the strengthening of existing monopolies. In order for the medical labor market recommendations to achieve their intended results, the physical and technical conditions of primary care facilities must be improved, and the development of a properly equipped secondary care level, accelerated.

As discussed in Chapter I, a number of reforms are under discussion within the Government to address problems and inequities in how the ISAPREs operate, particularly with respect to their coverage and benefits for persons with non-communicable illnesses. It will be important that the **Superintendencia de ISAPRE** follow through on these reforms and consider additional measures such as the elimination of existing public subsidies to the ISAPREs in order to curtail cost-shifting to the public sector. The Government must also ensure that regulatory and financing reforms create clear incentives for cost containment in the private sector, as well as the public sector. Additionally, as done in some OECD countries,[13] a risk structure equalization scheme should be contemplated for the ISAPRE

---

12. Giaconi, J., Valdivieso, V., and Guiraldes, E. 1994. Algunas Ideas Para Contribuir A La Reforma Del Sector Salud En Chile. Rev. Med. Chile 122: 346-350.

13. Henke, K-D., Ade, C., and Murray, M.A. 1994. The German Health Care System: Structure and Changes. J. Clin. Anesth. 6(May/June):252-262.

system as a whole (e.g., ISAPREs with low-risk/high-income memberships would subsidize those with high-risk/low-income profiles) to remove the economic incentive to discriminate among potential affiliates, and to control costs due to external factors, such as the risk structure of individual ISAPREs' memberships.

Additionally, the Government will need to redouble its efforts to develop and implement strategies for primary prevention of risk factors. As shown in Chapter VI, substantial health benefits could be derived from these efforts. Chile can learn from the experience of many OECD countries which have achieved success with mass information campaigns and other interventions to change lifestyles. The successful experience with maternal and child care programs, and more recently with the population-wide education campaign launched to control the spread of cholera, indicate that the Chilean population responds well to health promotion initiatives. The Government must also ensure that the new payment system provides appropriate incentives to both consumers and providers for cost-effective preventive care. Legal and fiscal measures must also be considered for confronting both individual (e.g., restrictions on smoking in public places, higher taxes for cigarettes) and community-wide (e.g., enforcement of safety guidelines in the work place, anti-pollution traffic restrictions) health risk factors.

Reforms in health care financing that are now being promulgated by the Government should take into account the future demand for long-term care (e.g., nursing home care, catastrophic care) and advanced home health care (e.g., post-operative care, intravenous infusion therapy, home dialysis) by the chronically ill, the elderly, and the disabled and how such services will be financed. For example, in most countries of the European Union, nursing home care and homes for the aged are financed by a separate budget of local government or social security or are largely left to the private sector (e.g., in the Netherlands, nursing home care is financed under a national insurance scheme, and in Germany a new tax-based system of social insurance is being phased in to replace financing of long-term care from welfare funds).[14][15] The eligibility and benefits of public long-term care insurance, however, vary greatly among major industrialized countries.[16] In countries such as Belgium, France, and the United States, eligibility depends on a means test (i.e., after beneficiaries have "spent down" their income and assets to levels where they become eligible for a means-tested program), while in others such as Canada, Japan, and the United Kingdom, cost sharing is required, usually in a progressive way. In most of these countries,

---

14. Abel-Smith, B. and Mossialos, E. 1994. Cost Containment and Health Care Reform. A Study of the European Union. The European Institute. London School of Economics Occasional Paper in Health Policy No. 2. London: LSE.

15. United States General Accounting Office. 1994. Long-Term Care. Other Countries Tighten Budgets While Seeking Better Access. Washington, D.C.: GAO/HEHS-94-154.

16. Norton, E.C. and Newhouse, J.P. 1994. Policy Options for Public Long-term Care Insurance. JAMA 271(19):1520-1524.

housing and medical benefits are provided jointly, except in Belgium and France, where the residents are responsible for housing costs and the government for medical costs.

While long-term care and advanced home health care have not been a major concern heretofore in Chile, the growing aged population, the increasing life expectancy, and the projected increases in non-communicable illnesses all signal the likelihood of rapid increases in the demand for such services. As discussed in Chapter VI, the future costs of health care are somewhat ominous. The demographic and epidemiological trends analyzed in this study are likely in the future to raise financing problems for both public and private health programs in Chile since they have traditionally been financed on a "pay-as-you-go" basis in which current contributions are used to meet current expenditures. Early planning efforts would offer the opportunity to prefund, on an individual or social basis, higher consumption of services which otherwise would be financially burdensome if the entire cost had to be paid upon their delivery. For public sector beneficiaries (i.e., FONASA's affiliates), this would mean beginning to set aside now a portion of the payroll deduction earmarked for health, in order to cover anticipated future long-term care costs. As a result, a policy issue facing FONASA is whether the current level of 7 percent payroll deduction is adequate to finance long-term care benefits along with acute health care benefits. To this end, a careful assessment is needed to determine whether fluctuations in consumption may be compensated for over time by an internal reallocation of funds and thus covered by the 7 percent payroll deduction, or whether the global cost of the system, given the new epidemiological profile, require an increase above the current 7 percent payroll level. In order to determine whether adequate financing is available in light of the epidemiological transition further simulation work should be conducted to examine likely future revenues and expenditures in the NHSS.

In the private sector, advanced "savings" approaches similar to Individual Retirement Accounts (IRAs) or other capitalization schemes, whereby an individual pays contributions which accumulate in a technical reserve and are paid out after a number of years, together with a guaranteed interest rate, should be considered, particularly for providing and financing nursing home and advanced home health care, which remain a gap in the Chilean health system. In some countries, since approximately 70 percent of an average person's health expenses occur in the later years of his life, private health insurance companies have adopted capitalization schemes to provide long-term benefits. For example, private health insurance companies in Germany have built up technical reserves charging actuarial premiums that are higher than the age-related costs for younger people and lower than the age-related costs for the elderly.[17]

The urgency of developing alternative financing schemes for long-term care needs will increase in direct relation to the aging of the Chilean population. Given the public/private interactions in the financing and delivery of health care services in Chile, there is substantial

---

17. Normand, C. and Weber, A. 1994. Social Health Insurance. World Health Organization/International Labour Office.

potential for growth of private sector financing mechanisms for long-term care. However, as shown by the United States' experience,[18] these approaches may be unaffordable for a large segment of the elderly for financing a significant share of total nursing home and home health care expenditures. Other considerations discussed in Box IX-3 also indicate that the issue of how to finance long-term care should be of utmost importance to both FONASA and the ISAPREs. The Government's role in the financing of long-term care and advanced home health care should be guided by equity and efficiency considerations, i.e., subsidizing low income groups. In addition, as has been proposed in developed countries,[19][20] the Government should assume leadership in bringing these issues to the fore in a public policy debate, including public information campaigns. Overall, as argued for alternative financing and managerial arrangements for old age security,[21] the establishment of financing schemes for long-term care would help the Chilean elderly mainly by: (a) shifting some of their income from their active working years to old age; and (b) providing insurance against the many health risks to which they are especially vulnerable.

Finally, the organizational and management capacity of the NHSS should be strengthened, since it is indispensable for the development and implementation of public policies. The effectiveness of many cost containment measures will depend upon the capability of the MOH to monitor both costs and the relationships between inputs, outputs, and outcomes of care (e.g., service quality and efficacy) to ensure that goals of equity and efficiency are being met. Since information systems are not well developed in the Chilean public health sector, a central ingredient of the reform effort would have to be the modernization of medical records and cost accounting systems at the different levels of care. The training of human resources to carry out management functions should be of high priority to substitute more professional management and technical skills for the traditional medical administration that characterizes the present system. This approach would follow worldwide trends to apply business techniques to medical care financing and administration. To achieve results from such training, there would need to be an effort to ensure that individuals who receive specialized training are put in positions of status and authority. The present situation, in which HSA or hospital directors have responsibility for major institutional decision-making without necessarily possessing the requisite management skills, needs to be replaced with a system of professional specialists (e.g., management specialists, statisticians, financial officers). This does not mean that physicians cannot continue in their present roles if they have appropriate skills, but rather that efforts are needed to significantly upgrade and professionalize the management of health services in Chile.

---

18. Rivlin, A.M. and Wiener, J.M., with Hanley, R. J., and Spece, D.A. 1988. Who Should Pay for Long-Term Care for the Elderly? The Brookings Review Summer 1988:3-9.

19. Burke, T.R. 1988. Long-term care: The public role and private initiatives. Health Care Financing Review Annual Supplement: 1-5.

20. De Lissovoy, G. and Feustle, J. A. 1991. Advanced home health care. Health Policy 17: 227-242.

21. The World Bank. 1994. Averting The Old Age Crisis: Policies to Protect the Old and Promote Growth. New York: Oxford University Press for the World Bank.

**Box IX-3**

## SOME ISSUES IN THE FINANCING OF LONG-TERM CARE IN CHILE

One of the challenges facing the ISAPRE system is how it will cover the health expenses of younger beneficiaries once they age. If in the future the cost of health plan premiums absorbs a large share of retirement pensions, many ISAPRE beneficiaries will be forced to drop their ISAPRE coverage and seek care in the public sector.

As the elderly ISAPRE beneficiaries begin to return to the public sector two problems may arise. The first is that these beneficiaries may become dissatisfied with public sector service after being accustomed to the amenities of the ISAPREs, such as shorter waiting times and more elegant facilities. Second, this will put a strain on the public sector which will be forced to provide care for beneficiaries who contributed their 7 percent health care payroll tax solely to the ISAPREs when they were younger and needed less medical care, but, who no longer contribute much to their care through the payroll tax.

In order to circumvent these problems the Superintendency of ISAPREs proposed in 1991 that 0.9 percent of the 7 percent health care payroll tax be set aside in a special individual account to cover the cost of health care during old age. These funds, which would accumulate in each individual's name, could be used to pay a higher ISAPRE premium or to purchase additional health coverage. If the beneficiary left the ISAPRE system and returned to the public sector the savings would be available to the health sector.

Before this type of plan can be implemented, several issues which gave rise to a great deal of controversy in Chile need to be resolved. One of the most serious concerns is that by diverting 0.9 percent of the payroll tax for future health expenses beneficiaries will be contributing less money (6.1 percent of the health care payroll tax) to their present health care and as a result may have to pay greater out of pocket expenses or accept a cheaper policy with less service coverage. Other potential problems include: the possibility that this savings will not cover the increased health care expenses of the elderly; and the impact this plan could have on the ISAPREs if a large number of their beneficiaries decided to return to the public sector as opposed to paying more for their coverage once their payroll tax contribution is reduced.

Nevertheless, given the potential cost of long-term care and advanced home health care, and the difficulty of every society to ration or mandate limits on health care, new means must be explored to begin to pre-fund these future obligations, on an individual or social basis. It is worth noting that firms in the United States are now being forced by the Financial Accounting Standards Board (Reg. 106) to acknowledge and fund the future liabilities of their retirees and the World Bank has recently set aside US$630 million to pre-fund its future liabilities for its 10,000 current and retired employees. In the private sector, individuals may consider this future liability and evaluate capitalization schemes to pre-finance future obligations.

Source: Sánchez, H. 1991. Proceso de Privatización en el Sector Salud de Chile. Report prepared for PAHO; and Musgrove, P. 1991. Financial Balance in Chile: The ISAPREs (Instituciones de Salud Previsional) Health Care System and the Public Sector. A View from LATHR No. 4. Human Resources Division, Technical Department, Latin American and Caribbean Region, The World Bank.

## CHAPTER X

## *SUMMARY OF POLICY ISSUES AND RECOMMENDATIONS*

On the basis of the analysis of the likely implications of Chile's changing demographic and epidemiologic profile, recommendations are presented in five major areas of concern to policymakers: the consolidation of current reforms in the delivery of health care services; strengthening health promotion, disease prevention, and health protection programs and interventions; the efficient use of critical health care inputs; containing health care costs; and regulation of health care.

### Consolidation of Current Reforms for Reorganizing, Improving, and Managing the Delivery of Health Care Services

The deteriorated condition of much of the country's public hospital infrastructure and equipment compromises the public sector's ability to meet the clinical needs of those persons already suffering from non-communicable illnesses and injuries, and without significant improvement now, the country will be ill-equipped to meet the needs of the increasing numbers of persons with these conditions that were projected by the forecast model.

It is recommended that:

- The public hospital infrastructure be revamped and the quality of public hospital services upgraded. The MOH's TAHRP and HSRP Projects, as well as those financed by other multilateral and bilateral agencies provide a mechanism for advancing this agenda.

- The planned reform of the health care delivery model being supported under the MOH's HSRP Project to create ambulatory Referral and Diagnostic and Treatment Centers be implemented to make specialized services more widely available and reduce the use of higher cost hospital-based services, thus, significantly increasing the efficacy of the health delivery system.

- Procurement of technologies and equipment as well as physical plant rehabilitation place emphasis on ensuring the availability of cost-effective equipment and technologies to support timely diagnosis and treatment of non-communicable illnesses and injuries.

A key aspect of the ongoing health sector reforms in Chile is a redefinition of the role of the MOH and the concomitant decentralization of the management of health services delivery to the HSAs.

It is recommended that:

- The management information and epidemiological monitoring systems of the MOH be strengthened to enable the MOH to guide efforts to improve health services efficiency and efficacy and resource allocation decisions.

- Appropriate information systems be developed to facilitate implementation of the proposed new resource transfer mechanisms for primary care facilities at the municipal level and hospitals in the HSAs.

- The proposed annual service provision agreements between the HSAs and the MOH be structured so as to provide a mechanism for periodic, systematic review of the quality, effectiveness and efficiency of services to monitor the relationships between resources used and services produced, and between services and outcomes to ensure that goals of equity and efficiency are being achieved.

- Training and technical assistance be provided to MOH staff to develop the capacity to undertake cost-effectiveness analysis in order to increase the efficiency in the resource allocation process, as well as to the HSAs to develop their own internal capacity to prepare program budgets, monitor expenditures, and assess productivity and quality.

### Strengthening Health Promotion, Disease Prevention and Health Protection Programs and Interventions

It is recommended that the Chilean Government adopt an aggressive, multisectoral approach to reducing common risk factors throughout the population, focussing on smoking, dietary and nutritional habits, sedentarism, alcohol and drug use, and mental health. In view of Chile's epidemiological profile and the potential impact of available treatments, the priority areas for early secondary prevention and diagnosis should be cardiovascular diseases, cancer and diabetes, to prevent or slow the progression of disabling complications and death.

Specifically, it is recommended that:

- Prevention strategies address the control of multiple risk factors and target the social environment to facilitate and create greater support for individual decisions to make healthy lifestyle choices.

- Strategies be targeted to specific population groups on whom they can have the greatest impact. For many risk factors that are difficult to modify once they are firmly established, this means channeling resources toward primary prevention activities among school-age children and adolescents.

- More comprehensive data be gathered on the prevalence of risk factors and non-communicable illnesses and on the characteristics of groups at highest risk to facilitate targeting.

- Specific measures which appear promising for Chile include increasing the early detection of hypertension and diabetes and testing of alternative strategies to increase compliance with treatment regimens; expanding coverage of cervical cancer screening and continuing to upgrade capabilities for cytological diagnosis as proposed in the MOH's HSRP Project; increasing education on breast cancer self-diagnosis; and educating patients on the benefits of risk factor modification.

Currently, activities to combat non-communicable illnesses and their risk factors are fragmented among different MOH programs which do not control the resources needed to implement the programs they plan. This situation has resulted in important gaps in adult health program priorities and impeded the dissemination of standards and guidelines and the organization of integrated control efforts.

It is recommended that:

- The MOH strengthen its approach to the management of non-communicable illnesses and injuries so as to facilitate greater integration of prevention strategies and coordination of resources to address multiple risk factors.

- The development of program priorities and intervention strategies be based on consideration of the magnitude of the problem (both prevalence and severity), susceptibility to modification, and the technical and financial feasibility of the interventions proposed.

Health protection activities related to occupational health, injuries, and environmental contamination are diffused among various government agencies and have been constrained by lack of coordination and data for decision-making.

It is recommended that:

- The MOH strengthen its capabilities to collect and monitor data on occupational and environmental risks to guide planning and priority-setting.

- The pilot program to carry out, at the HSA level, targeted occupational health actions in high-risk industries be extended throughout the country, and the necessary training provided to HSA personnel to implement monitoring and health education activities.

- With respect to non-occupational injuries, the MOH play a leadership role in injury prevention initiatives and ensure coordination with police and judicial agencies as well as with its own alcohol and drug programs.

- Systems be established to track and evaluate the linkages between environmental exposures and diseases. To this end, health workers should be encouraged to work closely with the agencies involved in pollution control.

- The model of successful inter-agency coordination that has been developed to fight pollution in the Santiago Metropolitan Area be replicated in MOH-led efforts to address other health protection priorities.

The MOH will need to continue to exercise a leadership role while finding ways to strengthen coordination with other ministries and government institutions. By the same measure, the MOH must find ways to enlist greater cooperation and participation of the private sector (i.e., ISAPREs, NGOs, private practitioners) in health education concerning non-communicable disease risk factors. Given the decentralized nature of the Chilean health system, the role of the MOH should be to foster the development and implementation of appropriate and timely disease prevention efforts by local governments, HSAs, municipal health authorities, NGOs, and practitioners.

To this end, it is recommended that:

- A national constituency-building initiative on health prevention and promotion priorities be launched to raise public awareness of individual, community, and societal responsibilities in health. To this end, the following steps should be considered: (a) the development of national health goals, including specific targets for selected preventable conditions and their risk factors; (b) the creation of popular and political consensus on these goals; and (c) the development of a plan to achieve these goals, incorporating regulation, public education, and appropriate incentives to individuals, businesses, and providers.

- The Government, with private sector support, establish a demand-driven funding mechanism to channel resources to implement cost-effective interventions and facilitate funding of intersectoral activities. The fund should be managed by an intersectoral group headed by the MOH and should allocate resources to NHSS and other public agencies, NGOs, private providers and community groups. Activities that could be financed by such a fund include pilot interventions or their replication at the community level, media campaigns, and applied research on risk factor prevalence and effectiveness of interventions.

## Increasing the Efficient Use of Medical Inputs: Technology, Drugs and Personnel

The treatment of non-communicable illnesses is characterized by the intensive use of technological inputs, including drugs, sophisticated equipment and specialized personnel. Experience in Chile and OECD countries has shown that these inputs are a major source of cost escalation for health care. In view of the projected rapid growth in the demand for adult health services, limits on health care resources will place increasing pressure to enhance efficiency in the use of these inputs.

It is recommended that:

- The methodology used by the Government to guide the acquisition of sophisticated medical technology be redesigned to address efficiency, equity and cost control concerns. The large amount of procurement of medical equipment contemplated under ongoing investment projects lends urgency to this need.

- Institutional responsibilities for medical technology assessments be reassessed (i.e., whether the MOH, MIDEPLAN and the Ministry of Finance along with private sector agencies together be responsible for conducting technology assessments), as well as the adequacy of resources currently available to carry them out.

- Mechanisms be developed for the participation of the HSAs and of practitioners in the process of identifying technology needs and priorities and in assessing effectiveness of practices and technologies. To this end, the medical technology inventory conducted in 3 HSAs should be extended to the entire country, to serve as the baseline for future procurement decisions.

In view of rising drug costs and the predominance of pharmaceutical therapies in the management of many non-communicable conditions affecting adults, it is recommended that the MOH identify ways of controlling drug expenditures while at the same time improving the availability of efficacious drugs for early treatment and management.

Specifically, it is recommended that:

- The MOH focus attention on the design and implementation of policies and strategies to improve the selection, procurement and use of pharmaceuticals. Emphasis should be given to promoting the use of generic equivalents.

- A public information campaign be developed to educate providers and consumers about the efficacy of generic drugs.

Given the sizeable share of public health resources that are channeled to private providers, a larger issue for the Government is how to manage competition and/or coordination with the private sector with respect to the acquisition of sophisticated medical equipment in order to avoid duplication and to contain the escalation of health care costs resulting from the increasingly intensive use of technological inputs.

It is recommended that:

- The MOH develop approaches to leverage government investment in medical technology to generate additional revenues through the sale of diagnostic and therapeutic services in public facilities to private providers.

- In those areas where private institutions already possess sophisticated medical technology unavailable in public facilities, public providers should be encouraged to purchase services from private providers to avoid duplication of investment.

- Given the well developed public/private mix in Chile for the financing and delivery of health services, it should be explored in the future mechanisms for establishing integrated high technology reference centers for certain specialized procedures.

Another issue with profound financial implications that merits in-depth assessment is the current skewed health personnel mix. A striking aspect of Chile's physician market is the low number of general practitioners and the growing supply of specialists. A related issue is the geographical maldistribution of physicians and the low number of available nurses vis-a-vis the evolving needs of the primary care system.

It is recommended that:

- The MOH-administered scholarship programs for young physicians who have served in rural areas should be continued, to provide incentives for recent medical graduates to locate in underserved areas.

- Medical schools give greater importance to the training of general practitioners that can better respond to the country's health care needs and demands.

- Health promotion and disease prevention strategies give explicit consideration to the use of nursing personnel in providing care related to non-communicable adult illnesses. The MOH should develop incentives to encourage the training and employment of nurses and auxiliary personnel to fulfill these roles.

## Containing Health Care Costs

The increasing demand for medical care engendered by the projected relative increases in persons suffering from non-communicable illnesses will further strain public sector health resources and create resource allocation tensions between health promotion and protection efforts on one hand, and treatment and rehabilitation services on the other. It is imperative that Chile begin implementing strategies now that will contain the escalation of health care costs and mitigate the financial burden of the increased demand for health services.

It is recommended that:

- The Government implement the proposed health financing reforms mechanisms to use a prospective payment based on overall treatment of a diagnosis at the hospital level and capitated payments for primary health care services. These reforms would help link the planning process to resource allocation in the production and delivery of health services. Also, they would positively affect the country's ability to use health resources more efficiently.

- The revised reimbursement mechanisms should provide appropriate incentives to both providers and consumers for cost-effective preventive care, especially at the primary level.

- Disease prevention and management strategies must direct resources to those interventions proven to be cost-effective. Efficiency criteria should receive greater explicit treatment in decision-making about resource allocation and technology acquisition.

- Since standardized cost-effectiveness data for most health interventions are lacking in Chile, a pending activity is the gathering of appropriate and reliable local data to adequately carry out a comparative assessment of the cost-effectiveness of health interventions under the NHSS to rationalize the allocation of public health resources.

- Chilean policymakers should examine in more depth the experience of OECD countries with diagnostic-related groups (DRGs) and global budget instruments to identify ways of overcoming pitfalls in implementing these types of reimbursement systems.

- The ISAPRE system should assess the underlying factors of cost escalation and devise strategies to control them in the medium and long term.

Wider cost recovery in public sector facilities is needed to mobilize additional resources to complement budgetary allocations.

It is recommended that:

- Existing fee schedules for services must be revised to reflect actual production costs. The NHSS should establish a mechanism for periodic updating of price lists to take into account inflation and changes in production costs, and strengthen cost recovery for services rendered to ISAPRE patients.

- The boundaries of the four income categories used to classify FONASA beneficiaries should be redefined so that those who cannot afford copayments effectively do not pay them and those who can afford them do. Given the current low level of cost recovery, the overall effect would be to increase financing through copayments but drawing from a wider, more equitable base.

- Rules governing cost recovery at the individual hospital level should be reviewed to ensure that undue restrictions and disincentives are removed. However, because of differences among public hospitals in their opportunities to capture fee-paying clients, a mechanism should be introduced for redistributing some portion of revenues from "high profit" hospitals to those serving primarily low-income populations where cost recovery potential is not as great.

While long-term care and advanced home health care have not been a major concern heretofore in Chile, the growing aged population and the increasing life expectancy, as well as the projected increases in non-communicable conditions, all signal the likelihood of rapid increases in the demand for such services.

It is recommended that:

- Reforms in health care financing take into account the future demand for long-term care and advanced home health care and how such services will be financed both in the public and private systems. Early planning efforts would offer the opportunity for prefunding, on an individual or social basis, higher consumption of services than would be difficult to afford if the entire cost had to be paid upon their delivery.

- Ways be explored to begin to develop the financing needed to cover future health care costs, perhaps considering new schemes based on a prefunded system in the public sector or advanced "savings" approaches in the private sector, particularly for providing and financing long-term care and advanced home health care, which are still a gap in the Chilean health system.

## Enhancing the Regulation of Health Care

For many of the adult health problems discussed in this report, the intervention strategies used by the MOH have not fully utilized the range of mechanisms available to promote and protect health and prevent non-communicable disease, particularly those regulatory measures which extend beyond the traditional boundaries of the health sector. In areas such as occupational health and safety where adequate legislation already exists, the MOH's efforts at enforcement of laws have often been lax and lacked the necessary resources.

It is recommended that:

- The Government make greater use of fiscal and regulatory tools to control tobacco and alcohol use, including taxes on cigarettes and greater restrictions on cigarette and alcohol advertising.

- Laws be extended and strictly enforced for the widespread use of seat belts in cars and helmets when driving motorcycles, as well as to deter driving while under the influence of alcohol and drugs.

- The Government actively enforce compliance with existing occupational safety legislation and increase its efforts, in cooperation with the HSAs, to educate and inform managers and workers about occupational health risks and protective measures, as well as to assist small firms to set up occupational health and injury prevention programs.

- Revisions be made in the primary law covering Occupational Health (Law No. 16.744) to extend its coverage to workers currently not protected.

The trend toward rapid growth in number of beneficiaries and total expenditures of the ISAPREs underscore the increasingly predominant role that the private health insurance plans will have in responding to Chile's emerging epidemiological profile. Competition for new patients will increasingly lead to cost escalation in the private sector as ISAPREs try to maintain their edge by offering state-of-the art medical equipment. The Government's interest in controlling the growth of health care spending must necessarily address spending in the private sector.

It is recommended that:

- Cost-shifting to the public sector, such as from denial of coverage or benefits to persons with pre-existing conditions, be discouraged through enactment of proposed reforms of the ISAPRE Law and the elimination of existing public subsidies to the ISAPREs. Also, a risk structure equalization scheme should be contemplated for the ISAPRE system as a whole (e.g., ISAPREs with low-risk/high-income memberships would subsidize those with high-risk/low-income profiles) to remove the economic incentive to discriminate among potential affiliates, and to control costs due to external factors, such as the risk structure of individual ISAPREs' memberships.

- The Government create appropriate incentives for the private sector to adopt medical technologies of proven cost-effectiveness.

# *ANNEXES*

# ANNEX A

## SPECIFIC TRENDS IN MORTALITY AND SERVICE UTILIZATION FOR EACH MAJOR ILLNESS GROUP

### Cardiovascular disease (CVD)

CVD involves a group of infectious and degenerative diseases that affect the heart, brain, and the circulatory system.[1] The most important modifiable risk factors, termed primary risk factors, that can independently produce clinical complications due to cardiovascular arteriosclerotic disease are: hypertension, high cholesterol levels, and smoking. Other risk factors like obesity, diabetes, and sedentary life contribute to cardiovascular morbidity and mortality in conjunction with primary risk factors.

According to data from the Pan American Health Organization (PAHO/WHO),[2] CVD is the principal cause of death in 26 of 36 countries in the Americas, including Chile. In Chile of the 78,443 total deaths in 1990, 21,568 or about 27 percent were due to CVD. This figure is higher than the average for developing countries where CVD accounts for approximately 16 percent of all deaths, but is lower than in North America and Europe where it accounts for almost 50 percent of all mortality.[3] The age-adjusted death rate from CVD in 1990 was 155.8/100,000. Of the various types of CVD, coronary heart disease and cerebrovascular are the main killers in Chile, accounting for approximately 36 percent and 32 percent of all CVD deaths respectively. In comparison with other countries in the Americas, Chile shows an intermediate risk. The age-adjusted death rate in Chile from coronary heart disease (59.1/100,000) is much lower than the rates in Argentina (120.6/100,000) and the United States (102.9/1000), yet is higher than rates in Peru (36.6/100,000) and El Salvador (44.3/100,00). Similar trends are seen for cerebrovascular disease where the age-adjusted death rate in Chile is 34.3/100,000 compared to Brazil (46.5/100,000), Paraguay (60.6/100,000), the United States (18.7/100,000) and Canada (13.0/100,000).

As shown in Figure A-1, the importance of death from CVD increases with age. In the adult population, mortality from ischemic heart disease occurs predominately among older men. In contrast, women have higher mortality rates from cerebrovascular disease than men because of their longer life span (deaths caused by stroke tend to be more frequent among persons aged 75 years and older). The mortality rate for ischemic heart disease and cerebrovascular disease is three times higher among persons aged 15 and older with no

---

1. The codes for CVD under the Ninth Revision of the International Classification of Diseases (ICD9) are in Chapter VII.

2. Pan American Health Organization. 1990. Health Conditions in the Americas. Washington D.C.: Pan American Health Organization.

3. Pearson T.A, D.T Jamison, and J. Trejo-Gutierrez. "Cardiovascular Disease." In Dean T. Jamison, W. Henry Mosley, Anthony R. Measham, and José-Luis Bobadilla, eds. 1993. Disease Control Priorities in Developing Countries. New York: Oxford University Press.

formal education or only primary education than those with secondary or university education. In Chile, as elsewhere, educational levels are correlated with socioeconomic and heath status.

## Figure A-1

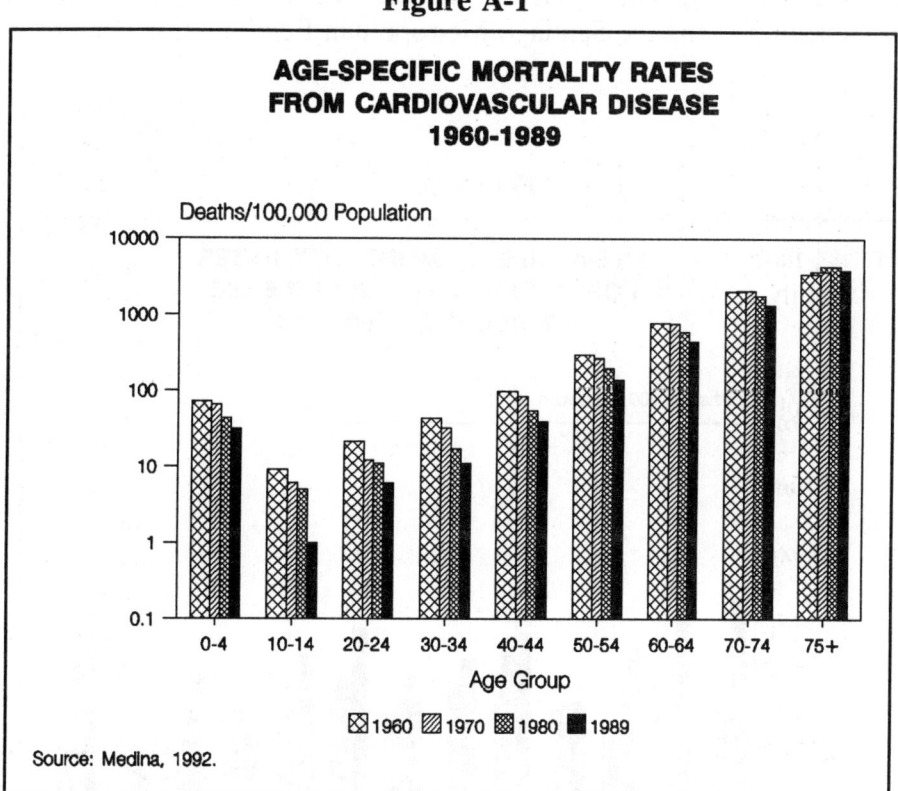

Surveys performed in Santiago and other Chilean cities indicate that slightly more than 3 percent of the population suffers from some cardiopathy or hypertension.[4][5] This figure is equivalent to about 400,000 persons and only includes diagnosed patients. In 1989, there were 65,593 hospitalizations due to CVD, equivalent to about 5 percent of the total hospital discharges that year, representing a hospitalization rate of 5/1,000. In adults 15 to 44 years old CVD is the eleventh cause of hospitalization; it is the second in the 45-64 age group; and is the first in people over 65 years. The average length of hospital stay for cardiovascular disease is about 10 days, above the national average for all causes of 6 days. CVD accounts for about 2.5 million or 6 percent of all consultations in the public health system.

4.  Medina, E. and Kaempffer, A.M. 1979. Morbilidad y atención médica en el Gran Santiago. Rev. Méd. Chile 107:155-164.

5.  Medina, E., Kaempffer, A. M., Martínez, L., et al. 1988. Estudio de morbilidad en la población de 12 ciudades chilenas. Rev. Méd. Chile 116:476-483.

While the relative importance of CVD as the leading cause of death increased in the last 20 years, there was a 30 percent decrease in the age-adjusted death rate for CVD, from 221.5/100,000 in 1968 to 155.8/100,000 in 1990. This decrease reflects the high drop in death rates between the ages of 15 and 64 years, and it has been more pronounced in those regions with a large urban population, such as in Tarapaca (Region I), Antofagasta (Region II), Valparaiso (Region V), and the Santiago Metropolitan Region (RM) (Figure A-2).

### Figure A-2

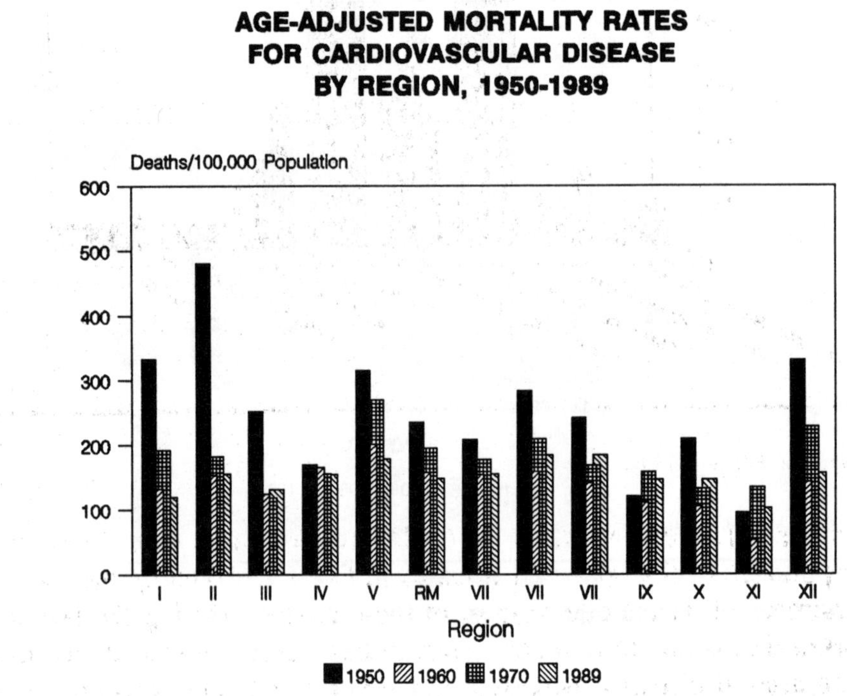

AGE-ADJUSTED MORTALITY RATES
FOR CARDIOVASCULAR DISEASE
BY REGION, 1950-1989

Source: Medina, 1992.

As shown in Figure A-3, when mortality for CVD is disaggregated by type, a declining trend is consistently seen only in rheumatic cardiopathy, due to reduction in morbidity. The variation in other causes makes it difficult to establish a trend. A slight increase is observed in the last 10 years in mortality due to hypertensive disease. The decline in arterial disease may be due to a more specialized diagnosis in recent years. The virtual stability of mortality rates for coronary heart and cerebrovascular diseases and for congenital cardiopathies are probably real, particularly in the case of the former diseases, given the high prevalence of hypertension in the country.

**Figure A-3**

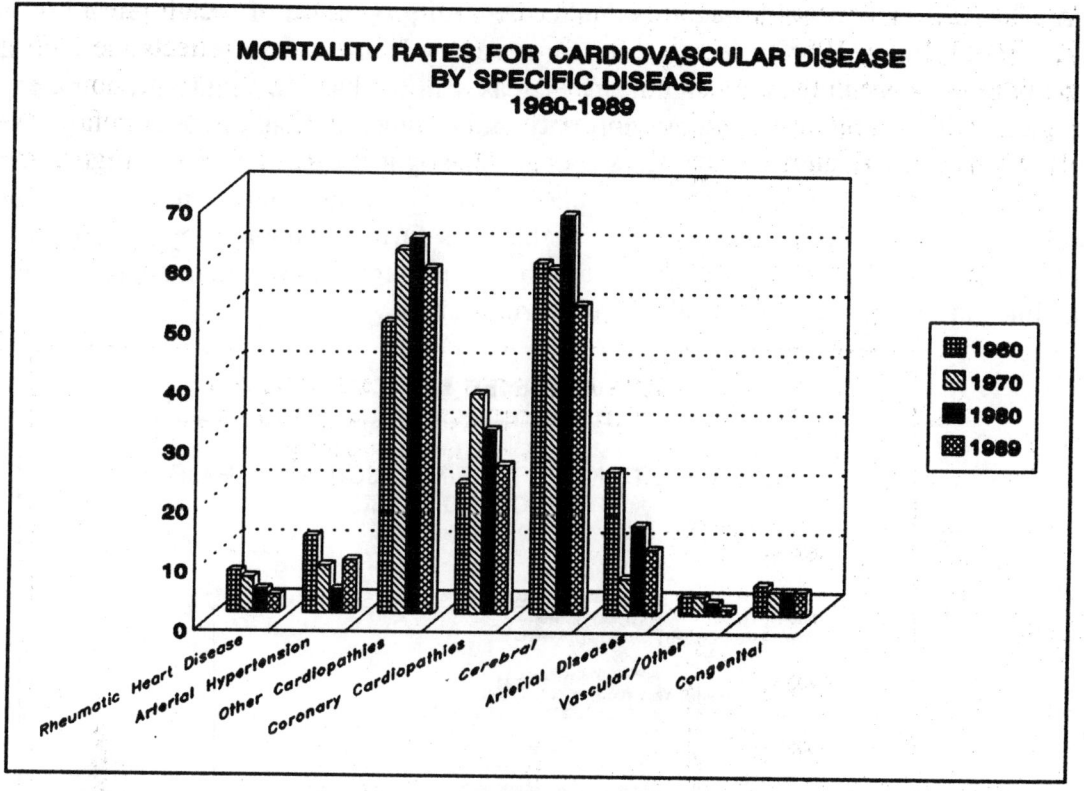

Source: Medina, 1992.

Although age-adjusted death rates for CVD have decreased over time, the continued public health importance of this group of diseases in Chile is shown by the increasing trend in the absolute number of deaths due to most of these causes. During the last 40 years, the number of reported deaths due to coronary heart disease, cerebrovascular disease, arterial hypertension, and arterial diseases increased by 1,400 percent, 117 percent, 10 percent, and 9.8 percent, respectively.

There are no data in Chile to assess trends in ambulatory visits for CVD in the last 30 years. Nevertheless, hospitalization data for cardiovascular illnesses provide information about the prevalence of this disease over time. Between 1950 and 1989, hospitalization rates for CVD increased from 243 to 501/100,000 inhabitants, a 106 percent global and a 2.1 percent annual increase. Also, throughout this period, hospitalization rates for CVD increased for most age groups, and they increased with age.

The historical evolution of hospitalizations by type of CVD is shown in Figure A-4. The decreasing trend observed for rheumatic cardiopathy is related to improved access to primary care services which has permitted the identification and treatment of infections associated with the onset of this condition. The decrease for arterial hypertension in the 1980's could be the result of the use of new antihypertensive drugs on an outpatient basis, which reduces the need for hospitalization. The increase in congenital cardiopathies is probably due to improved diagnosis due to the high proportion of deliveries in hospitals (99 percent in 1990). Hospitalization rates for coronary heart disease, cerebrovascular disease, and other cardiopathies show significant increases in the past 40 years. An apparent paradox is observed in Chile as increasing morbidity rates from CVD -as gauged from trends in hospitalizations- are contrasted with stationary or slight increases in CVD mortality rates. This disparity might be in large part explained by significant improvements in the medical care of many types of CVD. This interpretation is further supported by the observation that the sharpest decline in CVD mortality took place in large cities, where sophisticated medical facilities are more readily available than in rural areas.

**Figure A-4**

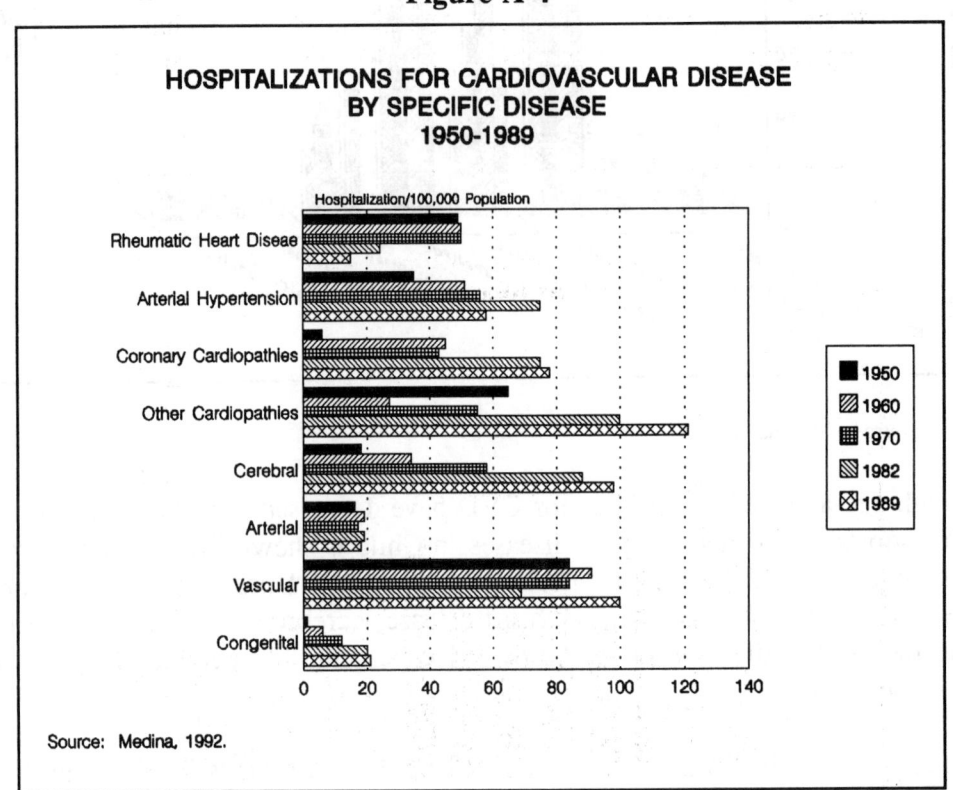

**Cancer**

Cancer is a group of diseases characterized by the uncontrolled growth and spread of abnormal cells.[6] Based on the most recently available information, PAHO estimates that cancers accounted for 16.4 percent of all deaths in the Americas and are the second leading cause of death in the majority of these countries, including Chile. Of a total of 78,434 deaths in Chile in 1990, 14,163 were due to cancer, up from 9,515 in 1968. The relative

---

6. The codes for cancer under the ICD9 are in Chapter II.

contribution of cancer as a cause of death has increased from 15 percent in 1960 to 18 percent in 1990. The age-adjusted mortality rate from cancer reached 102.6/100,000 in 1990. This is higher than the age-adjusted rates in Uruguay (92.0/100,000), Canada (82.2/100,000) and the United States (77.1/100,000).

As shown in Figure A-5, regional cancer mortality rates above the national average of 149.9/100,000 are found in Antofagasta (Region II, 195.4/100,000), Tarapaca (Region I, 158.5/100,000), Magallanes (Region XII, 157.9/100,000), Maule (Region VII, 157.6/100,000), and Atacama (Region III, 156.2/100,000). Information is limited on the prevalence of risk factors in these regions that may help to explain the above mortality rates. The high mortality rates in the norther regions of the country such as in Atacama and Antofagasta, may be associated with smoking as well as exposure to environmental and occupational hazards such as mining. In Santiago, the pollution, which has a weak but significant relationship to lung cancer, may impact upon the prevalence of cancer.

**Figure A-5**

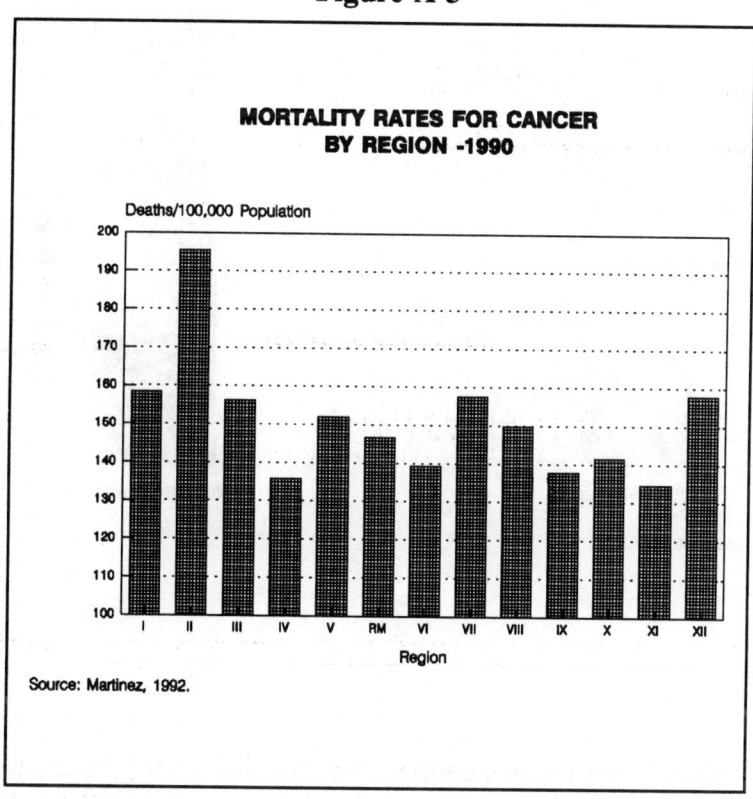

Source: Martinez, 1992.

Approximately one-quarter of all the cancer deaths in Chile are preventable, either corresponding to tumors susceptible to primary prevention (such as those associated with smoking), or those susceptible to screening and early treatment (like cervical and breast cancer). Another group of tumors has good chances for treatment with a high rate of survival (e.g., skin cancer, which is associated with exposure to sunlight). Health care activities related to cancer in Chile are predominantly those of diagnosis and treatment performed at the secondary or tertiary level. Rehabilitation of patients after surgery or other treatment activities and management of terminal ill-patients are performed to a lesser extent. Primary prevention is incipient and occurs only for some types of cancer.

Chile does not have a cancer registry but information is available from cancer notifications by the HSAs throughout the country, though these are assumed to be subject to underreporting. Figure A-6 presents the number of reported cancer cases by site in men and women in 1990. For the population as a whole, the five most frequently diagnosed cancers in 1990, accounting for approximately 60 percent of all cases, were those of the cervix (15 percent); stomach (13 percent); breast (10 percent); skin (6.4 percent); gallbladder (6.1 percent); prostate (5 percent); and lung (4.7 percent).

**Figure A-6**

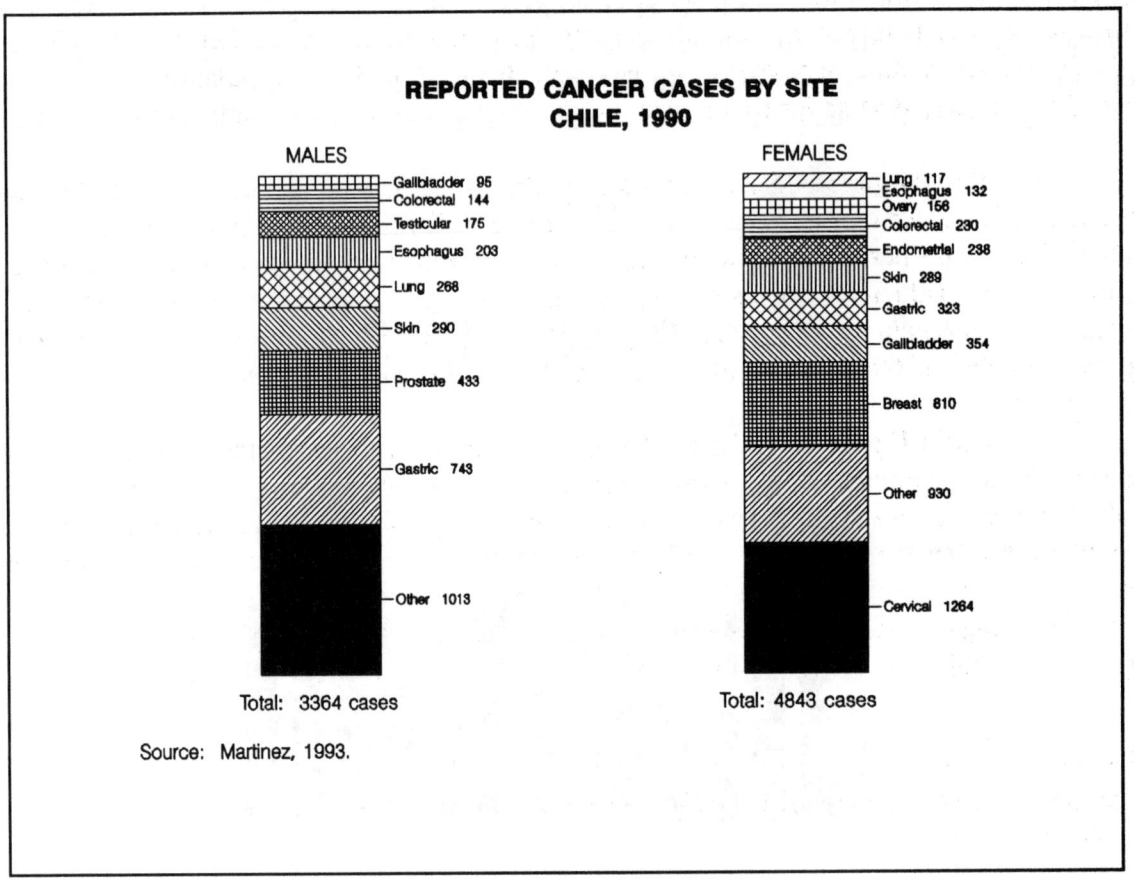

The high prevalence of cervical and breast cancer, which together represented more than one-fourth of all cancer cases reported in the country in 1990, reflects the heavy burden imposed by cancer on women's health. The prevalence of cervical cancer, which has an incubation period that varies between 10 to 20 years before it reaches an invasive stage, is highest in females between the ages of 30 and 44. The high incidence of cervical tumors in Chile is likely associated with the high and early onset of fertility. The prevalence of breast cancer is greatest among women 45 years of age or older. Menstrual and reproductive history are associated with the onset of breast cancer. High consumption of animal fat intake and the presence of obesity may also increase the risk of breast cancer.

Stomach cancer is the leading cancer diagnosed among men, particularly after the age of 40 years. Among women, stomach cancer ranked third after cervical and breast cancer. Stomach cancer in Chile shows special characteristics in relation to its prevalence, which is higher than in other countries, and its geographical distribution. Several epidemiological studies in the country have shown that men have a higher risk than women of gastric cancer, and its prevalence is higher in low-income rural areas and among people with limited education and manual workers.[7][8] The highest prevalence is observed in the Maule and the Araucania regions which are rural and have lower socioeconomic levels. The pathogenesis of stomach cancer is unknown. Attempts to correlate this disease with dietary habits have not been conclusive although several studies have demonstrated that populations exposed to nitrates used in fertilizers may be at a higher risk of developing stomach cancer.[9]

Both skin and gallbladder cancers are on the rise in Chile. A number of studies have found that gallbladder cancer is much more common in Chile than in other countries although the reason has not been identified. The high prevalence of pathologies that precede the onset of gallbladder cancer such as biliary disorders, particularly among women, may explain this phenomenon. More than 90 percent of all prostate cancer cases occur among men over the age of 60 years. Lung cancer is also on the rise in both sexes.

As shown in Figure A-7, for the Chilean population as a whole the leading causes of cancer death are: stomach, lung, gallbladder, cervical, breast, and esophageal tumors. Deaths from cancer are highest among the 45 to 64 age group and are relatively evenly distributed between men and women (51 percent of all deaths from cancer occurred among females and 49 percent among males). While in men the most fatal cancer is stomach cancer followed by lung, prostate and esophageal cancer, in women the leading cause of cancer mortality is gallbladder cancer followed by stomach, breast, and cervical cancers.

---

7.  Medina, E. 1973. Variaciones Geográficas y Cronológicas del Cáncer Gástrico en Chile. Rev. Méd. Chile 101:574.

8.  Armijo, R., et al. 1981. Epidemiología del Cáncer Gástrico en Chile. Rev. Méd. Chile 109:551-556.

9.  Armijo, R. y Coulson, A. H. 1975. Epidemiología del cáncer gástrico en Chile. Rol de los fertilizantes nitrogenados. Int. J. Epidemiol. 4:301-309; Zaldivar, R. y Wetterstrand, W. H. 1975. Evidencia de correlación positiva entre exposición a fertilizantes nitrogenados y tasas de mortalidad por cáncer gástrico: nitritos y nitrosaminas. Experiencia 31:1354-1355; Zaldivar, R. y Wetterstrand, W. H. 1978. Niveles de nitratos nitrogenados en agua de bebida en áreas de alto y bajo riesgo para cáncer gástrico. Z Krebsforsh 92:227-234; Armijo, R., González, A., Orellana, M., y Coulson, A. H. 1981. Epidemiología del cáncer gástrico en Chile. Exposición a nitratos y frequencia de cáncer gástrico en Chile. Int. J. Epidemiol. 10:57-62; Armijo, R., Orellana, M., Medina, E., y Coulson, A. H. 1981. Epidemiología del cáncer gástrico en Chile: Estudio de casos y controles. Int. J. Epidemiol. 10:53-56.

**Figure A-7**

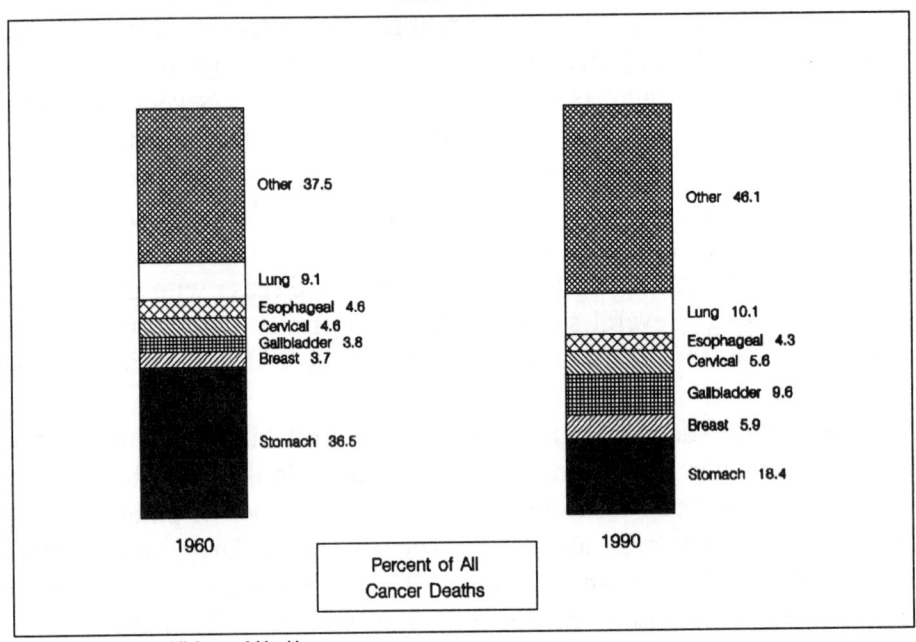

LEADING CAUSES OF DEATH FROM CANCER
1960 AND 1990

Percent of All
Cancer Deaths

Source: Chilean Ministry of Health.

As has occurred in the rest of the world, the age-adjusted mortality rate from stomach cancer has decreased in Chile, from 35.8/100,000 in 1960 to 12.8/100,000 in 1990 (Figure A-8). This decline parallels similar but unexplained trends in other western countries and is independent from changes in diagnostic methods or improved survival after treatment. At present the age-adjusted rate in Chile is similar to the rates in Japan, Hungary, and Poland, but is much higher than the rate in the United States, particularly among whites.[10] An important increase in the age-adjusted death rates for gallbladder cancer in both sexes took place in the last 20 years (from 6.2 to 13.8/100,000). Lung cancer mortality has also shown an increasing trend over time for both sexes, from 3.8/100,000 to 5.4/100,000. In comparison with more industrialized countries, such as the United Kingdom and some northern European countries, where rates among males are 115/100,000 and 75/100,000 respectively, the rate in Chile is relatively low. Among women, the death rate from cervical cancer has stabilized since 1970 at around 10/100,000. This is comparable to the rates found in Mexico (9.2/100,000) and Paraguay (6.8/100,000), but is much higher than the rates in Canada (1.6/100,000) and the United States (1.7/100,000). There is strong evidence that the lower rates in the United States and Canada are the result of the widespread use of Pap

10. Barnum H. and E.R. Greenberg. Cancers. In Dean T. Jamison, W. Henry Mosley, Anthony R. Measham, and José-Luis Bobadilla, eds. 1993. Disease Control Priorities in Developing Countries. New York: Oxford University Press.

testing. The death rate from breast cancer in Chile has increased in the past 30 years from 7.5 to 11.4/100,000. This is lower than rates in more developed countries such as Canada (14.8/100,000) and the United States (13.6/100,000). While early detection in Chile may have helped to hold down the death rate from cervical cancer, this strategy is less feasible for breast cancer because of the considerable infrastructure and cost required to perform screening mammography.

**Figure A-8**

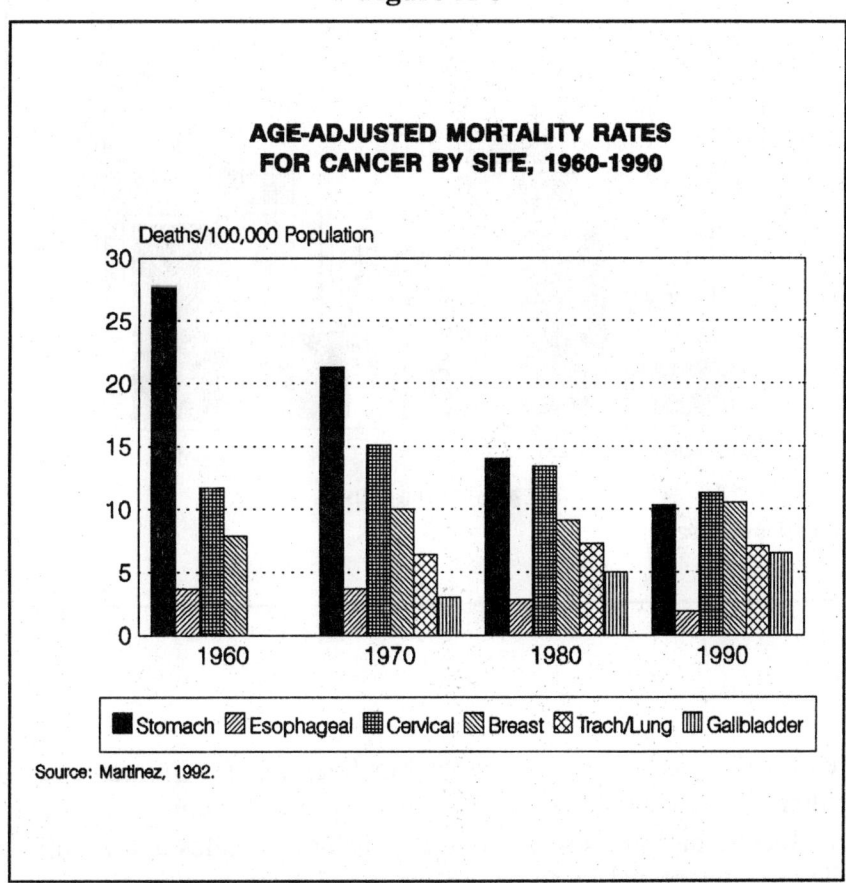

Source: Martinez, 1992.

Due to the underreporting of cancer diagnoses, hospital utilization data provide a more realistic picture of cancer morbidity in Chile because they are less prone to underestimation. Hospitalization rates due to cancer increased by 38 percent, from 1970 to 1989, from 247.4/100,000 to 341.3/100,000. A remarkable increase took place in the 55-64 year old group. About 37 percent of all hospitalizations for cancer occur in patients over the age of 65. In the same period, the number of hospital discharges due to cancer went from 14,322 to 30,645, a 114 percent increase (Figure A-9). The largest increase was observed in breast cancer (130 percent). Most smoking-related cancers, including lung cancer, show an increasing trend in the number of hospital discharges starting after age 35.

**Figure A-9**

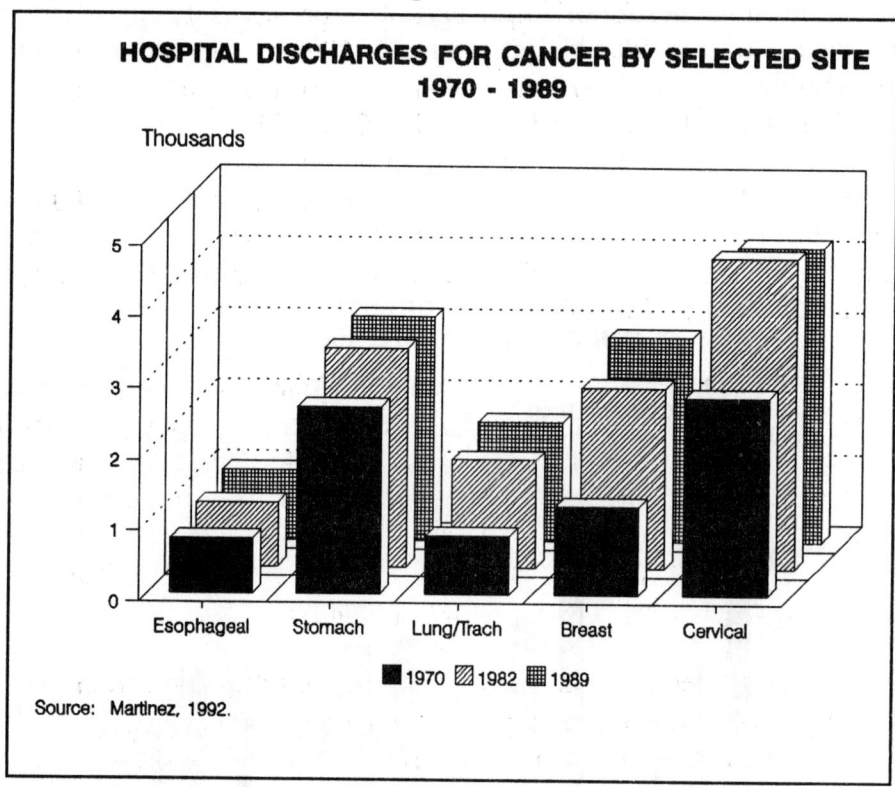

**HOSPITAL DISCHARGES FOR CANCER BY SELECTED SITE
1970 - 1989**

Thousands

1970 ▨ 1982 ▦ 1989

Source: Martinez, 1992.

## Injuries

Injuries are classified as either unintentional or intentional. Unintentional injuries include traffic accidents, poisonings, falls, fires, asphyxiation, drowning, and accidents involving firearms. Intentional injuries, or violence, include suicides and homicides.[11] Injury data in Chile are constrained by the poor quality of death certification in terms of specifying types of trauma and poisons causing death, possible biases in hospital discharge statistics, and exclusion from police statistics of all deaths caused by injuries which occurred after accidents.

In Chile, injuries ranked third among the leading causes of death in 1990, accounting for 9,587 deaths or 12 percent of total deaths. In 1990, the age-adjusted mortality rate from injuries was 70.2/100,000 persons. The age-specific mortality rate from injuries in Chile is comparable to the rates in Brazil (63.7/100,000), Mexico (77.4/100,000), and Ecuador

---

11. The codes for all injuries under the ICD9 are in Chapter XVII.

(63.1/100,000), but is higher that rates in the United States (48.4/100,000), Canada (38.6/100,000), and Argentina (44.8/100,000).

Of all injuries in Chile, the principal cause of mortality is traffic accidents, with an age-adjusted mortality rate of 7.9/100,000 persons in 1990. This rate is much lower than the average of 11.3/100,000 reported for Latin America, as well as the rates reported for the United States (17.2/100,000) and Canada (13.2/100,000). The second leading cause of injury deaths in Chile are suicides with and age-adjusted mortality rate of 5.5/100,000, which is similar to rates found in Argentina (5.4/100,000) and Uruguay (5.3/100,000) and somewhat lower than rates in Canada (10.0/100,000) and the United States (8.9/100,000). This is followed by homicide (3/100,000), falls (3/100,000), fire (2.2/100,000), and asphyxiation and drowning (0.4/100,000).

Men are more prone to injuries than women in Chile, particularly from traffic accidents, drownings, suicides, and homicides. The disparity between the sexes has become even greater in the last 30 years. This is particularly true for the 25 to 34 age group where the mortality for males is 7.5 times greater than for females. The occurrence of injuries has been much higher in regions which are predominately agricultural and rural, such as O'Higgins, Maule, Bio-Bio, Araucania, and Los Lagos, probably due to lack of or limited safety measures affecting housing, labor, and transportation.

While the age-adjusted mortality rate for injuries has decreased from the 1960 rate of 91.5 persons (Figure A-10), injuries as a percent of all deaths has increased in the past 30 years from 7 percent to 12 percent. Among the specific causes of injury deaths there has been a remarkable reduction in the age-adjusted mortality rate for asphyxiation and drowning from 14.3/100,000 in 1960 (about 16 percent of all accident deaths) to only 0.4/100,000 (about 0.6 percent of all accident deaths) in 1990.

**Figure A-10**

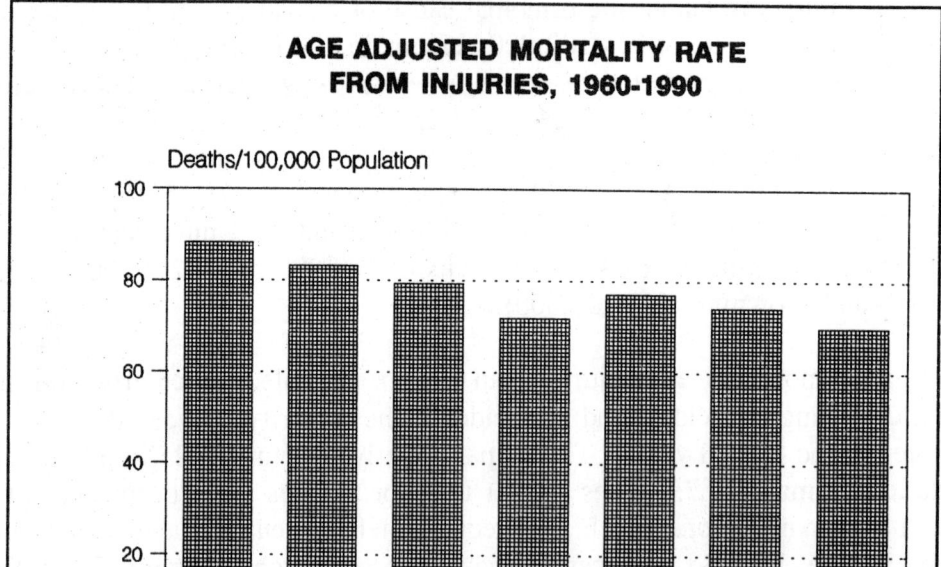

Age-specific mortality rates have generally declined since 1960 with the exception of rates for children under the age of 5 and adults 55-65 years of age, which have registered slight increases (Figure A-11). As shown elsewhere, the increase in child injuries may be due to the greater availability of household electrical appliances, which are potential causes of household injuries, particularly in crowded living spaces, and poor supervision of children that may result from the increasing number of working mothers who work outside the home and the limited availability of day care centers for low socioeconomic groups.[12]

---

12. Stansfield, S.K., Smith, G.S., and McGreevey, W. "Injury." In Dean T. Jamison, W. Henry Mosley, Anthony R. Measham, and José-Luis Bobadilla, eds. 1993. Disease Control Priorities in Developing Countries. New York: Oxford University Press.

**Figure A-11**

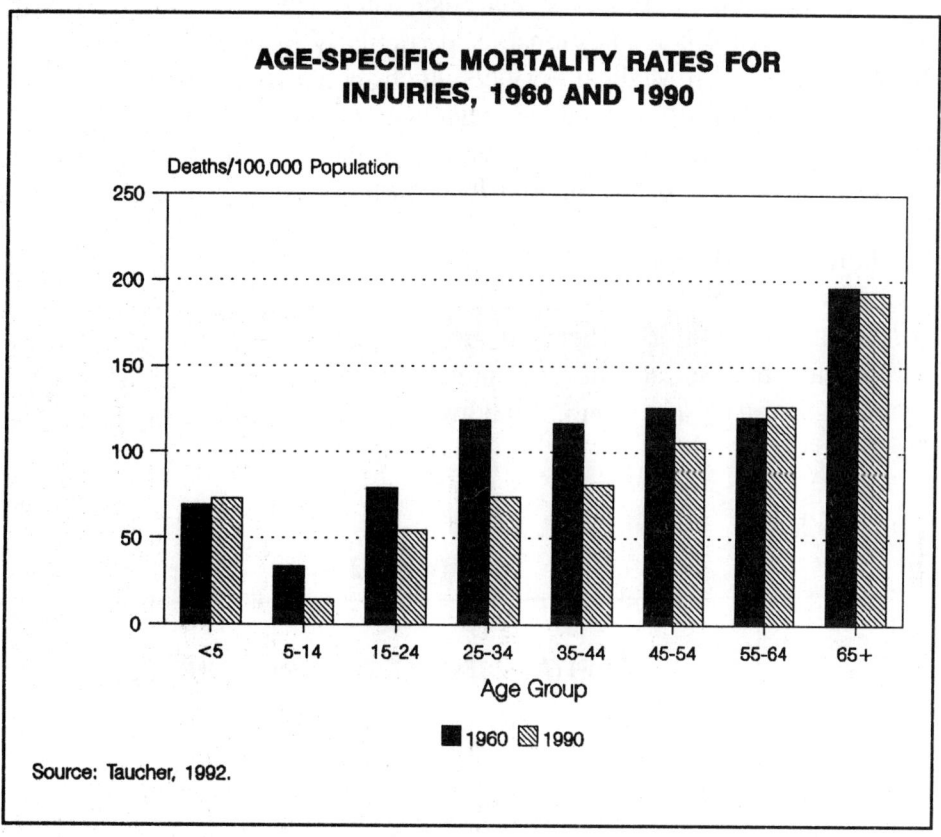

**AGE-SPECIFIC MORTALITY RATES FOR INJURIES, 1960 AND 1990**

Deaths/100,000 Population

Age Group

■ 1960 ▨ 1990

Source: Taucher, 1992.

Police records provide detailed information on traffic accidents since 1977. Historical trends, however, have to be interpreted with caution because they are likely to be influenced by changing criteria for reporting accidents to the police. The number of traffic accidents per 100,000 persons increased significantly in the last two decades, from 184,6/100,000 in 1977 to 287,1/100,000 in 1989; the greatest increases were in crashes (from 58 to 115,5/100,000) and collisions (from 56,2 to 78/100,000). Buses are most often involved in traffic accidents as measured by crashes per vehicle. Traffic accidents are more prevalent in more urbanized regions. However, these tend to be minor accidents as compared to those in rural locations, where the rate of injury and death per accident are higher, mainly due to high speed driving on highways and bicycle riders being overrun by motor vehicles.

The increase in traffic accidents may be attributed in great part to the sharp increase in the overall number of vehicles in Chile, particularly since the latter part of the 1970's. The total number of vehicles increased by 94 percent in 12 years, from 529,911 in 1977 to 1,032,147 in 1989. As the number of cars in the country increased, the rate of traffic accidents reached an all-time high in 1982 of 61/1,000 vehicles before declining again to levels that prevailed in the 1970's. Identification of specific causes of motor vehicle accidents is difficult. Official registration of "other" as the main cause of the accident has decreased from 60 percent in 1985 to 20 percent in 1989, suggesting possibly better documentation, but making comparisons difficult. In addition, the category "not obeying traffic laws" is not specific enough for analysis. There are also few alcohol- and speed-related accidents listed; this is questionable, particularly in view of data from the Metropolitan Region Legal Medical Service which indicate that during the 1980's between one-third and one-half of all fatal traffic accidents, suicides, and homicides in Santiago were associated with excessive alcohol intake. Although there are no reliable data, it is assumed that a similar proportion of drowning and fatal burn accidents are related to alcohol abuse.

The burden of injuries is growing. The number of hospital discharges for injuries per 100,000 persons has steadily increased since 1962 (Figure A-12), accounting now for 133,281 or about one-tenth of all hospital discharges. A breakdown of rates by age group for 1990 illustrates that the rates have remained steady among the 25 to 64 age group, while increasing for the over 65 age group. The average hospital length of stay is highest for burn victims (15.6 days).

**Figure A-12**

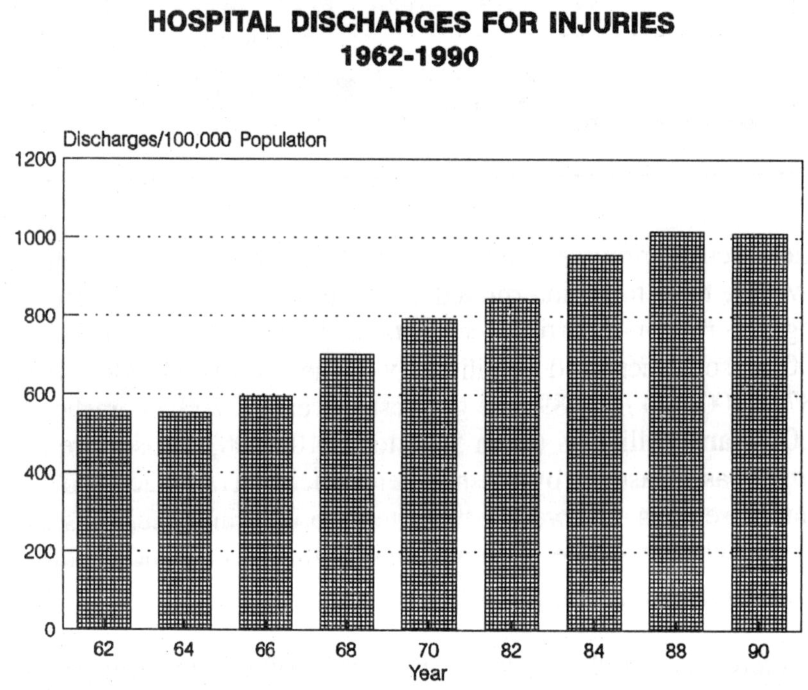

HOSPITAL DISCHARGES FOR INJURIES
1962-1990

Source: Taucher, 1992.

## Chronic Obstructive Pulmonary Diseases (COPD)[13]

COPD is a family of diseases whose main characteristic is the obstruction of air flow to the lungs because of resistance in the air passages or a loss of lung elasticity. Chronic bronchitis and emphysema are included in this group of diseases, but bronchial asthma is not. The principal risk factors in COPD are smoking (by far the most important), pollution (which acts as an exacerbating factor), and some occupational exposures. In the natural history of COPD there is a lapse of 20 to 40 years from the appearance of the first symptoms to respiratory insufficiency and death, which means that actions on risk factors take years in exert their effect.

In Chile, the mortality due to COPD has risen in the last few decades, a worrisome trend which signals the importance of preventive measures to combat the disease, particularly for controlling modifiable risks such as smoking. Among the Chilean adult population, it is estimated that 78 percent of COPD in men and 72 percent of COPD in women can be attributed to smoking. About 1,000 Chileans aged 15 years or older died in 1990 of COPD-related complications, up from 177 in 1960. Figure A-13 shows the age-adjusted rates for mortality due to COPD among the adult population, where an increase is observed in the last 30 years from 4.1/100,000 in 1960 to 19.4/100,000 in 1990.

## Figure A-13

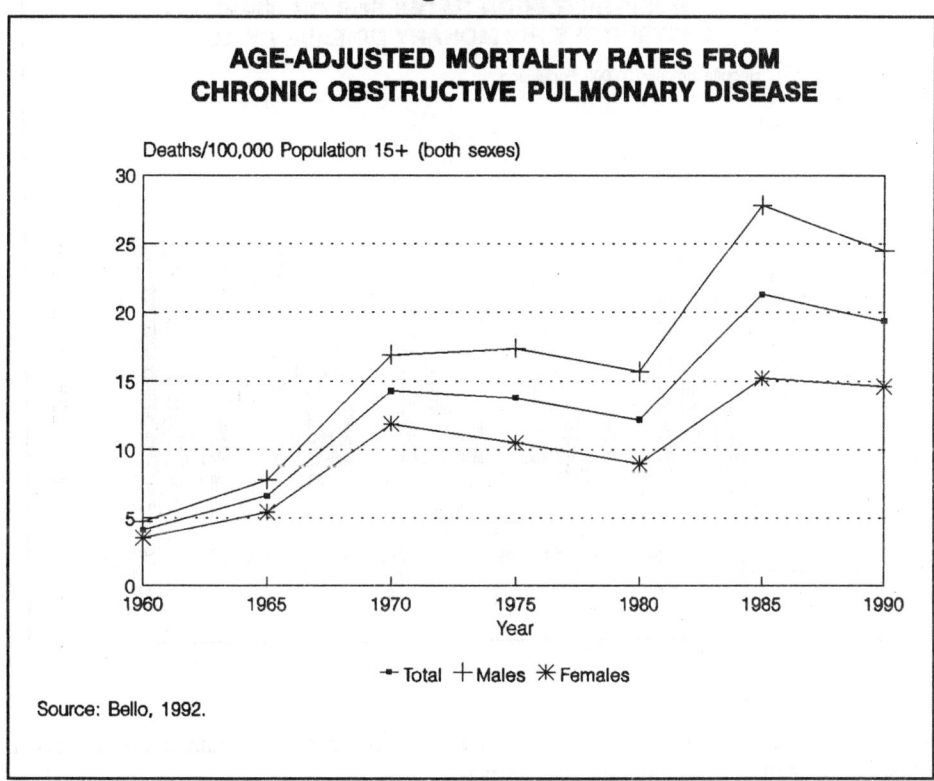

---

13.  The codes for COPD under the ICD9 are in Chapter VIII.

Mortality rates in men due to COPD are 1.6 times higher than in women and progress with age, particularly after the age of 55 years, reflecting a longer and heavier smoking experience among men. There seems to be an inverse relationship between socioeconomic status and COPD. Although information on risk factors for COPD in Chile is scarce, some studies do permit inferences for the relationship between COPD and environmental contamination. For example, one epidemiological study showed a relatively higher risk for irritative lung disease, bronchial obstruction, and pneumonia in Santiago, a city with high contamination levels as compared with Los Andes, a city with low environmental contamination.[14] Also, there is a documented relationship between certain occupations and COPD, such as miners and those working in the chemical industry, metal foundries, and glass and ceramic industries.[15/16/]

Since COPD patients cannot be cured, this condition contributes significantly to the disability burden of the country, particularly among the older age groups. Treatment can only relieve the symptoms and improve the quality of life of the patient. As shown in Figure A-14, a decrease is observed in hospitalization rates from 1970 to 1989. This trend may be explained by improved outpatient care, including home care. Most hospitalizations are of individuals older than 55 years of age.

**Figure A-14**

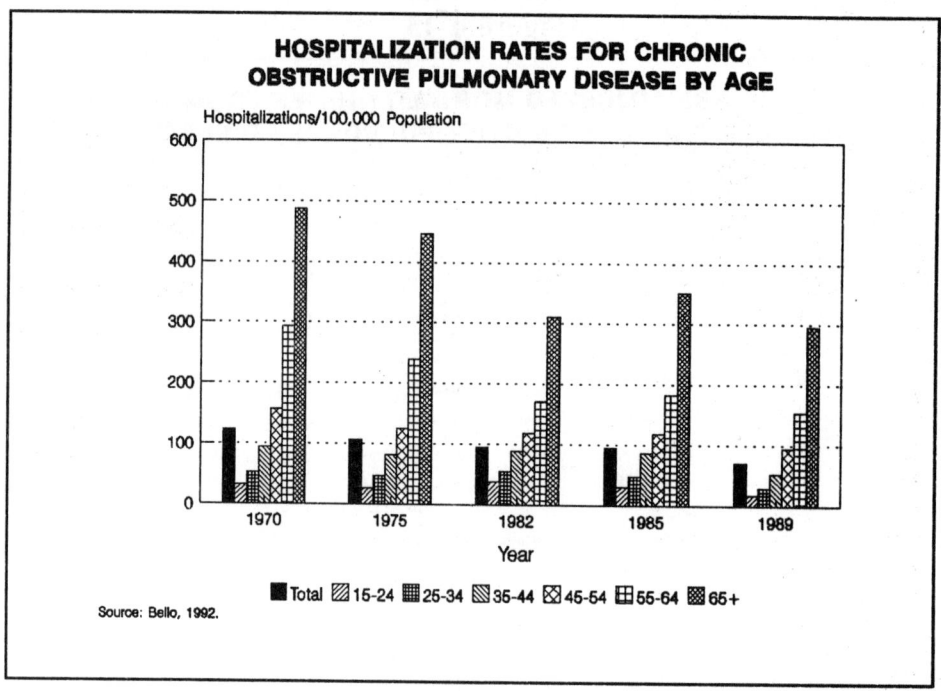

14. Belmar, R., et al. 1990. Estudio epidemiológico sobre efectos de la contaminación atmosférica. Informe para la Intendencia Regional Metropolitana de Santiago.

15. Oyanguren, H., Donoso, H., Busel, J., et al. 1979. Bronquitis crónica y contaminación atmosférica. Rev.Méd. Chile 107:858-864.

16. Espinosa, R. 1988. Prevalencia de bronquitis crónica en residentes de la Provincia El Loa, II Región, Chile. Tesis para optar al grado de Magister en Salud Pública. Escuela de Salud Pública, Universidad de Chile.

## Diabetes[17]

Diabetes is a group of diseases that have in common high blood sugar levels due to an absolute or relative insulin deficiency. Insulin dependent diabetes mellitus (IDDM) or Type I, which may appear at any age, is seen most frequently in children and young adults (<30 years of age) and requires insulin; its most common cause is the destruction of pancreatic cells. The most common form of diabetes is non-insulin dependent diabetes mellitus (NIDDM), which usually appears after age 40 and is generally associated with obesity and genetic factors and modern lifestyles like sedentary life, dietary factors such as an overload of simple carbohydrates, and stress.

NIDDM is an important public health problem because it is a predisposing factor for a number of other non communicable conditions such as coronary heart disease, hypertension, arteriosclerosis, blindness, kidney disease, and neuropathy. It also contributes to pregnancy complications and infections. Together these conditions translate into a high number of years of productive life lost, reduction in the quality of life, disability, and a high demand for costly health services.

There are few studies on the prevalence of NIDDM in Chile. A sample study[18]/[19]/ conducted in the late 1970's in Santiago found a prevalence of diabetes of 5.3 percent and that about 44 percent of those diagnosed as diabetics did not know their condition. Prevalence increased with age and obesity and was similar in both sexes. No differences were observed among socioeconomic groups. In the 1980's, another sample study[20] in Santiago found a prevalence of diabetes of 2.3 percent, with a higher prevalence among low income persons.

In Chile, the increase in the life span of the population, the adoption of sedentary lifestyles, and an increase in the prevalence of obesity may have contributed to the rise in the relative importance of diabetes in the past two decades as a cause of mortality. In 1990, diabetes accounted for 2 percent of deaths and was the underlying cause of death for more than 1,300 Chileans, up from 542 in 1960. Although the quality of the Chilean data is good, there is likely underreporting of diabetes as a cause of death since often its complications are listed as the primary cause of death. During the 1965-85 period, there was a steady increase in mortality for diabetes among adults, with a leveling of rates at 14.6/100,000 after that

17. The codes for diabetes mellitus under the ICB9 are in Chapter III.

18. Covarrubias, A. 1979. Prevalencia de Diabetes Mellitus en el Gran Santiago. Tesis para optar al grado de Magister en Nutrición Humana, INTA, Universidad de Chile.

19. Mella, I., García de RM, et al. 1981. Prevalencia de la Diabetes en el Gran Santiago. Rev. Méd. Chile 109:869-875.

20. Berrios, X., et al. 1990. Prevalencia de factores de riesgo de enfermedades crónicas. Estudio en población general de la región metropolitana, 1986-1987. Rev. Méd. Chile 118:597-604.

year (Figure A-15). As opposed to what is observed in other countries, with higher rates among women than in men, in Chile the risk is about similar in both sexes for people 15 years of age and older, and even higher for men 65 years of age and older. Mortality rates increase progressively with age reaching the highest levels among those 65 years and older, triple the rates for the 55-64 age group.

**Figure A-15**

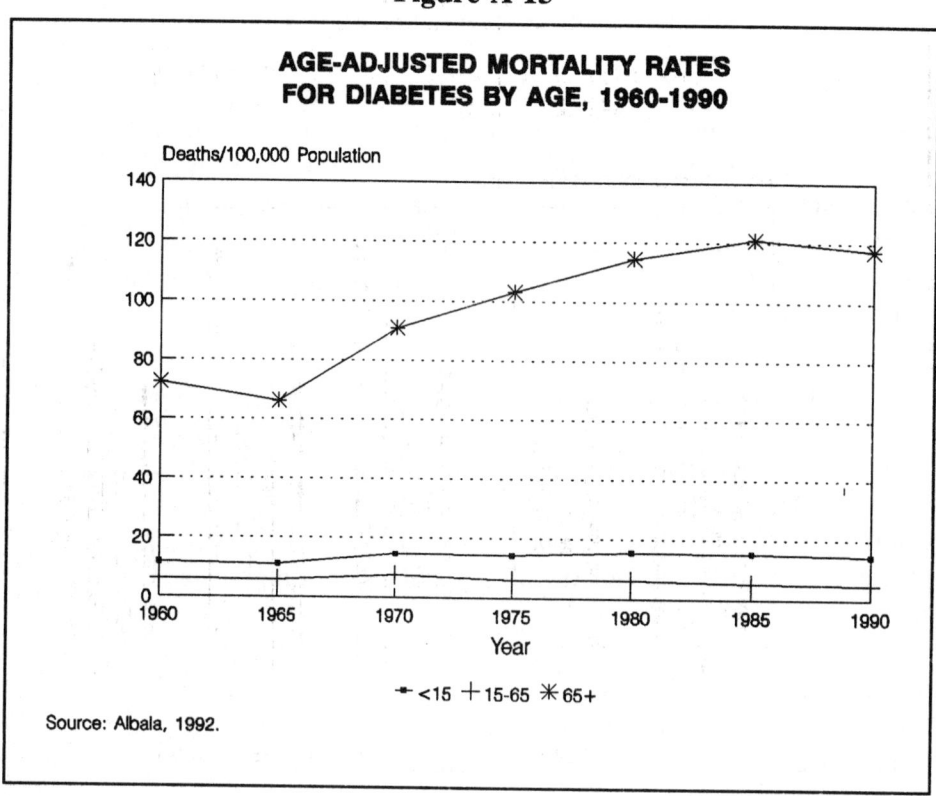

There is a substantial difference in diabetes mortality in the population according to urban or rural living, with a clear predominance in more urbanized regions. Although there is no reliable information, it is presumed that the prevalence of obesity is also higher in urban areas. Mortality rates due to diabetes above the national average are observed in the northern and central regions of the country (Antofagasta, Valparaiso, Maule, O'Higgins, and Santiago), while the lowest rate appears in the southern regions, probably due to rural living conditions that require a higher level of physical activity in a less stressful environment. Among socioeconomic groups, recent data indicate that mortality due to diabetes tends to be higher among low income uneducated groups than those with secondary and higher education. This situation may be explained by the higher prevalence of obesity among low income women.

Hospitalizations for diabetes have increased among all age groups (Figure A-16). Estimations by surgeons and ophthalmologists indicate that in people older than 40 years of age diabetes is the main cause of amputations and blindness in Chile. These estimations suggest that early diagnosis and treatment of diabetes are not carried out.

**Figure A-16**

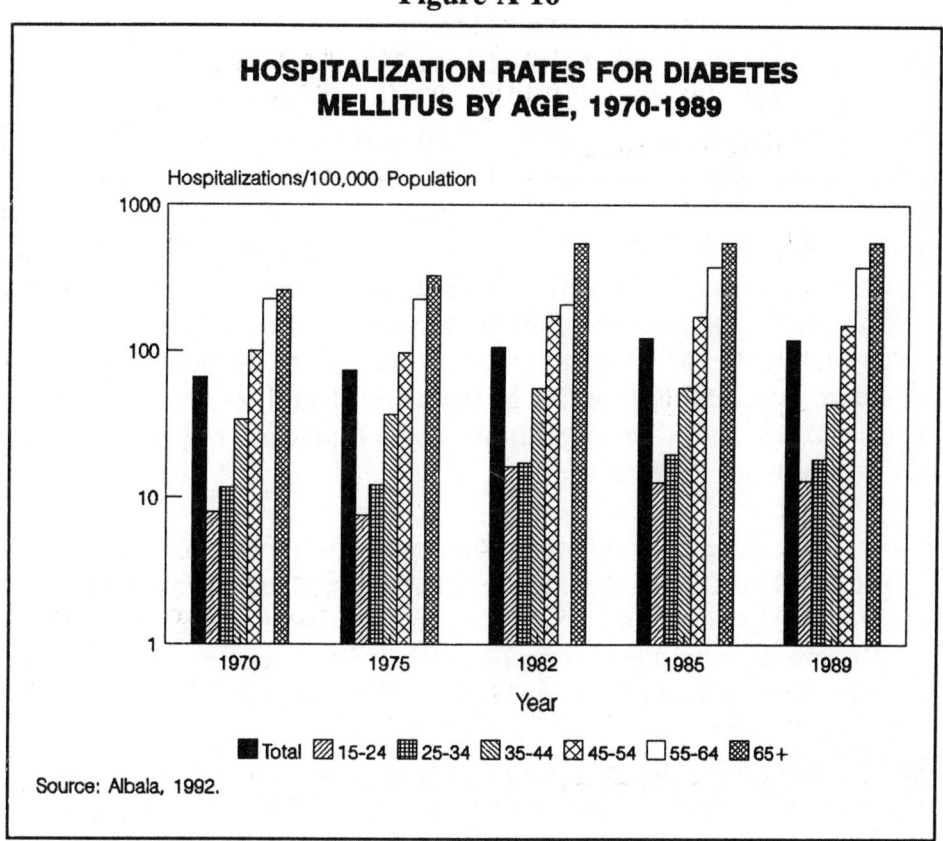

## Mental Illness

Most mental illnesses share the characteristics of the chronic conditions discussed above: they are multifactorial, of predictable evolution, and their prevention and treatment require both behavioral changes in the affected individuals and medical intervention.[21] Advances in recent decades in the understanding of mental disorders have enabled the identification of psychological, psychosocial and neurological factors that play an important role in their onset.

---

21. Mental illness is covered under Chapter V of the ICD9.

The poor quality of the information on mental illnesses in developing countries reflects the low priority given to this problem in past decades. Even though pioneering studies in mental health in some countries of Latin America have shown that about 20 percent of the adult population has some type of recognizable mental disorder, no mechanisms have been established for their registration. Problems with the classification and reporting of mental disorders are also present in Chile. Even when it is the major mortality cause, mental illness is not reported as the cause of death except in those cases where an intoxication (e.g., alcohol) is present.

Whether psychological, psychosocial or neurological in origin, mental illnesses constitute an important public health burden in Chile, contributing substantially to disability and suffering among adults and the elderly. Studies on the prevalence of mental disorders in Chile have been scarce and based mainly in Santiago. A 1983 study conducted in 12 cities showed that mental disorders represented 5 percent of the total number of ambulatory visits.[22] In the ISAPREs, 4.7 percent of all consultations in people 15 to 65 years of age were for psychiatric reasons (equivalent to 88,322 consultations out of a total of 1,871,996 for 432,981 affiliates of the system). Preliminary results of a sample survey performed in 1991 in Concepción by the MOH indicate that 37 percent of the people studied showed at least one symptom of mental disorder. The most prevalent disorder was neurosis accounting for 17 percent of cases studied, alcoholism for about 6 percent, organic brain syndrome for 5 percent, and psychosis for 3 percent.

In 1989, there were 25,469 hospital discharges for mental illness, equivalent to 2 percent of the total discharges in the country. The hospitalization rate that year for mental illness was 277/100,000 inhabitants. Sixty percent of these discharges were from psychiatric services and 40 percent from other clinical services. The average stay for mental disorders is estimated to be 98 days, utilizing about 6 percent of all hospital bed-days.

Since the mid-1980's, the proportion of deaths due to mental disorders among Chilean adults has increased reaching 1.5 percent of all deaths in 1990. This represents 1,108 deaths, up from about 400 in 1960. Age-adjusted mortality rates excluding deaths from alcohol or drugs show an increase in this period in both sexes (Figure III-17); this increase has been particularly important in the group above 75 years of age. The highest mortality for both sexes was seen in the Valparaiso, Maule, and Antofagasta regions.

---

22. Medina Cárdenas, E. 1983. Salud Mental en Chile: Estado actual y perspectivas. Rev. Chil. Neuropsiquiat. 21:77-90.

**Figure A-17**

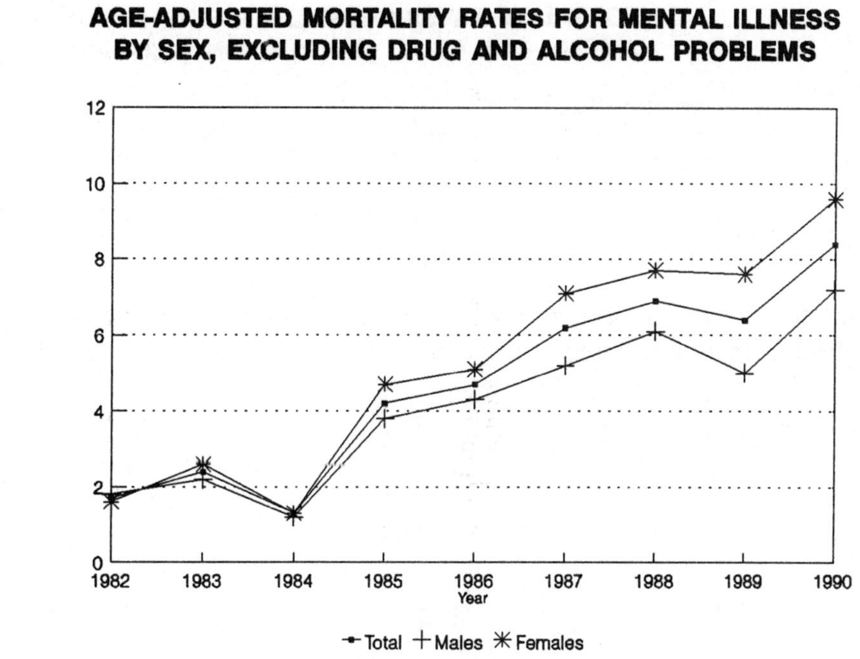

**AGE-ADJUSTED MORTALITY RATES FOR MENTAL ILLNESS BY SEX, EXCLUDING DRUG AND ALCOHOL PROBLEMS**

Source: Penjam, 1992.

## Cirrhosis of the Liver

Alcohol abuse is a major public health problem in Chile. One of the manifestations of this problem is the high prevalence of cirrhosis of the liver,[23] which is largely attributable to heavy alcohol consumption, particularly among men. As shown in Figure A-18, in the last 40 years, cirrhosis death rates among adults in Chile have remained at relatively high levels (about 40/100,000) compared with other Latin American and Caribbean countries with rates ranging from 24.2/100,000 to 2.5/100,000. In 1990, there were more than 3,749 deaths attributed to cirrhosis; among persons 45 to 64 years of age, cirrhosis is the third most frequent cause of death. The current age-adjusted death rate from cirrhosis among men 15 years of age or older (61.8/100,000) is three times the rate for women (19.3/100,000). This disparity represents significant differential drinking patterns by sex in Chile and is similar to that found in the majority of other Latin American countries such as Uruguay and Mexico, where the mortality rate is over four times as high for men than women.

---

23. The codes for cirrhosis of the liver under the ICD9 are in Chapter IX.

**Figure A-18**

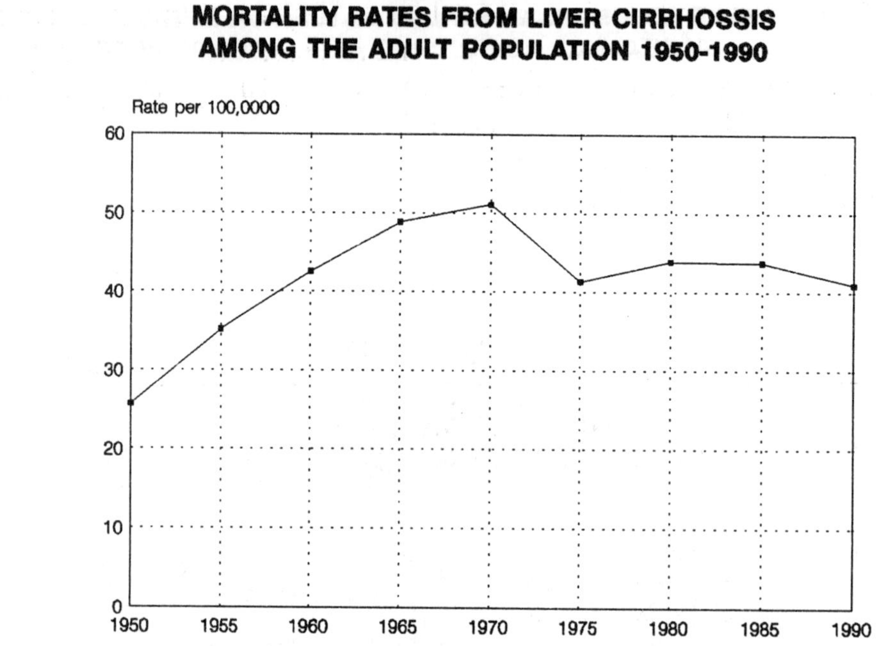
MORTALITY RATES FROM LIVER CIRRHOSSIS
AMONG THE ADULT POPULATION 1950-1990
Rate per 100,0000
60
50
40
30
20
10
0
1950
1955
1960
1965
1970
1975
1980
1985
1990

Source: Medina, 1992.

## AIDS

The Acquired Immunodeficiency Syndrome (AIDS) epidemic has expanded worldwide at an alarming rate since the 1980's. In Latin America, it has flourished amid haphazard prevention. Although on a much smaller scale than more populous countries such as Brazil (9,500 cases), Mexico (3,500 cases), or Argentina (2,700 cases), Chile has not been immune to this problem. By 1991, reported cases of AIDS reached 517. Of current AIDS patients, more than 90 percent are men, usually between the age of 20 and 50 years, and about 70 percent are male homosexual and bisexuals. Heterosexual sex is the third leading means of transmission in Chile, accounting for 17 percent of the reported AIDS cases, with the victims are again mostly men (77 percent of the heterosexual cases). The regions that have the larger number of reported AIDS cases are the Santiago Metropolitan Region (about 70 percent of the total) and the port region of Valparaiso (about 18 percent of the total). Although the survival period of AIDS patients worldwide has been lengthened as a result of therapeutic advances, at present no treatment exists to prevent death.

Currently, it is reported that 804 people in Chile are infected with the human immunodeficiency virus (HIV) and of these, approximately 80 percent became infected between 1988 and 1991. The magnitude of the AIDS epidemic in Chile is quite small when compared with the approximately 1 million infected persons in Brazil and in the United States with total populations of 150 million and 255 million, respectively, and 200,000 infected persons in Colombia and 100,000 infected persons in Argentina, with a similar total population of approximately 33 million. As shown in Figure A-19, groups at special risk, which account for more than 90 percent of the infected cases, are homosexual and bisexual men (65 percent); heterosexual men (14 percent); women (10 percent); and intravenous drug-abusers (5 percent). About one-half of those infected with HIV tend to develop AIDS within 10 years of infection if no treatment is provided, and about 40 percent develop other medical complications associated with HIV infection.

**Figure A-19**

**REGISTERED CASES OF HIV INFECTION BY RISK FACTOR AND BY SEX, AS OF MAY 1992**

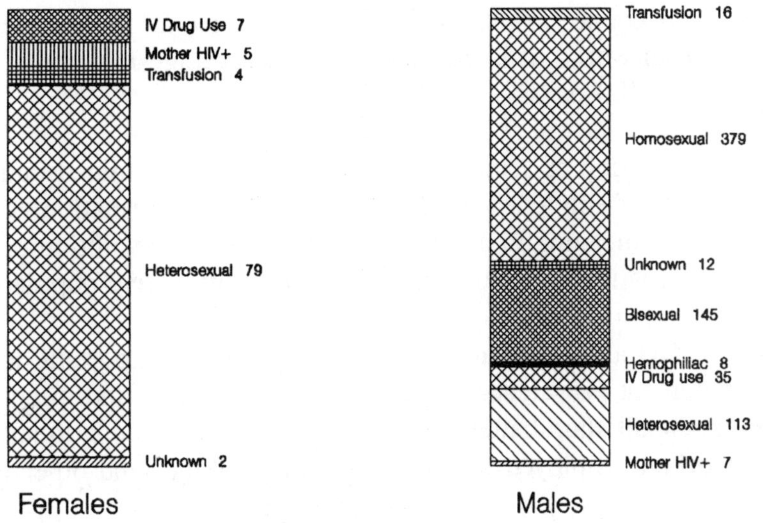

Females

IV Drug Use 7
Mother HIV+ 5
Transfusion 4
Heterosexual 79
Unknown 2

Males

Transfusion 16
Homosexual 379
Unknown 12
Bisexual 145
Hemophiliac 8
IV Drug use 35
Heterosexual 113
Mother HIV+ 7

Source: Chilean Ministry of Health.

## Occupation-related health conditions

Under current Chilean legislation (Law No. 16.744 of 1968), occupation-related health conditions are defined as those caused directly by the performance of a profession or a work activity that might produce disability or death. These conditions encompasses occupational injuries and occupational diseases. The law also establishes maximum permissible concentrations of toxic pollutants and physical agents in the work environment, but has not yet established top limits for chemical substances.

There is no epidemiological surveillance system for occupational health conditions. Information published in the Annals of Occupational Injuries and Diseases refers only to the protected 60 percent of the labor force and is often incomplete. A background analysis carried out for this study estimated that in recent decades the underreporting of work-related injuries by employers may be in the 80 to 90 percent range. This is largely due to the limited monitoring and supervisory capacity of the NHSS and the limited awareness of legal protection on the part of employers and insured workers. Between 1982 and 1988 the rate of work-related injuries per 100,000 protected workers increased by 138 percent (from 2,072 to 4,926) in Chile.

In 1988, the last year with available information, more than 2.2 million accidents were reported among insured workers; more than two-thirds of these injuries were concentrated in the industrial, construction, agricultural, and mining sectors. The highest rates of occupational injuries were found in the group aged 25-44 years. The Santiago Metropolitan Region and the mining region of Atacama had the highest rates of occupational-related injuries in the country. Occupational injuries have an immediate cost in terms of reported absence from work. It is estimated that the average number of days lost per accident in 1988 was 13.3 days.

The high proportion of accidental injuries with undetermined outcome, in addition to the known 40 percent of employed workers for whom no information is available, are factors that jointly preclude a meaningful analysis of the extent and evolution of mortality and disability due to occupational hazards in the economically active population as a whole.

Available MOH and INE data indicate that the most important occupational diseases are silicosis (4-5 percent prevalence among industrial workers and miners), lead intoxication (50 percent among small shop battery repair workers), and occupational deafness (19 percent hearing loss in workers employed in mills, furniture making, and other high noise level occupations).

## Aging-related nutritional problems: Osteoporosis

Osteoporosis is a complex disease characterized by a reduction in the amount of bone mass per unit volume among adults and the elderly. When bone mass becomes too low, fractures of the bone can occur. Bone loss is present in all individuals after age 50, accelerating in women after menopause. Calcium intake correlates directly with bone mass and inversely with the rate of bone fractures.

Current information on the prevalence of osteoporosis in Chile is scarce. Therefore, the severity of the problem is not know, although a substantial increase has been observed in recent years in the rate of fractures with age. The rate of bone fractures at later ages provides an indication of the final consequences of a process of bone mass loss that can continue for several decades before being diagnosed. A study in Chile of all bone fractures in public hospitals in one year (1985) found 33,544 hospitalizations for fractures in Chile, amounting to 3.3 percent of all hospital admissions.[24] The proportion of fractures advances with age. Twenty-three percent of the most common fractures occur in the population above 55 years of age, although this age group amounts to only about 12 percent of the total population. The group above 65 years of age had 15 percent of the total fractures, although equivalent to only 6 percent of the population.

24. Contreras, L. G., Kirshbaum, A. K., and Pumarino, H. C. 1991. Epidemiología de las fracturas en Chile. Rev. Méd. Chile 119:92-98.

# ANNEX B

## METHODOLOGY USED FOR CALCULATING
## DISABILITY-ADJUSTED LIFE YEARS (DALYs)

### Measuring Loss and Years of Life Lost

In order to assess the effect of an intervention or to compare the morbidity/mortality experience of various countries (or the same country over time) the concept of "cost" or "loss of human capital" is often used. One method of measuring loss is to establish a natural age of death and then fix a loss to any death that preceeds this age. Such a death is considered a "premature" death. In this case, the number of years lost (or days lost) for each premature death is defined as the difference between the age at death and the natural age. Thus, for each death at a particular age, a loss equal to the total years that could have been lived is tallied. The result is a total number of years lost for each age at each point in time.

The number of years lost is simple but still implicitly includes a weight for the loss of life that is a function of the age at death. Heuristically, a premature death at age 25 should be greater than the loss associated with a premature death at age 55. However, the years of life lost index has a couple of drawbacks. First it provides no loss for disability only. Second, it values each year the same regardless of when the year occurs in the future and the age of the individual when it occurs. In an effort to resolve this problem, the World Bank in cooperation with outside researchers and consultants, developed the "disability adjusted life years" (DALYs) concept. The three points of concern mentioned above are all explicitly addressed in the definition of DALYs.

### Adjusting for Disability

First, a disability score was determined for each disability. This score is a number between 0 and 1 that reflects the degree of disability. As regards societal loss, a score of 1 for a disability is synonomous with death. A score of 0.25 is similar to the loss of a fourth of a life. These scores were determined by a professional board.

Unfortunately, in order to use these scores one needs to know the disability incidence at each year. Such data were not available for Chile. To get a disability score, it was assumed that each cause-specific death indicated a fixed (unknown) number of disabilities in the population. Since both disability-specific and mortality-specific DALYs are available for all of Latin America, under this assumption, the ratio of the disability DALYs to mortality DALYs is constant for any specific age. If the ratio is the same for Chile as for the whole of Latin America, one can calculate the disability DALYs from the age-specific mortality DALYs for Chile. Such was done in the report.

## Adjusting for the Value of a Year

As noted above, the value of a year lost depends on the age of the individual. The definition of DALYs specifies a function for determining the value of a year by age. This function is given as Value=0.16243*age*exp(-0.04*age), where exp is the exponential function. This function gives the highest value for ages in the mid twenties and tapers off for older ages. Ages prior to the mid twenties are also valued less.

## Adjusting for the Future Value

Just as the value of money in the future is less than the value of money at present, the value of a year saved in the distant future is less than the value of one saved now. This is captured in the definition of DALYs by using a discount function. The discount rate used in the definition of the DALYs (and also the one used in this study) is 0.03 percent per year.

Thus an individual who dies at say, 62, when a natural age of death of say, 75, is used saves one current year, valued as above, one year that is a year away valued at age 63 and then discounted by 3%, a year valued at age 64 and then discounted by 3 percent for each of two years and so forth. The total of these valued, discounted years will equal the mortality DALY for the premature death. On the other hand, if a disability with a score of 0.25 onset at age 62, the disability DALY would be determined in the same way as the mortality DALY except that it would be multiplied by 0.25 at the end.

## Calculation of DALYs

DALYs consist of two components: loss due to premature death and loss due to disability. These components are calculated separately in the model as follows:

### Mortality Loss:

- Maximum age is assumed to be 85.
- For each death of an individual in an age group below 85, the discounted loss is calculated as (see Murray, *Bulletin of WHO*, 72 No. 3, 1994):

$$\text{Loss} = \frac{.16243\,e^{-.04a}}{.0049}\left[-e^{-.07L}(1 + .07 \times 85) + (1 + .07a)\right]$$

where a = age at death or onset of disability and L = 85 - a.
- Implicit in the above formula are the following assumptions:
  - Each person who dies in a five year age group has age equal to the middle of the age range
  - interest is at 3%
  - value of a year lost at age a is $.16243ae^{-.04a}$.
- Total annual mortality loss is the sum of the losses overall deaths over all age groups.

**Disability Loss:**

- The ratio between cause-specific disability loss and mortality loss for all of Latin America for each age and gender is assumed to be the same as in Chile and that this ratio will remain constant.
- For each age and gender, this cause-specific ratio is calculated using total DALYs for Latin America.
- Disability DALYs are calculated for each cause in Chile by multiplying this ratio by the cause-, age- and gender-specific mortality loss.
- Total disability DALYs are calculated by summing over cause, age and gender.

# Distributors of World Bank Publications

**ARGENTINA**
Carlos Hirsch, SRL
Galeria Guemes
Florida 165, 4th Floor-Ofc. 453/465
1333 Buenos Aires

Oficina del Libro Internacional
Alberti 40
1082 Buenos Aires

**AUSTRALIA, PAPUA NEW GUINEA,
FIJI, SOLOMON ISLANDS,
VANUATU, AND WESTERN SAMOA**
D.A. Information Services
648 Whitehorse Road
Mitcham 3132
Victoria

**AUSTRIA**
Gerold and Co.
Graben 31
A-1011 Wien

**BANGLADESH**
Micro Industries Development
    Assistance Society (MIDAS)
House 5, Road 16
Dhanmondi R/Area
Dhaka 1209

**BELGIUM**
Jean De Lannoy
Av. du Roi 202
1060 Brussels

**BRAZIL**
Publicacoes Tecnicas Internacionais Ltda.
Rua Peixoto Gomide, 209
01409 Sao Paulo, SP

**CANADA**
Le Diffuseur
151A Boul. de Mortagne
Boucherville, Québec
J4B 5E6

Renouf Publishing Co.
1294 Algoma Road
Ottawa, Ontario
K1B 3W8

**CHINA**
China Financial & Economic
    Publishing House
8, Da Fo Si Dong Jie
Beijing

**COLOMBIA**
Infoenlace Ltda.
Apartado Aereo 34270
Bogota D.E.

**COTE D'IVOIRE**
Centre d'Edition et de Diffusion
Africaines (CEDA)
04 B.P. 541
Abidjan 04 Plateau

**CYPRUS**
Center of Applied Research
Cyprus College
6, Diogenes Street, Engomi
P.O. Box 2006
Nicosia

**DENMARK**
SamfundsLitteratur
Rosenoerns Allé 11
DK-1970 Frederiksberg C

**DOMINICAN REPUBLIC**
Editora Taller, C. por A.
Restauración e Isabel la Católica 309
Apartado de Correos 2190 Z-1
Santo Domingo

**EGYPT, ARAB REPUBLIC OF**
Al Ahram
Al Galaa Street
Cairo

The Middle East Observer
41, Sherif Street
Cairo

**FINLAND**
Akateeminen Kirjakauppa
P.O. Box 128
SF-00101 Helsinki 10

**FRANCE**
World Bank Publications
66, avenue d'Iéna
75116 Paris

**GERMANY**
UNO-Verlag
Poppelsdorfer Allee 55
53115 Bonn

**GREECE**
Papasotiriou S.A.
35, Stournara Str.
106 82 Athens

**HONG KONG, MACAO**
Asia 2000 Ltd.
46-48 Wyndham Street
Winning Centre
7th Floor
Central Hong Kong

**HUNGARY**
Foundation for Market Economy
Dombovari Ut 17-19
H-1117 Budapest

**INDIA**
Allied Publishers Private Ltd.
751 Mount Road
Madras - 600 002

**INDONESIA**
Pt. Indira Limited
Jalan Borobudur 20
P.O. Box 181
Jakarta 10320

**IRAN**
Kowkab Publishers
P.O. Box 19575-511
Tehran

**IRELAND**
Government Supplies Agency
4-5 Harcourt Road
Dublin 2

**ISRAEL**
Yozmot Literature Ltd.
P.O. Box 56055
Tel Aviv 61560

**ITALY**
Licosa Commissionaria Sansoni SPA
Via Duca Di Calabria, 1/1
Casella Postale 552
50125 Firenze

**JAMAICA**
Ian Randle Publishers Ltd.
206 Old Hope Road
Kingston 6

**JAPAN**
Eastern Book Service
Hongo 3-Chome, Bunkyo-ku 113
Tokyo

**KENYA**
Africa Book Service (E.A.) Ltd.
Quaran House, Mfangano Street
P.O. Box 45245
Nairobi

**KOREA, REPUBLIC OF**
Pan Korea Book Corporation
P.O. Box 101, Kwangwhamun
Seoul

Korean Stock Book Centre
P.O. Box 34
Yeoeido
Seoul

**MALAYSIA**
University of Malaya Cooperative
    Bookshop, Limited
P.O. Box 1127, Jalan Pantai Baru
59700 Kuala Lumpur

**MEXICO**
INFOTEC
Apartado Postal 22-860
14060 Tlalpan, Mexico D.F.

**NETHERLANDS**
De Lindeboom/InOr-Publikaties
P.O. Box 202
7480 AE Haaksbergen

**NEW ZEALAND**
EBSCO NZ Ltd.
Private Mail Bag 99914
New Market
Auckland

**NIGERIA**
University Press Limited
Three Crowns Building Jericho
Private Mail Bag 5095
Ibadan

**NORWAY**
Narvesen Information Center
Book Department
P.O. Box 6125 Etterstad
N-0602 Oslo 6

**PAKISTAN**
Mirza Book Agency
65, Shahrah-e-Quaid-e-Azam
P.O. Box No. 729
Lahore 54000

**PERU**
Editorial Desarrollo SA
Apartado 3824
Lima 1

**PHILIPPINES**
International Book Center
Suite 1703, Cityland 10
Condominium Tower 1
Ayala Avenue, H.V. dela
    Costa Extension
Makati, Metro Manila

**POLAND**
International Publishing Service
Ul. Piekna 31/37
00-677 Warszawa

*For subscription orders:*
IPS Journals
Ul. Okrezna 3
02-916 Warszawa

**PORTUGAL**
Livraria Portugal
Rua Do Carmo 70-74
1200 Lisbon

**SAUDI ARABIA, QATAR**
Jarir Book Store
P.O. Box 3196
Riyadh 11471

**SINGAPORE, TAIWAN,
MYANMAR,BRUNEI**
Gower Asia Pacific Pte Ltd.
Golden Wheel Building
41, Kallang Pudding, #04-03
Singapore 1334

**SOUTH AFRICA, BOTSWANA**
*For single titles:*
Oxford University Press
    Southern Africa
P.O. Box 1141
Cape Town 8000

*For subscription orders:*
International Subscription Service
P.O. Box 41095
Craighall
Johannesburg 2024

**SPAIN**
Mundi-Prensa Libros, S.A.
Castello 37
28001 Madrid

Librería Internacional AEDOS
Consell de Cent, 391
08009 Barcelona

**SRI LANKA AND THE MALDIVES**
Lake House Bookshop
P.O. Box 244
100, Sir Chittampalam A.
    Gardiner Mawatha
Colombo 2

**SWEDEN**
*For single titles:*
Fritzes Fackboksforetaget
Regeringsgatan 12, Box 16356
S-106 47 Stockholm

*For subscription orders:*
Wennergren-Williams AB
P. O. Box 1305
S-171 25 Solna

**SWITZERLAND**
*For single titles:*
Librairie Payot
Case postale 3212
CH 1002 Lausanne

*For subscription orders:*
Librairie Payot
Service des Abonnements
Case postale 3312
CH 1002 Lausanne

**THAILAND**
Central Department Store
306 Silom Road
Bangkok

**TRINIDAD & TOBAGO**
Systematics Studies Unit
#9 Watts Street
Curepe
Trinidad, West Indies

**UNITED KINGDOM**
Microinfo Ltd.
P.O. Box 3
Alton, Hampshire GU34 2PG
England

**ZIMBABWE**
Longman Zimbabwe (Pvt.) Ltd.
Tourle Road, Ardbennie
P.O. Box ST 125
Southerton
Harare

72°  Ovalle  70°  **B**  74°  72°  **C**

44°

**REGION
DE
COQUIMBO**

**IV**

*Limari*

32°

EE INSET D

Illapel

*Choapa*

San Felipe

Quillota

Viña Del Mar
ALPARAISO    Los Andes    Andina

San Antonio

SANTIAGO

San
Bernardo

*Cardenal
Caro*    *Cachapoa*    El
Teniente
RANGAGUA

34°

San Fernando    San
Vicente

*Colchagua*

Curico    *Curico*

*Talca*

TALCA

San Javier    Linares

aquenes    *Linares*

Carlos

Chillan
*Ñuble*

*BioBio*

Los Angeles

Victoria
Curacautín

Lautaro

Villarrica

S o u t h
A m e r i c a

Pacific Ocean    Atlantic
Ocean

A
B
C

*Aisén*

1000

Pto. Aisén
**COIHAIQUE**

*Coihaique*

1000

**REGION AISEN DEL
GENERAL CARLOS
IBANEZ DEL CAMPO**

**XI**

*Buenos
Aires*

*General
Carrera*    Chile
Chico

2000

Cochrane

*Gulf
of
Penas*

*Capitán Prat*

Lake
Higgins

1000

*Ultima Esperanza*

Puerto
Natales

52°

*Magallanes*    **PUNTA
ARENAS**

Porvenir

*Tierra
Del Fuego*

**REGION DE MAGALLANES Y
DE LA ANTARTICA CHILENA**

**XII**

*Antártica Chilena*

1000

**CHILE**

A R G E N T I N A

Pacific Ocean

Atlantic
Ocean

——————— MAIN ROADS
+———+———+ RAILWAYS
~5000~ CONTOURS (1000m intervals)
RIVERS
SALINE LAKES
ICE FIELDS
✕ MINES
✈ INTERNATIONAL AIRPORTS
⚓ PORTS, THROUGH-PUT
EXCEEDING 300,000 TONS
PER YEAR
✪ NATIONAL CAPITAL
● REGION CAPITALS
——————— PROVINCE BOUNDARIES
▨▨▨▨ REGION BOUNDARIES
**IV** REGION NUMBERS
—·—·—·— INTERNATIONAL BOUNDARIES

0   50   100   150   200

KILOMETERS

PERU

BOLIVIA

72°  70°  A

*Parinacota*

Arica

*Arica*

Rio Camarones

**REGION
DE
TARAPACA
I**

18°

20°

*Iquique*

IQUIQUE

22°

*Tocopilla*

Tocopilla

*Chuquicamata*

Chuquicamata

María
Elena

*Exótica*

Calama

*El Loa*

**REGION
DE
ANTOFAGASTA
II**

ARGENTINA

22°

*Salar
de
Atacama*

ANTOFAGASTA

24°

*Antofagasta*

24°

Taltal

*El Salvador*

26°

Chañaral

*Chañaral*

**REGION
DE
ATACAMA
III**

*Copiapó*

COPIAPO

26°

28°

Vallenar

*Huasco*

28°

**REGION
DE
COQUIMBO**

LA SERENA
Coquimbo

*Elqui*

30°

Ovalle

30°

72°  70°  68°

The boundaries, colors, denominations
and any other information shown on
this map do not imply, on the part of
The World Bank Group, any judgment
on the legal status of any territory, or
any endorsement or acceptance of
such boundaries.

---

**REGION
DE
VALPARAISO
V**

72°  D

*Petorca*

La Ligua

*San Felipe
De Aconcagua*

San
Felipe

*Quillota*

Los Andes

Quillota

*Los Andes*

VALPARAISO

*Chacabuco*

ARGENTINA

*Valparaiso*

*Santiago*

SANTIAGO

*San Antonio*

*Talagante*

Puente Alto
San Bernardo

San Antonio

Melipilla

Talagante

*Cordillera*

*Melipilla*

*Maipo*

**REGION
METROPOLITANA
DE SANTIAGO**

34°

72°

---

**REGION DEL LIBERTAQDOR
GENERAL BERNARDO O'HIGGINS**  VI

Constitución

**REGION
DEL
MAULE
VII**

*Cauquenes*

Ca

San

36°

**REGION DEL
BIOBIO
VIII**

Talcahuano

*Concepción*

CONCEPCION
Lota

Lebu

Angol

*Arauco*

*Malleco*

38°

TEMUCO

**REGION
DE
LA ARAUCANIA
IX**

*Cautín Rio*

Valdivia

40°

La Unión

*Vale*

Osorno

*Osorno*

**REGION
DE
LOS LAGOS
X**

*Llanquihue*

Pto. V
PUER
MON

42°

Ancud

Castro

*Chiloé*

*Pale*

74°